D0076702

The New Foreign Policy

NEW MILLENNIUM BOOKS IN INTERNATIONAL STUDIES

SERIES EDITORS
Eric Selbin, Southwestern University
Vicki Golich, California State University, San Marcos

FOUNDING EDITOR
Deborah J. Gerner, University of Kansas

NEW MILLENNIUM BOOKS issue out of the unique position of the global system at the beginning of a new millennium in which our understandings about war, peace, terrorism, identity, sovereignty, security, and sustainability—whether economic, environmental, or ethical—are likely to be challenged. In the new millennium of international relations, new theories, new actors, and new policies and processes are all bound to be engaged. Books in the series are of three types: compact core texts, supplementary texts, and readers.

EDITORIAL BOARD
Maryann Cusimano Love, Catholic University of America
John Freeman, University of Minnesota
Nils Petter Gleditsch, International Peace Research Institute, Oslo
Joshua Goldstein, Brown University
Ole Holsti, Duke University
Christopher C. Joyner, Georgetown University
Margaret Karns, University of Dayton
Marc Levy, Columbia University
James McCormick, Iowa State University

Karen Mingst, University of Kentucky
Laura Neack, Miami University
Jon Pevehouse, University of Chicago
Anne Sisson Runyan, University of Cincinnati
Gerald Schneider, University of Konstanz, Germany
Philip A. Schrodt, University of Kansas
Timothy M. Shaw, University of the West Indies
Thomas G. Weiss, City University of New York Graduate Center
Michael Zürn, Hertie School of Governance, Berlin

The New Foreign Policy

Power Seeking in a Globalized Era

Second Edition

Laura Neack

ROWMAN & LITTLEFIELD PUBLISHERS, INC.
Lanham • Boulder • New York • Toronto • Plymouth, UK

ROWMAN & LITTLEFIELD PUBLISHERS, INC.

Published in the United States of America
by Rowman & Littlefield Publishers, Inc.
A wholly owned subsidiary of The Rowman & Littlefield Publishing Group, Inc.
4501 Forbes Boulevard, Suite 200, Lanham, Maryland 20706
www.rowmanlittlefield.com

Estover Road, Plymouth PL6 7PY, United Kingdom

Copyright © 2008 by Rowman & Littlefield Publishers, Inc.

All rights reserved. No part of this publication may be reproduced, stored
in a retrieval system, or transmitted in any form or by any means, electronic,
mechanical, photocopying, recording, or otherwise, without the prior permission
of the publisher.

British Library Cataloguing in Publication Information Available

Library of Congress Cataloging-in-Publication Data
Neack, Laura.
  The new foreign policy : power seeking in a globalized era / Laura Neack. —
2nd ed.
    p. cm. — (New millennium books in international studies)
  Includes bibliographical references and index.
  ISBN-13: 978-0-7425-5631-7 (cloth : alk. paper)
  ISBN-10: 0-7425-5631-X (cloth : alk. paper)
  ISBN-13: 978-0-7425-5632-4 (pbk. : alk. paper)
  ISBN-10: 0-7425-5632-8 (alk. paper)
  eISBN-13: 978-0-7425-5744-4
  eISBN-10: 0-7425-5744-8
  1. United States—Foreign relations—2001–2. September 11 Terrorist Attacks,
2001. 3. Globalization—Political aspects. 4. United States—Foreign relations—
1989–5. United States—Foreign relations—Philosophy. I. Title.
  E895.N43 2008
  973.93—dc22

                                                                    2008005813

Printed in the United States of America

∞™ The paper used in this publication meets the minimum requirements of
American National Standard for Information Sciences—Permanence of Paper
for Printed Library Materials, ANSI/NISO Z39.48-1992.

In loving memory of
Charles William Neack
1923–2001
and
Agatha Isabel Liedel
1932–2005

Contents

Preface

This is a book on foreign policy analysis—that is, a book that discusses and describes what analysts do when they study foreign policy—as well as a book that analyzes foreign policy. Foreign policy analysis, like the conduct of foreign policy itself, happens in a political context. Foreign policy scholars do not work with test tubes inside sterile laboratories; instead, they view the world around them, examining real foreign policy choices and outcomes for the lessons to be learned. Ultimately, foreign policy scholars want to offer the world a better understanding of the real-life stuff of foreign policy, and some scholars even hope to make the world a better place as a result.

The world today is as chaotic as it is predictable, as dangerous as it is familiar. The meta-level trends in the world that were present during the writing of the first edition of this book remain and have intensified for the worse. And so I offer here an updated version of the preface from the first edition of *The New Foreign Policy*, emphasizing that we are in an era of globalization, global violence, and American overreach.

On September 11, 2001, terrorists hijacked four commercial airplanes in the United States and turned three of them into weapons of mass destruction. Two planes were flown into the towers of the World Trade Center in New York City and a third was flown into the side of the Pentagon in Washington, D.C. The fourth hijacked plane went down in a field in rural Pennsylvania as the passengers and crew fought the hijackers to regain control of the plane. The people on that flight used cell phones to communicate with their families after the plane was hijacked. Those brave citizens knew the fate of the other hijacked planes and were determined not to let a fourth plane wreak such death and destruction.

September 11, 2001, will be one of those days that we'll never forget; we will remember always where we were and what we were doing when we heard the incredible news. On that morning, I was working on the first edition of the book you are holding now, at home in southwestern Ohio. My husband called from a classroom at Miami University right before ten o'clock to say he had heard something about a plane hitting one of the World Trade Center towers, and to ask what I had heard. Then my father called and said, "Are you watching the news, someone has *attacked* the World Trade Center and the Pentagon; turn on your TV." I asked him to repeat what he said; it seemed incredible. I turned on the television and watched the live pictures of the WTC towers billowing smoke. Then one of the towers collapsed. I had trouble understanding that what I was watching was not some imagined reality but *was* reality. Within moments of the collapse of the second tower, my son called from high school—was I watching and could I believe it? As so many people did that day—even people who were claimed ultimately as victims of the attacks—we were reaching out to loved ones to try to make some sense of what we were watching and hearing.

My father was a World War II vet, serving four years in the Marine Corps in the South Pacific and China. When I called him back that dreadful September morning, my father said this was just like Pearl Harbor, but so much worse. He was in shock, like me, like so many others. Later that day, as my teenage son and I were watching nonstop television coverage of the attacks, we heard former U.S. secretary of state Henry Kissinger use the same analogy my father had—that this attack was another Pearl Harbor. Kissinger said that once we learned who perpetrated this attack we should do to them what we did to the Japanese. My son looked at me with wide, horrified eyes and said, "Kissinger thinks we should *nuke* them?" We knew that an American response was in order, but *what kind*?

September 11, 2001, *was* like December 7, 1941, in that the United States, a country that luxuriated in its geographical isolation, found it was not so isolated after all. But September 11, 2001, was more *unlike* December 7, 1941, than it was like it. On September 11 (1) the continental United States was attacked; (2) the perpetrators used commercial aircraft as their weapons of choice, taking charge of those aircraft by wielding cardboard cutters and no "typical" weapons; and (3) the perpetrators *represented no government*. The political "game" *seemed* to have shifted dramatically in September 2001.

We should keep in mind, though, that a far less "successful" attack occurred in 1993 when persons alleged to be loosely affiliated with the September 11 hijackers bombed the World Trade Center. Had Americans been paying closer attention, we might have been aware that a new "game" had been upon us for a number of years. Still, humans are creatures locked in what they know. The response to September 11 was in many respects predictable: the United States went to war. But in other respects the U.S. response was not predictable: the United States launched *two* wars—one against the Taliban government of Afghanistan and two years later another against Saddam Hussein's regime in Iraq. Both wars resulted in regime change; both wars continue through 2008.

My son is now in graduate school and my father passed away before the first edition of this book went to press. My mother passed away a few years later, but not before living to see one of her oldest grandchildren permanently disabled early in the U.S. war in Iraq. So much has happened in the world since September 11, 2001, and so much for the worse. Since March 2003, between 130,000 and 160,000 U.S. troops, some 150,000 private military contractors, and a small and steadily diminishing number of allied troops have been engaged in the war in Iraq. This war has lasted longer than World War II, and George W. Bush seems determined not to end the war before he leaves office in January 2009.

The war goes on and on. As of April 2008, 4,019 American troops have been killed in Iraq, and over 29,000 wounded. The financial costs are estimated to be over $400 billion and growing. More than four years after the United States invaded and toppled the dictatorship of Saddam Hussein, a civil war simmers, with 160,000 U.S. troops caught in a quagmire in which enemies are multiple and friends are uncertain. This war, a *war of choice* for the U.S. administration, has unleashed unending miseries on the Iraqi people. In testimony before the U.S. House Armed Services Committee in July 2007, Jessica T. Mathews, president of the Carnegie Endowment for International Peace, depicted the misery in these words: "More than 4 million Iraqis are refugees, internally displaced, or dead from violence. *In per capita US terms, that would be 50 million people forced out of their homes, sitting in Mexico or Canada, or dead.*"[1] Imagine that, Mathews implored, empathize with that, understand the challenges of that. Different nongovernmental organizations (NGOs) estimate that between 78,000 and 1,000,000 Iraqis have died as a result of the U.S.-led invasion and subsequent chaos and fighting.

The war in Afghanistan continues, too, at midyear 2008, as Taliban and al Qaeda elements regroup in the border areas of Afghanistan and Pakistan. The Iraq war didn't just leave the war in Afghanistan unfinished—it has also contributed to greater overall insecurity for the United States. In a 2007 survey by *Foreign Policy* magazine of the American "foreign policy establishment"—Republicans and Democrats, "people who have served as secretary of state, national security advisor, senior White House aides, top commanders in the U.S. military, seasoned intelligence professionals, and distinguished academics"—91 percent of those polled believe that "the world is becoming more dangerous for Americans and the United States."[2] The survey found that 84 percent of the foreign policy establishment "do not believe the United States is winning the war on terror," and 92 percent believe that "the war in Iraq negatively affects U.S. national security." The policies of the Bush administration—regarding the war in Iraq, the war on terrorism, Iranian nuclear ambitions, and Pakistan—were blamed for this increased insecurity. A different survey of U.S.-based international relations scholars also published by *Foreign Policy* produced similar results: 89 percent believe the Iraq war will decrease U.S. security in the long run, 96 percent say the United States is far less respected today than in the past, and a "scant 1 percent rank Bush among the most effective foreign-policy presidents of the past century."[3]

The Bush administration will not change directions; the wars in Iraq and in Afghanistan will become the legacy of the next U.S. president. Thus, we should expect that this American military overreach will have a continuing toll for U.S. and global security.

The New Foreign Policy presents some of the tools and lessons developed by scholars over the last half of the twentieth century and at the start of the twenty-first century, honed to the shifting landscape of the twenty-first century and new millennium. The meta-level phenomena of globalization, global violence, and American overreach shape the discussion of the scholarship presented here. Within this framework, *The New Foreign Policy* is constructed on the proposition that foreign policy is best understood as a "nested game" in which national leaders attempt to "play" the two games of domestic and international politics to their advantage. Foreign policy *analysis*, then, is best undertaken as a study of this nested game, or, as a multilevel study.

This revised edition of *The New Foreign Policy* has been reorganized into smaller chapters with old and new scholarship and cases to consider. Chapter 1 discusses the study of foreign policy and provides some general terms and theories that will set the stage for the chapters that follow. Chapters 2, 3, and 4 focus on the individual level of analysis. In chapter 2, I examine rational actors and the national interests, for a first take on the "individual" level. In chapter 3, I discuss cognitive studies that focus on the beliefs, perceptions, and misperceptions of national decision makers, for a second take on the "individual" level. In chapter 4, I focus on small-group decision-making dynamics. Chapters 5, 6, and 7 are set at the state level of analysis. Chapter 5 analyzes the impact of national self-image and culture; chapter 6 analyzes the impact of domestic politics; and chapter 7 discusses the impact of public opinion, elites, interest groups, and media on states' foreign policies. Chapters 8 and 9 shift the focus to the international system level of analysis. In chapter 8, I discuss what great powers are and what American grand strategy has been in this era of global hegemony. In chapter 9, I discuss the foreign policies of non–great powers, including secondary powers, middle powers, small powers, and the European Union as a "normative power." Finally, in chapter 10, I bring the levels of analysis and multiple actors back together in a discussion of foreign policy as a nested game with many players, particularly nonstate actors.

I again wish to thank Professors Ole Holsti and Robert J. Beck for their reviews of the first edition of this book. I also wish to thank former Rowman & Littlefield executive editor Jennifer Knerr and Renee Legatt. For the second edition, my gratitude goes to Professors Susan Penksa and Melanie Ziegler, whose dedicated and critical use of the first edition helped shape this second edition, and to Professor Pat Haney, who answered random e-mail questions from me. Special thanks go to Melanie Ziegler and Roger Knudson for reading and commenting on the full manuscript. Without Melanie and Roger, my endnotes might not match up, and my thinking would be much fuzzier than it is on some topics! Rog deserves special kudos for reading the entire manuscript in less than twenty-four hours and passing a pop quiz. Finally, thanks are owed to many, many Miami University students who have helped me focus and refocus this second edition.

At Rowman & Littlefield, I want to express thanks to Susan McEachern, editorial director, Jess Gribble, and Alden Perkins. Susan has demonstrated unlimited patience with me through two books, having inherited my last book midway through. The Editorial Board of New Millennium Books in International Studies are hard, hard critics to please, but somehow I did so, and thus they charged me with another edition of this book. Eric Selbin, Margaret Karns, and Karen Mingst all earn special "shout-outs" for their roles on the Board and for helping me think about, shape, and stick with this second edition. Thanks to Lindsay Mosser for constructing the glossary.

There would not be a New Millennium Books series without Deborah Gerner. The first time around I mentioned how daunting a task it was to write a foreign policy book for such a preeminent foreign policy scholar. This time around, I write this edition in her memory. I am still amazed and appreciative that Misty brought me into the New Millennium family.

I am grateful for the constant support and love of my guys—my husband Roger Knudson and my son Harry Neack. What a wonderful thing it is to be human and to love with such abandonment! Finally, this book is dedicated to my mother and my father.

1

Introduction:
The New Foreign Policy

IN THIS CHAPTER

- A Tangled Tale of Tibet
- The New Foreign Policy
- Defining the Subject: Foreign Policy
- Selecting Entrance Points: Levels of Analysis
- Worldviews and Theories
  Realism
  Liberalism
  Marxism
  Constructivism
- The Bridge between International and Comparative Politics
- A New Millennium
- Chapter Review

Cases Featured in This Chapter

- The tangled relations between Tibet, China, and the United States.
- The impact of the Cold War on the development of the comparative study of foreign policy.

A TANGLED TALE OF TIBET

Let's go back to 1989 and up to the top of the world—Tibet. In 1989, the Tenth Panchen Lama, one of two of the highest leaders of Tibetan

Buddhism, died under mysterious circumstances in his monastery. By Buddhist tradition, the soul of the Panchen Lama would be reincarnated, returning to Earth to teach others the path to enlightenment. Also according to Buddhist tradition, the former friends and teachers of the late Panchen Lama would begin a series of divinations designed to determine where he would be reincarnated so they could locate the living Buddha and ensure his proper religious training and preparation.

What does this have to do with *The New Foreign Policy*? This is one entrance into a tangled tale that involves many countries strong and weak, key international figures, transnational human rights and religious groups, the United Nations, and even Hollywood. We could open the tale years earlier—decades and centuries earlier—or in the year 2000. If we fast-forwarded to 2007, we would find the Dalai Lama in Washington, D.C., receiving a Congressional Gold Medal. Meanwhile, the Chinese government would be registering its anger over congressional meddling in Chinese internal affairs. Changing the starting point would change the issues somewhat, but the tangled nature of the tale would not change, nor would its entanglement in the foreign relations of some powerful states. Indeed, the fate of Tibetan Buddhism is inextricably enmeshed in the foreign policy choices of several important countries and presents us with a perfect case study on *The New Foreign Policy*.

In early 1995, the Panchen Lama search party narrowed its search to a short list of boys, in and outside Tibet, and assembled photos and evidence to present to the highest holy figure in Tibetan Buddhism, the Dalai Lama. The search party would offer its opinion on which boy was most likely to be the reincarnate lama. The Dalai Lama would make the final decision regarding the recognition of the Eleventh Panchen Lama, taking into account the evidence and opinion of the search party. So here's where we'll bring foreign policy in—the Dalai Lama is the spiritual and temporal leader of the government of Tibet in exile. The Dalai Lama and his government reside in Dharamsala in northern India, where they sought refuge from the Chinese occupation of Tibet. The Chinese army invaded Tibet in 1950 in order to incorporate it into the new communist regime. This incorporation required eliminating the independence-minded Tibetan government led by the young Dalai Lama. By 1959, brutal Chinese efforts to eradicate Buddhism and the culture of the Tibetan people led the Dalai Lama to flee Tibet in the hope of maintaining in sanctuary some semblance of the true Tibet. Of course, this is not the story the Chinese government told—then or now.

Regardless of whether one takes the position that Tibet was part of China for centuries or that Tibet was always independent, since 1950 Tibet has been part of the country called the People's Republic of China. Ever since he fled Tibet, the Dalai Lama has frustrated and angered the

Chinese government because of his persistent work for the liberation of his people and culture. Since his flight from Tibet, the Dalai Lama has been accorded head of state treatment by governments around the world, including the executive and legislative branches of the U.S. government, and been praised and supported by international human rights and religious freedom groups. As an advocate of nonviolence, the Dalai Lama was awarded the Nobel Peace Prize in 1989. The Dalai Lama was but a single individual who caused the Chinese government considerable consternation and bad international publicity. Further, the Dalai Lama's government in exile was/is located in the territory of one of China's competitors, if not enemies—India.

The Panchen Lama chose to be reincarnated inside Tibet, it turned out. The Dalai Lama, worried about the reaction of the Chinese authorities, carefully weighed the options about announcing who the reincarnate lama was. In April 1995, the Dalai Lama decided to name the boy to start the process of his training and preempt any efforts by the Chinese to thwart the process. The Chinese government formed its own naming team and chose a different boy as the reincarnation. In December, the Chinese government (which is officially atheist) staged a grand ceremony at which its designate assumed the position of the Eleventh Panchen Lama. The Dalai Lama's choice, Gedhun Choekyi Nyima, and his family disappeared into Chinese custody and have not been seen since the spring of 1995. The Dalai Lama, human rights groups such as Amnesty International, and religious groups declared the boy to be the world's youngest political prisoner. The Chinese government, when its spokespersons even acknowledged Gedhun Choekyi Nyima's existence, only said that he "is where he is supposed to be."[1]

How does this tale become a foreign policy issue? The Chinese government has declared many times that this tale or any tale about Tibet should never be a foreign policy issue, since it involves the domestic affairs of China. As a foreign ministry spokesperson said in 1993 regarding Tibet, "The business of the United States should be addressed by the American people, and the business of the Chinese people should be handled by the Chinese people."[2] But the domestic affairs of any country are often a source of contention with other countries. How and to what extent the tale of the Panchen Lama gets entwined in foreign policy depends on the decisions and actions taken and the "power" held by various interested actors in various countries. Let's switch sites and see how this plays out.

Since the Chinese government's violent crackdown on the prodemocracy demonstrators in Tiananmen Square on June 3, 1989, the George H. W. Bush (Bush 1) administration had been open to criticism for its policy toward China. (A few months prior to Tiananmen, the Chinese had used violence to quell an uprising in Lhasa, Tibet.) President Bush's view was that the best way to influence China, avoid future Tiananmens, and end other alleged human rights violations was to remain "constructively engaged" with China, offering incentives rather than disincentives to change.

A majority in Congress disagreed with constructive engagement, as did human rights and religious interest groups. When an attempt by Congress to pass a tough sanctions bill to punish China was defeated by presidential veto, congressional critics decided to place human rights conditions on the yearly renewal of China's most favored nation (MFN) trading status.[3] Constructive engagement remained U.S. policy during the remainder of the Bush 1 administration, but the 1992 presidential elections would keep a prosanctions coalition alive and hopeful.

After meeting with members of Congress and leaders of various interest groups opposed to the Bush 1 policy, Democratic presidential candidate Bill Clinton came out in favor of attaching human rights conditions to any future granting of MFN status to China. Clinton announced his position: "I do not want to isolate China . . . but I believe our nation has a higher purpose than to coddle dictators and stand aside from the global movement toward democracy."[4] This statement was repeated many times by Clinton on the campaign trail. Upon Clinton's election, Chinese authorities signaled their unhappiness with the results of the U.S. election by suspending further human rights talks. But the complexities of the China policy soon became clear to the president-elect, who announced a moderated view in late November 1992: "We have a big stake in not isolating China, in seeing that China continues to develop a market economy. . . . But we also have to insist, I believe, on progress in human rights and human decency."[5]

Before his inauguration, Clinton hosted several conferences in his hometown of Little Rock, Arkansas, to clarify key issues for the new administration. At the economic conference, the chief operating officer of toy manufacturer Mattel raised worries about Mattel's ability to stay on top of the world toy market if human rights conditions were attached to renewing China's MFN status. Voices within the United States—such as the aircraft and wheat industries—and voices outside the United States—such as the governments of Japan and Hong Kong—were similarly urging Clinton to back away from his campaign stand on China.[6]

Right before the Clinton inauguration, two different groups of Democratic senators visited China and Tibet in December 1992 and January 1993, at the invitation of the Chinese government. This Chinese effort to influence the domestic political debate within the United States—and thereby shape U.S. foreign policy in the new administration—reaped some benefits, as several of the senators declared that it would be shortsighted to link trade and human rights.

A new U.S. policy on China was formulated in 1993 by the new administration in which the president, acting under executive orders authority, attached some pro–human rights conditions to the U.S.-Chinese relationship, but not on trade issues. This compromise policy was hammered out by talks on many levels between administration officials and various members of Congress, and with their respective domestic groups engaged behind the scenes. The compromise allowed voices on both sides to be partially satisfied and partially dissatisfied. Farm and business groups and their supporters in Congress were glad to keep trade off this particular table, while human rights groups and their congressional supporters were glad to see some official pronouncement privileging human rights and democracy. Even in this age of globalization, where market forces seemed to drive so much international activity, it appeared that key noneconomic values would remain central to U.S. foreign policy. At the signing ceremony for the executive order, leaders of human rights groups, business leaders, prodemocracy Chinese students, and members of the Tibetan government in exile stood behind President Clinton.[7] The president warned that the next year's renewal of MFN status would be subject to human rights conditions and conditions designed to curtail Chinese weapons sales (an increasingly troublesome issue). Concurrently, demonstrations in Lhasa, Tibet, were being ended with force.[8]

There were others in the Clinton administration and Congress who favored a tough China policy for reasons other than Tibet or the treatment of prodemocracy advocates. Chinese weapons sales to "rogue" states were causing worries among some security analysts. Adding to these worries, in October 1993, the Chinese conducted an underground nuclear weapon test. In response, Clinton ordered the Department of Energy to prepare for its own test.[9]

The compromise China policy would not last and the threat about the following year would not be carried out. Internal divisions within the Clinton administration—reflecting divisions in American society—led to a reevaluation of policy over the year to follow. "On the one side were the economic agencies, Treasury, Commerce, and the National Economic Council (NEC), who favored developing ties with China and pursuing human rights concerns only secondarily. . . . On the other side were State Department officials . . . who favored continuing a tough stance on human rights."[10] The economic agencies gained the upper hand on the issue, with support from corporate leaders and increasing numbers of members of Congress, all of whom were interested in tapping into China's enormous potential market. This coalition was able to change the Clinton policy and avoid future annual threats to link MFN status with human rights issues. As Clinton explained the change in policy in May 1994, "linkage has been constructive during the last year, but . . . we have reached the end of the

usefulness of that policy."[11] Human rights groups went along with this
delinking in order not to lose their potential leverage on the rest of the
China policy.[12]

By the next year, 1995, the controversy over the reincarnation of the
Panchen Lama came to a climax of sorts with the naming of the two com-
peting "soul boys." That December, as the Chinese-favored Panchen
Lama was ceremoniously installed, the Chinese government also sen-
tenced a prominent democracy advocate to fourteen years in prison.
These events caused some members of Congress and human rights
groups to attempt to force a Clinton policy reassessment on trade with
China. Yet even in the face of this pressure, the deputy U.S. trade representative reassured all that the president's previous decision to delink
MFN status and human rights "remains fixed and unchanged."[13] Although human rights problems in China might temper the climate of talks
somewhat, the president was committed to helping China gain entry into
the World Trade Organization, unless, the trade rep warned, the Chinese
leaders continued to make no progress on opening their markets.

THE NEW FOREIGN POLICY

This saga demonstrates several important observations about foreign policy that will be explored in detail in this book:

- Foreign policy is made and conducted in complex domestic and international environments.
- Foreign policy results from the work of coalitions of interested domestic and international actors and groups.
- Foreign policy issues are often linked and delinked, reflecting the
  strength of various parties and their particular concerns.
- The "stuff" of foreign policy derives from issues of domestic politics
  as well as foreign relations.
- Foreign policy analysis needs to be multilevel and multifaceted in order to confront the complicated sources and nature of foreign policy.

How each of these key features pertains to the tangled tale of Tibet is summarized below.

*Foreign policy is made and conducted in complex domestic and international
environments.* The "tangled tale of Tibet" illustrates that decision makers—
here, Bill Clinton and the members of his administration in charge of
China policy—operate in at least two different environments, domestic
and international. Bill Clinton the candidate was focused primarily on the
domestic environment, with very little attention paid to the international

environment. Bill Clinton the newly elected president had to give attention to both the domestic and international environments. Political scientist Robert Putnam has described this situation that national leaders find themselves in as a "two-level," "dual," or "nested" game.[14] Leaders cannot afford to focus exclusively on one level but must try to play both to some advantage. Sometimes issues on one level will cause a leader to put greater emphasis there, and sometimes leaders will use issues on one level to pursue goals in the other, but no leader can afford to ignore the reality of this nested game.

Foreign policy results from the work of coalitions of interested domestic and international actors and groups. Coalitions are, by nature, in constant flux. The coalition of interests and groups that might get a politician elected is not necessarily the coalition that will get that leader's programs legislated or executed. Leaders come to power "owing" some groups yet often intent on "wooing" others. As the environments shift, the issues shift and the nature of coalition building shifts. Leaders often need to pay more attention to those who form the opposition—trying to entice them into forming policy coalitions to get favored programs passed—than to their loyal constituents. The human rights and religious groups inside the United States and human rights and democracy advocates outside the United States (such as the Tibetan government in exile, Chinese students studying in the United States, and the governments of other countries) could not pose any significant threat to the Clinton presidency if Clinton were to "water down" his China policy somewhat. Indeed, we might say that these groups needed the Clinton presidency more than the Clinton presidency needed them—especially the coalition of non-U.S. actors who were not very "powerful" international actors. In order to pursue his broader list of goals—both domestic and international—Clinton needed to garner key support from groups that opposed linking trade with human rights.

Foreign policy issues are often linked and delinked, reflecting the strength of various parties and their particular concerns. Because of the "nested game" leaders play and the necessity of building various policy coalitions, issues cannot help but be linked and delinked. Politics is a game of bargaining and compromising, and this involves trade-offs. The politics of foreign policy making is no different. Although the Chinese government insisted that human rights should not be linked to trade issues, by this very demand China made it clear that the United States could not hope to achieve its goals vis-à-vis China unless it quit talking about human rights. That is, the Chinese linked favorable relations with the United States on a broad array of issues to the requirement that human rights stay off the table. The Chinese government and the U.S. domestic interests that wanted entrance into the potential Chinese market commanded the greatest influence over the Clinton policy, and this informal "coalition" was able to win the day and get trade policy delinked from human rights. The domestic and international groups in favor of using trade as a way to compel China to follow a better human rights standard found themselves with less leverage, perhaps because their issues were more narrowly focused, and so they could not link their desired China policy to other issues over which they had control.

The "stuff" of foreign policy derives from issues of domestic politics as well as foreign relations. Despite Chinese insistence that domestic politics was off-limits to outsiders, the line between domestic politics and international politics is blurry. Issues go across national borders, and coalitions supporting or opposing certain policies on those issues also form across national borders. Some have called this blurring of the distinction between international and domestic politics "intermestic," combining the words to indicate the combining of issues and interests. Others prefer to use the terms transnational actors and transnational forces to indicate the linking of interests and actions across national lines. Since the mid-1990s, most observers have suggested that the line between domestic and international politics is not just blurry but is quickly disappearing because of globalization. Globalization is a term that refers to "the increasing internationalization of culture and economics."[15] As national markets are increasingly opened to the global market, national cultures similarly are opened to the global culture. National sovereignty is eroded in terms of both control of the national economy and—perhaps more importantly—preservation of national culture. When the Clinton administration took human rights conditions off its China trade policy, the justification was that opening up China for trade would open up China for other influences, ultimately changing the behavior of the Chinese government in the way that human rights and democracy groups wanted. Put another way, the Clinton policy was based on the idea that, ultimately, the forces of globalization would compel changes in Chinese human rights behavior, and U.S. policy should facilitate those forces.

Further emphasizing this "intermestic" quality of politics, leaders have been known to use foreign policies to promote domestic agendas, and vice versa. In the U.S. presidential election of 1992, Bush 1 attempted to convince American voters to reelect him—a domestic agenda—by pointing to his foreign policy accomplishments. This can be turned around the other way—sometimes domestic credentials are used to promote foreign policy goals. The Chinese government has released political prisoners from time to time as a demonstration of its cooperative nature in order to garner greater U.S. investment, U.S. support for Chinese membership in the World Trade Organization, and international support for hosting the 2008 Olympic Games in Beijing.

DEFINING THE SUBJECT: FOREIGN POLICY

Before we go any further we need to be clear about our subject: foreign policy. Charles Hermann calls foreign policy a "neglected concept."[16] He asserts, "This neglect has been one of the most serious obstacles to providing more adequate and comprehensive explanations of foreign policy." Hermann thinks that part of the reason for this neglect is that "most people dealing with the subject have felt confident that they knew what foreign policy was."[17] To put it colloquially, we know it when we see it. Ultimately, Hermann defines foreign policy as "the discrete purposeful action that results from the political level decision of an individual or group of individuals. . . . [it is] the observable artifact of a political level decision. It is not the decision, but a product of the decision."[18] Hermann defines foreign policy as the behavior of states.

Hermann rejects the idea that the study of foreign policy is the study of policy, but his is a minority view. Bruce Russett, Harvey Starr, and David Kinsella take an opposite and broader view: "We can think of a policy as a program that serves as a guide to behavior intended to realize the goals an organization has set for itself. . . . Foreign policy is thus a guide to actions taken beyond the boundaries of the state to further the goals of the state."[19] Although these scholars define foreign policy as a program or statement of goals, they also stress that the study of foreign policy must involve study of both the "formulation and implementation" of policy.[20]

Deborah Gerner takes foreign policy further when she defines it as "the intentions, statements, and actions of an actor—often, but not always, a state—directed toward the external world and the response of other actors to these intentions, statements and actions."[21] Gerner combines Hermann's interest in behavior with Russett, Starr, and Kinsella's emphasis on programs or guides. Note that in Gerner's definition the emphasis is on states but does not have to be on states. Other actors—such as international cause groups, businesses, religions, and so forth—in the international system formulate guidelines and goals that direct their actions toward other international actors. In this book, the emphasis is primarily on states, but other actors will appear from time to time as well.

We will use a broad definition of foreign policy that includes both statements and behaviors or actions. The study of foreign policy, however, needs to consider more than what states declare to be their goals and how they attempt to achieve them. The study of foreign policy needs to consider how certain goals arise and why certain behaviors result. Thus our focus is on how goals are decided upon. We will explore the factors that cause a state to declare and embark on a certain foreign policy course. Our emphasis will be on determining these factors and the processes by which policy (statements and behaviors) is made. In summary, the "stuff" of our foreign policy study includes processes, statements, and behaviors.

SELECTING ENTRANCE POINTS: LEVELS OF ANALYSIS

This book rests on the assertion that studying foreign policy is a complicated undertaking requiring multilevel, multifaceted research. This is not meant to imply, though, that we need to study every foreign policy case in all of its varied aspects. Indeed, this quickly could become an unmanageable task. Instead, foreign policy analysts disaggregate or break down each case into different component parts in order to study and understand select aspects. The knowledge generated by many such studies—studies conducted in the same way, asking the same questions, in similar and different contexts and cases—begins to accumulate and form a body of knowledge.

As the case of the tangled tale of Tibet demonstrates, we can enter a case and study it at many different points. For example, we might want to study the change that occurred in Bill Clinton's stance from the perspective of Bill Clinton the individual decision maker. Was Clinton inclined to see the world through a particular "lens" that somehow altered what he saw to fit what he believed? Did he have some weakly held beliefs about the Chinese, allowing him to be open to new thinking about China policy? Were there key advisers whose opinions shaped his, or did his opinion or preferences shape the views of his closest advisers? Were there some group dynamics at play that gave the economics-focused Cabinet members greater leverage over those who privileged human rights? Did this lead to an imbalanced consideration of the policy and, therefore, a policy recommendation that did not leave Clinton much room for choice? We could conduct a study of this case using any of these questions to guide our research. Each of these is posed at what scholars call the *individual level of analysis*—a focus on individual decision makers, how they make decisions, what perceptions and misperceptions they hold, the ways key decision makers interact in small, top-level groups, and so on.

We might, instead, decide to explore the involvement of interest groups and Congress in the changing nature of the Clinton China policy. We could explore the lobbying of Congress and the Executive branch by groups on the pro–human rights and protrade sides. We could explore the "turf" problems between the Executive and Legislative branches on the defining of the U.S. China policy. We could ask whether the Pentagon, worried about potential Chinese military threats, lobbied the White House and Congress for a certain stand against the Chinese. We could investigate the rise and fall of the fortunes of the pro–human rights groups and the rise of the protrade groups, charting their different strategies, arguments, and overall effectiveness. Entering the case in this way involves study at the *state level of analysis*. At the state level, we examine those societal and governmental factors that contribute to the making of foreign policy in a particular state.

If we expanded our focus, we could investigate the following questions. Did changes in the overall balance of power between countries in the Asia Pacific region convince American leaders that accommodating China was the most prudent way to have some influence over China? Were there some international mechanisms for pursuing human rights separately from trade, thus allowing the United States to delink the issues and still pursue both? Was there some consensus among key allies that China would need to be enticed into being a "good international citizen" rather than bullied into such a role? These questions about state versus state, or geostrategic concerns about regional power tilts, or states acting through international organizations, are all posed at the *system level of analysis*. The system level explores bilateral (state-to-state) relations, regional issues and interactions, and global issues and multilateral interactions between states. At this level we also consider the role played by regional and international organizations and by nonstate actors such as transnational nongovernmental organizations (NGOs) that have a direct influence on the foreign policies of states.

The levels of analysis are tools—heuristic devices—that help us study our subject. All disciplines employ levels of analysis, although the levels vary depending on the discipline. The levels might be better understood by thinking about the lens on a camera and the detail we desire in our subject. At each level of analysis, we gain a particular understanding of our subject. Our understanding may be quite thorough for that level but will necessarily exclude information that can only be attained using one of the other levels of analysis. When we pose our questions at a single level, we acknowledge that our understanding will be limited. Recall that the case study detailed above revealed complexities across the levels of analysis. One level of understanding will not yield a complete picture. Yet we take such a risk and emphasize a single level because we are curious about questions at that level and, perhaps, we are convinced that one level gives a better explanation than the others. It is also true that choosing to frame our study at a single level helps us better manage what we study.

This book is organized around the three levels of analysis. Just as these can help make a single research project more manageable, the levels are useful ways to divide the study of foreign policy. We could divide our subject using more levels of analysis. One of the "pioneers" of foreign policy study, James Rosenau, suggests five levels or sources of foreign policy making: individual, role, governmental, societal, and systemic.[22] The levels used

in this book encapsulate these five. Another important international relations scholar, J. David Singer, describes two broad levels: system and sub-
system. This scheme collapses our individual and state levels into the sub-
system category.[23] It is important to reiterate that we'll use a
levels-of-analysis approach in this book as a way to manage the study of
foreign policy. It is, though, impossible to truly isolate one level from the
other levels, as we'll see when we discuss each. Not only is it analytically
impossible to isolate one level from another, it would also be foolhardy to
make pronouncements or policy decisions using but a single-level analysis
in an era of globalization.

WORLDVIEWS AND THEORIES

In some important ways, the number of levels described is related to what
the individual scholar thinks is important. Every one of us holds a view
of "how things work" or "human nature." These views might be very
elaborate or very simple, but they set the stage for how we act in the
world. These "worldviews" don't have to apply to politics; generally a
personal worldview can be used to explain why your best friend won't
talk to you today, how to play the stock market or pick lottery numbers
(or whether to bother playing the market or picking lottery numbers), or
why countries choose peace over war.

The study of foreign policy derives, in large part, from the discipline
called international relations. There are three worldviews or grand theories that dominate the study of international relations: realism,[24] liberalism,[25] and Marxism.[26] Although there are variants and even disagree-
ments within each of these worldviews, these offer three fairly
straightforward explanations of "how things work" in the world. Scholars and foreign policy makers all have identifiable worldviews, although
from time to time, individuals may use one or the other or borrow key
concepts to fit particular circumstances.

An explanation of how something works is also known as a *theory*. We
can call realism, liberalism, and Marxism worldviews, traditions, or theories. At their most fundamental level, each offers what we call a *grand theory* of how the world of politics works. A grand theory purports to explain
how things are the way they are—or, how things *might be*. In this latter
sense, theories can be *prescriptions* for action to achieve the desired end-
point.

Theories are also used to help us tell the future, or predict. An explanation of a single incident in the past might be interesting, but it cannot tell
us anything about the future. This is a problem for scholars, but even
more so for foreign policy makers. Foreign policy makers need to be able

to confront new circumstances with decisive, effective responses, and they need to be able to be proactive when planning the course for their countries. Theories about how the world works can help policy makers generalize from the past to new experiences, thereby helping them know which policies to undertake and which to avoid.

When analysts apply their theories about the world to the study of particular aspects of foreign policy—such as why countries form alliances, why countries enter into trade agreements, why countries ban land mines or why they don't—they offer something of use to policy makers. The explanations of the world that result from these particularized studies are called *midrange theories*. These midrange theories don't claim to explain everything, just selected parts of world politics. In fact, midrange theories tend to do a better job of explaining parts of the world than the grand theories do in explaining all of the world. This should make sense on an intuitive level.

Theories explain the past and help predict the future. With predictive capability, policy makers can plan their own actions. Theories are of no use to analysts or policy makers if they are too particular, or overly specified. Theories need to go beyond single instances; they need to generalize across cases, events, incidents, and time frames. That is, theories should help in the development of generic knowledge.

How much do foreign policy makers consider the theories—grand or midrange—of scholars? Scholars around the world sit in foreign ministries (or state departments) and analyze the world and advise their governments. Sometimes these scholars are officeholders—such as U.S. president Woodrow Wilson, who was a professor of international relations and politics at Princeton University before he was president—or hold key ministerial/cabinet positions. Fernando Henrique Cardoso, the president of Brazil (1995–2003, serving two terms), was a leading scholar in the Marxist–dependency theory tradition studying asymmetrical power relations between rich and poor countries. In Canada, as another example, foreign policy and international relations scholars frequently spend part of their careers in universities, and part in the Department of Foreign Affairs and International Trade. Sometimes scholars write syndicated columns for newspapers or host talk shows that are broadcast around their countries. The work of scholars gets translated into the work of foreign policy makers, and that translation happens in many different ways. This is why there is an imperative that foreign policy studies have something to say about the world—something tangible and practical.

Scholars in different traditions can and do examine the same set of events and arrive at different explanations about why those events occurred and how best to deal with similar events in the future. These theories give us different answers to the puzzles of the world because they begin with different starting assumptions, stress different "critical" variables, and have different ideal endpoints. It is also important to note that an analyst working within a particular tradition will ignore evidence that another analyst using a different worldview would find indispensable. When a scholar comes up with an answer as to why an event occurred and whether it will occur again, we would be wise—especially as foreign policy makers—to ask ourselves: What tradition is this person applying? What factors did this person ignore, disregard, or downplay? Will we imperil our policy if we ignore other potentially important variables?

As foreign policy makers as well as students of foreign policy, we should read every study with caution—with a critical mind—remembering that each scholar's orientation has led her or him to choose some variables over others. We might learn a great deal from this scholar's work, but the things we are not learning might be just as important. We would be wise, then, to critically mix and match our studies, looking for scholars of different orientations to offer us competing explanations that we can assess critically on the path to a more comprehensive understanding of events.

Let's review the dominant grand theories in brief.

Realism

Classical realists start with a pessimistic view of human nature and from this they make key assumptions about the "nature" of states and state behaviors. Humans are essentially self-interested (some would say selfish) and exist in a social condition characterized by the constant struggle to maintain autonomy from other self-interested humans. States also are self-interested actors existing in an international system characterized by the constant struggle to maintain autonomy (sovereignty) from other states.

Whereas in a national society some legal limitations are placed on the ability of individuals to infringe on the autonomy of other individuals, in the international system any "society" that exists is loosely formed with no ultimate guarantor of the sovereignty of states except the states themselves. Indeed, the dominant characteristic of the international system is anarchy. Neorealists or structural realists emphasize this, rather than human nature, as the starting point for their explanation of world politics.

Because of anarchy, states are compelled to be constantly vigilant, watching out for impositions on their autonomy. The best way to protect a state's autonomy—and thus ensure its survival—is to amass power resources that can be used to deter or defend against other states. All states are similarly motivated and thus can be expected to do what is necessary to survive—sometimes resorting to the use of armed violence against others to capture additional power resources that can be harnessed for the protection of the state. Power itself (or the things that together constitute power, such as military and economic might) is finite in the international system, so whenever a state lays claim to a certain amount of power resources, other states are deprived of those resources. For classical realists, international politics is a zero-sum game where the gains of one state equal the losses of another. International politics is also necessarily conflictual.

The realist perspective is state centered. States and only states are international actors, or the only international actors of note, privilege, and agency. International organizations and nongovernmental actors are only important to study as instruments of states pursuing their own national interests. What goes on within a state also is unimportant because all states have the same operating motivation—protect the state (the national interest) by acquiring greater and greater amounts of power. The important topics to study from a realist perspective include power balances, relative versus absolute power, and the multiple uses of power by one state over another (or a group of states over another group). More recent realist scholarship focuses on whether to balance power or threats and states' pursuit of relative and contingent gains over others.

Globalization is a process that realists meet with some suspicion. Globalization both poses a serious threat to national autonomy and control and creates interdependencies that impede the pursuit of national interests.

Liberalism

Liberals start from a different assumption about human nature and end up with a different view about international politics. Humans, in the liberal view, cherish autonomy but do not assume that their autonomy is threatened by other humans. Instead, humans exist within many networks of relationships that help them achieve collectively what they cannot achieve on their own. Humans who have the opportunity to exercise self-determination will respect others' rights to the same and will value the social fabric that assists all individuals in self-realization. Just as national society should result from a system that respects the rights of individuals and serves the collective will of those individuals, international society should also be founded on principles that respect the rights of individual, self-determining states and serve the collective good. International politics, then, is characterized by—or can be characterized by—harmony among international actors. Because of this expectation that the future might find countries in harmony with one another, the liberal view is sometimes called idealism.

Liberals are pluralists. They conceptualize politics as the interaction of multiple actors pursuing multiple interests and using different types of resources and methods of interaction (such as bargaining, coalition building, arm twisting, and so on). States and nonstate actors of all sorts are important in different ways, depending on the issues at hand. Liberals focus on the formation of international law, organizations, and cooperative arrangements of many sorts, as well as on coercive statecraft directed at preserving some greater, collective good such as international peace or the promotion of human rights. Liberals value multiplicity and norms that protect and encourage multiplicity, all in the service of a greater, collective good.

Liberalism has a corollary in liberal economic theory in which it is proposed that free and open trade between countries can decrease the possibility of conflict between them. Essentially, the argument is that the more people trade, the greater the ties that bind them together. And the more people trade, the more they reap the benefits of trade together. In time, interdependencies and mutual gains will make war and violent conflict less likely, as all countries benefit from—and understand that they benefit from—their open relationships with one another. Globalization is a phenomenon that liberals welcome, even as they acknowledge that aspects of globalization need to be tempered in order to accommodate different peoples' concerns and interests.

Marxism

Before I explain the Marxist view on international politics, let's consider whether this worldview is still relevant with the collapse of the Soviet-led communist world. In brief, it is! The Marxist view was established before the founding of the Soviet Union as a critique and response to capitalism. Both of the grand political theories discussed above, realism and liberalism, are compatible with capitalism. Marxism constitutes both a response to the problems inherent to capitalism—an economic system—and a response to realism and liberalism—which chiefly describe political systems.

As with realism and liberalism, there is more to Marxism than I will describe here. The foundation of the Marxist view is that the economic organization of a society determines the political and social system. A society founded on capitalism, with its free market and private ownership of wealth and property, is a society divided into economic/social classes. Essentially, there are two classes—owners and workers. The societal norms and political system built on a capitalist-based economy are designed to maintain the continued profit taking of the owner class. Politics will be dominated by elite interests, and the institutions of government will be designed and directed to keeping the workers in an exploited, dependent position in order to preserve and increase the wealth of the owners. An international system based on capitalism is also a system divided into the owners, or the "haves," and the workers, or the "have-nots." The institutions of the rich states—such as their militaries—are used to maintain the world capitalist system, which serves elite interests. International institutions, similarly, are used to maintain the system in favor of the wealthy class/states.

Communist or Marxist states attempted to build a different political/social domestic order by instituting an economic system that rejected private ownership and rejected wealth-based social classes. Instead, centrally planned economies were constructed to serve the interests of all citizens—theoretically. Internationally, these states—primarily the Eastern bloc led by the Soviet Union—attempted to remove themselves from the capitalist world system in order to protect themselves from the inherent distortions in that system. The Cold War conflict between the Soviet-led Eastern bloc and the American-led Western bloc was inevitable, according to the Marxist view, as capitalist states would use all means necessary to protect against the threat posed by communism.

Despite the collapse of the Soviet Union and the worldwide turn to liberal capitalism (a turn even manifested in the remaining communist states of China, Vietnam, North Korea, and Cuba), the Marxist critique of capitalism remains relevant. During and beyond the Cold War, Marxist discussions of international politics focus(ed) on how the world's rich states mobilize their resources and tools of statecraft to maintain and increase their wealth and predominance. International organizations, such as the United Nations, and international institutions, such as the World Bank and International Monetary Fund, serve as instruments of the rich (called the core or centre) states to maintain a world system that remains stratified into the rich few and the poor many on the periphery. Because this view stresses the structure of the world system and the structural determinants of power within the world economic system, it is also referred to as structuralism.

A Marxist or structuralist observer might focus on how the policies of international lending agencies keep the developing countries submerged in debt and dependent on the core states for trade and investment. Similarly, such an analysis might discuss how the terms attached to international loans coerce developing countries to enact domestic economic policies that increase poverty and human suffering in order to be able to make the service payments on external debt. Marxists also examine the patterns in the use of force—unilaterally and multilaterally—by core states against dependent states as continuing evidence of inevitable class conflict.

In this era of globalization, the Marxist/structuralist perspective on international politics remains an ongoing critique of the problems of a global free-market system. In an interesting twist, globalization provokes strong opposition among realists and Marxists alike. The realists reject globalization because, as mentioned above, it erodes national sovereignty. That is, the opening of national borders and markets diminishes the ways in which central governments traditionally exert power. The Marxists reject globalization because there appears to be no safe harbor for poor people in the free-market tsunami. The economic system being globalized is a wide-open liberal economic system; if states want to ride this wave to potential prosperity, they must disengage any "safety net" provisions designed to protect their poor and workers against the free market. Further, there is no countering force in globalization that will ensure a more equitable distribution of power in the system; thus globalization will only increase the structural power of the center at the expense of all others.

These worldviews don't focus on just different actors and issues but also on different levels of analysis. Realists are focused on the state—not on what's "in" the state but on relations between states based on differences in power. Thus realists study foreign policy at the system level—whether bilateral, regional, or global. Realists often conflate leaders and countries; for instance, a realist may examine the calculations of Egyptian president Gamal Abdel Nasser leading up to the 1967 war between Egypt and Israel, with reference to Nasser and Egypt as if they were one entity. A realist would never examine the personal beliefs of leaders—all leaders, like all countries, are the same: they all pursue the national interests (the protection of the state and its power) in a rational, strategic, calculating manner.

Liberals, being pluralists, focus on all the levels of analysis, depending on the subject of the study. Liberals borrow from comparative politics and look at the persons, groups, structures, cultures, and so on within a state that may lead it to take certain foreign policy stands. They may examine the workings of international organizations—which is a system-level international relations interest. Liberals also explore the interaction of nonstate actors across state boundaries. Or they may look at the belief sets or personalities of individuals who form the foreign policy elite.

Marxists look at foreign policy from the system and state levels. At the system level, the asymmetrical relations between states are important. At the state level, Marxists study the common interests of economic elites in one state with the elites in another. Or they study how military capitalist industrial interests push a state into war. Group politics is important to Marxists, so we can find such explanations of foreign policy posed at the state and system levels.

Constructivism

Is it true, as the realists say, that the world is a hostile place in which no other state can be trusted and every state must be constantly ready to prey or be preyed upon? Is anarchy a reality that states ignore at their own folly? If we start with realist assumptions about the world, we must go where the realists take us—to a self-help system in which violence is both natural and at times the preferred foreign policy instrument. If we change the starting assumptions, we can go to a differently constituted world. This idea has led scholars to use alternative grand theories to understand the world, such as liberalism and Marxism. Of course, all three world-views present starting assumptions that, if accepted, will lead us in certain intended directions.

There is an approach to understanding reality that, although not a grand theory per se, offers an alternative tool for analysis. This approach is called constructivism. Constructivists argue that there is no more or less objective social reality, but that reality is socially constructed from society's perceptions of it. Society projects a certain understanding of reality onto the world—such as the "reality" of anarchy—and from this identities and appropriate behaviors result. States/societies make the system anarchic and then the system they create makes the states self-interested and predatory by necessity. Constructivism can help us understand how certain views of the world have become predominant. But constructivism itself does not offer us an alternative vision of the world and so I choose to include it here as a tool rather than a worldview. Other scholars would disagree with this choice.

THE BRIDGE BETWEEN INTERNATIONAL
AND COMPARATIVE POLITICS

The study of foreign policy sits in the area of political science known as international politics, although you could say foreign policy sometimes jumps over the fence into comparative politics. As a "field" of study, foreign policy analysis is relatively new, coalescing more or less in the mid-1960s. There were, of course, scholars who studied foreign policy before this time, but their pursuit was one of many within the broader study of international politics.

The early study of foreign policy, like the study of international relations and comparative politics, reflected academic debates over the proper "ways of knowing" that dominated social science research in the 1950s and 1960s. Foreign policy study arose in this era as a bridge between international relations and comparative politics. To understand the construction of foreign policy study, we need to consider the development of international relations and comparative politics against real-world politics.

Prior to the twentieth century, Deborah Gerner explains,

> neither foreign policy nor international relations constituted a distinct field. Diplomatic history probably came the closest to what we now label as "foreign policy," and much of what we call international relations came under the rubric of international law, institutional analysis, or history.[27]

Although the post–World War I years marked the strong emergence of the idealist (liberal) worldview and witnessed tangible efforts to incorporate idealist notions into the newly established League of Nations, the study of international relations and foreign policy was dominated by realism. According to Gerner,

> For the study of foreign policy, this essentially meant the study of the international actions of individual state leaders—frequently monarchs—who were believed to have few constraints on their actions other than those imposed by the external situation.[28]

Real-world events, such as states' nationalistic responses to the Great Depression and the mobilization for World War II, reinforced the appropriateness of the IR (international relations) emphasis on political realism. Growing fascism on the European continent, as well as the entrenchment of Soviet-style communism, caused significant out-migration of political scholars. Many of these scholars made their way to the United States, bringing with them "new and often broader perspectives about international relations and foreign policy"[29] than typically had been found in American academic departments studying politics.

The study of comparative politics was established in the interwar period as a result of the same exodus of European scholars.[30] "Fascist Italy, Imperialist Japan, and Nazi Germany taught [these scholars] the dangers of mobilized masses from the extreme right end of the spectrum, while the politics of the Soviet Union taught them the dangers of mobilized masses from the left."[31] The new study of comparative politics was normative in its focus, exploring the development of "good" moderate participatory politics as found in the United States and some countries of Western Europe.[32]

In the post–World War II years, this new study of comparative politics coalesced around modernization theory (also called developmental economics), with its emphasis on state and economy building along the path of the Western model. In brief, this model proposed that all countries could develop into advanced industrialized countries with participatory democratic systems if they followed in the established footsteps of the United States and its Western friends. Moreover,

> as the Cold War emerged and deepened, the modernization/developmental model became the formula by which Western states, especially the United States, examined, judged, and intervened in developing states to protect them from the dangers of the mass politics of the left (communism) being exported by the Soviet Union.[33]

That is, the political cause and theoretical model that characterized the study of comparative politics was adopted with alacrity by Western policy makers as one of many tools to be used to fight the Cold War.

The politics of the day also influenced the broader study of politics, as Laura Neack, Jeanne Hey, and Patrick Haney explain,

> A principal strategy of the United States in the Cold War involved beating the Soviets through scientific advancements; academics were recruited to this cause. Federal funding for "scientific" research created a strong impetus among social scientists to become more "scientific" (and perhaps less "social" or "historical"). . . . This is also the era in which the majority of departments of politics or governments in the United States turned into departments of political science.[34]

International relations scholars joined this movement in political science, although Gerner tells us that those who focused on foreign policy were temporarily left behind:

> the fields of international relations and foreign policy, which had been intertwined, began to pull apart. International relations—or at least a significant subgroup of researchers represented after 1959 by the International Studies Association—became more scientific, with a goal of increasing knowledge through statistical tests and rational and dynamic modeling. Foreign policy theorists, however, were slower to adopt the behavioralist approach, and instead tended to continue in the classical tradition [derived from philosophy, history and law].[35]

As part of this positivist shift in international relations, a team of scholars produced two studies that proved critical to later foreign policy scholarship. In 1954 and 1963, Richard Snyder, H. W. Bruck, and Burton Sapin[36] presented a systematic decision-making framework in response to realism's privileging of national interest over human agency.[37] The emphasis for their framework was on decision makers:

> It is one of our basic methodological choices to define the state as its official decision makers—those whose authoritative acts are, to all intents and

purposes, the acts of the state. State action is the action taken by those acting in the name of the state.[38]

Snyder, Bruck, and Sapin rejected the realist notion that national leaders, regardless of individual differences, would make the same national interest-based foreign policy choices. Instead, they suggested that foreign policy choice derives from multiple sources, including the "biographies" of the individual decision makers as well as the organizational framework in which decisions are made. Snyder, Bruck, and Sapin pointed the way to studying foreign policy using multiple levels of analysis, a key theme of this book. Their work was taken up in James Rosenau's field-establishing work that appeared in the mid-1960s.

Charles Hermann and Gregory Peacock write, "If Snyder's framework invited scientific inquiry, Rosenau insisted upon it."[39] In his famous and foundational article, "Pre-Theories and Theories of Foreign Policy," James Rosenau sounded a clarion call to make the study of foreign policy into a science.[40] This is how Rosenau established the cause and scope of his call:

> To probe the "internal influences on external behavior" is to be active on one of the frontiers where the fields of international and comparative politics meet. Initial thoughts about the subject, however, are bound to be ambivalent; it would seem to have been both exhausted and neglected as a focus of inquiry. Even as it seems clear that everything worth saying about the subject has already been said, so does it also seem obvious that the heart of the matter has yet to be explored and that American political science is on the verge of major breakthroughs which will make exploration possible.[41]

Rosenau was frustrated because foreign policy study had remained behind the times and, without significant recasting, would fail to benefit from the "major breakthroughs" on the horizon.

> The nontheoretical state of foreign policy research is all the more perplexing when it is contrasted with developments elsewhere in American political science. In recent years the discipline has been transformed from an intuitive to a scientific enterprise, and consequently the inclination to develop models and test theories has become second nature to most political scientists.[42]

Foreign policy suffered, according to Rosenau, from the lack of a central theoretical framework (like realism in international relations) and the lack of a common methodology. He suggested that the common methodology be a commitment to comparative analysis, and that the central theory could be established through the subsequent efforts of scholars working within an agreed-upon framework. Rosenau offered his "pre-theory" framework—one in which he combined national attribute indicators to formulate "ideal nation-types." He hypothesized that factors at different levels of analysis might account for foreign policy differences that could be observed between these ideal nation-types. Using this "pre-theory," scholars could launch a systematic research program aimed at building a general body of theory that would, in time, define the scientific field of foreign policy. In response to Rosenau's call, a "self-conscious" field of foreign policy was begun by a more or less cohesive group of scholars whose collective efforts come under the heading of "Comparative Foreign Policy,"[43] or what Neack, Hey, and Haney call the "first generation" of foreign policy study.[44]

Real-world events in the late 1960s and into the 1970s again influenced the direction of international relations, comparative politics, and foreign policy study. By the mid-1960s, most of the world's colonies had become independent states, entering the United Nations as an emblem of their sovereign statehood. The countries of the "Third World" brought different issues to the United Nations and to discussions of world politics. They shifted the debate within the United Nations to issues of economic development, and in world politics oil exporters demonstrated a new kind of power when they withheld oil from the world market, causing the oil shocks of the 1970s. International relations scholars needed to develop frameworks for analyzing nonmilitary bases and definitions of power, as well as "find" a place for discussions of less-than-great power states. Further, the problems of Third-World countries were not primarily strategic or military, but also involved issues of economic development and dependency, as well as issues of state and nation building. International relations scholars had to develop more diverse theoretical and conceptual tools to study this altered reality.

Western and non-Western international relations scholars began exploring alternative theoretical frameworks to realism. Some scholars in the West resuscitated the old idealist school under a newer, more reality-based rubric of "complex interdependence," or "transnationalism."[45] Today, the umbrella category of liberalism is applied to various works in this tradition. Other scholars—in the West and especially from developing countries—proposed that the world should be understood in terms of the historical development of political and economic relations among states that has resulted in a world of "haves" and "have-nots." These scholars drew on Marxist understandings of politics. As these contending paradigms emerged in international relations to challenge the dominance of realism, so, too, was realism's insistence on positivist-behavioralist methodology challenged. By the end of the 1970s, more complex qualitative as well as quantitative research efforts were underway.

Similarly, the emphasis in comparative politics on modernization theory/developmental economics came under significant challenge. There were some early critics of modernization theory such as Raul Prebisch, head of the U.N. Economic Commission on Latin America (ECLA). Prebisch and ECLA proposed in the 1950s that economic development in the developing world—or, the periphery of the world economic system—would always be impeded by ever-declining terms of trade. That is, non-oil primary product exporters would keep falling behind because what they sold on the world market (coffee, rubber) would remain the same in price while what they bought on the world market (manufactured goods, petroleum products) would increase in price each year. Prebisch represented a Marxist variation called dependency theory, a theory with strong foundations in Latin America particularly and the broader developing world more generally. Although the dependency challenge to modernization theory was sounded in the 1950s, modernization theory remained dominant in comparative politics until the late 1960s and early 1970s. By this time, mainstream comparative politics had to make room for new voices and issues such as dependency theory.

Neack, Hey, and Haney describe the change in comparative politics in this time:

> Scholars from developing countries and Western "area specialists" who had rejected modernization theory were able to exploit the cracks in the crumbling modernization theory paradigm and assert the importance of studying complex domestic processes in comparative politics. . . . The study of domestic processes took a variety of forms in the 1970s, including the study of domestic class-based divisions caused by colonialism and perpetuated in post-independence dependent relations, political economy, state corporatism, and state-society relations. . . . The unifying feature of comparative politics from the 1970s onward was not a central theoretical core, but a central methodological agreement on the comparative method.[46]

Just as before, real-world political changes affecting international relations and comparative politics also affected the new field of comparative foreign policy. One result of the disequilibrium being felt in the fields of international relations and comparative politics was that divisions between the two were becoming less and less distinct. This was especially true in the case of political economy approaches to international and comparative politics. This blurring of divisions occurred precisely at the junction of these fields that foreign policy was supposed to bridge.

By the start of the 1980s, a variety of theoretical and methodological accountings from both international and comparative politics were adopted by foreign policy scholars. The impact of these accountings was evident in the growing number of contextualized, multilevel foreign policy analyses undertaken in the 1980s and into the early 1990s. This wave of scholarship has been called the "second generation" of foreign policy analysis by Neack, Hey, and Haney. A critical aspect of this second generation was the conscious choice by scholars to link their work to the major substantive concerns in foreign policy.

Second-generation foreign policy study reflected the complex issues of the times—the impact of the latest wave of democratization, the importance of the relative decline in U.S. economic power in the early to mid-1980s, the collapse of the Soviet empire and Soviet-style communism, the unprecedented international collaboration in the Persian Gulf War of 1991, and the December 1991 dissolution of the Soviet Union.

A NEW MILLENNIUM

The New Foreign Policy takes off from the second generation of foreign policy study, as the second generation was launched from the first. Just as the first and second generations reflected real-world politics, *The New Foreign Policy* reflects politics in this era of globalization. *The New Foreign Policy* is not necessarily a declaration of a third generation of foreign policy scholarship; instead, this book signals a refocusing of the rich research programs of the second generation on the politics of the new millennium.

The end of the last millennium and start of the new were marked by some monumental politics. From the mid-1990s until 2001, the American economy was in resurgence—a remarkable situation given relative American economic decline in the 1980s and a necessary boost to the world economy given the global economic downturn of the mid-to-late 1990s in Asia and Europe. The early 1990s saw another resurgence—in the use of the United Nations to address humanitarian crises and to promote human rights. In these tasks, the United Nations was not effective, doing little to stop genocide in Bosnia and Rwanda. As the 1990s wore on into the new millennium, the United Nations fell out of favor among some countries, and multilateral actions by groups such as the North Atlantic Treaty Organization (NATO) gained more favor. Still, some type of international response to conflict seemed in order with the outbreak of war and violence in the 1990s that only intensified into the 2000s. Refugee crises; HIV crises; sharp increases in illegal drug, human, and small arms trafficking—all these seem to have become the norm in this new era. Two countries pushed their way into the elite nuclear weapons club when India and Pakistan tested their own weapons in 1998. (A third attempted to do so less than a decade later when North Korea tested a low-yield nuclear device in 2006.) At the same time, the new era has not been without some significant advances in the promotion of democracy and protection of basic human rights. But the benefits of the new era have yet to be felt by all and have not been met by all with the same welcome and enthusiasm, as suggested by the frequency of Islamic fundamentalist attacks against U.S. military and diplomatic personnel in the late 1990s. The September 11, 2001, terrorist attacks against New York City and Washington, D.C., brought the dangers and frustrations of the new millennium home to the United States. Since then, interstate war has returned to center stage with the U.S.-led wars in Afghanistan and Iraq. Meanwhile, terrorist groups have responded to these wars with spectacular attacks in Indonesia, Spain, Saudi Arabia, and the United Kingdom, among other places.

Global politics in the new millennium include the following features that set the context for *The New Foreign Policy*. First, the American post–World War II grand strategy of building a liberal international trading order has succeeded. The economic and cultural currents that flow into and mold this order collectively can be called globalization. Yet, at the same time, the international system today is dominated by the single (hyper) power of the United States. This unipolarity itself might be the source of international instability (a topic considered in chapter 8), but certainly the Bush 2 administration's use of unilateralism and muscularity also have contributed to instability, backlash, and global insecurity. Second, globalization erodes the distinctions between domestic and foreign politics at the same time that it creates strong countercurrents among peoples attempting to assert their differences and their right to those differences. The example set by the United States in this period establishes the use of force as the norm rather than the exception in the pursuit of group goals. Those inclined to resist globalization take note of this example and modify their behaviors accordingly. Third, on a brighter side, democratization seems to be accompanying globalization into the new millennium. But, whereas democratization requires the protection of individual human rights, globalization gives governments an excuse to vacate their responsibilities to their citizens. Further, democratization can unleash dangerous demands on governments, many of which are inadequately prepared to manage the pace of globalization. Fourth, intrastate and interstate warfare as well as networked terrorism all are prominent and terrible features of the new landscape in the new millennium. *The New Foreign Policy* is intended as a guidebook for studying and considering state responses to globalization, global violence, and American overreach in the twenty-first century.

CHAPTER REVIEW

- "A Tangled Tale of Tibet" demonstrates how no policy issue is exclusively foreign or exclusively domestic in nature.

- "A Tangled Tale of Tibet" demonstrates, too, how state and nonstate actors try to build coalitions in support of their policy preferences, linking their issues with those of others.

- National leaders are said to play a two-level, dual, or nested game between the demands of the international system and those of domestic politics.

- The study of foreign policy is the study of both the statements or policies of decision makers as well as the behaviors or actions of states.

- The levels of analysis used in the study of foreign policy are the individual, state, and system levels. These are heuristic devices or tools that help us manage our subject matter. The levels of analysis also ask different questions of and provide different answers to foreign policy puzzles.

- The study of foreign policy is primarily situated in the field of international relations. International relations is dominated by three worldviews: realism, liberalism, and Marxism.

- Foreign policy is also a bridging discipline, taking lessons from both the study of international relations and the study of comparative politics.

2

✢

Rational Actors and the National Interests

IN THIS CHAPTER

- The Definition of "Leaders," Part One
- The Rational Actor Model
- Rationality, Deterrence, and "Irrationality"
- Poliheuristic Theory: A Bridge to the Next Chapter?
- Chapter Review

Cases Featured in This Chapter

- The strategic calculations made by Sudan, China, and the United States in their relations with one another, as played out in each country's policy on Darfur.
- Egyptian president Gamal Abdel Nasser's strategic calculations that led to the 1967 Arab-Israeli Six Days' War.
- The prisoners' dilemma and nuclear decision making.

THE DEFINITION OF "LEADERS," PART ONE

Here's another tangled foreign policy tale: In October 2007, China expressed anger toward the United States because the U.S. Congress (joined by the president) decided to give the Tibetan leader, the Dalai Lama, its highest civilian honor. Beijing was angry, but not so angry that it threatened to do anything of substance. Its displeasure might be used as leverage on

Washington for other and/or future foreign policy issues. For instance, China had been taking heat from nongovernmental organizations and the U.S. government for its unconditional backing of the Sudanese government. In the fall of 2007, Sudan, a key source of foreign oil for China, was dragging its feet rather than complying fully with U.N. Security Council resolutions regarding the violence and genocide in its Darfur region. So, too, was the Sudanese government not fully complying with a peace agreement with former southern rebels that had ended a decades-long civil war. One sticking point in that peace agreement was the control of rich oil fields. The U.S. government had been leaning on China to do more to bring its friend Khartoum in line with the international agreements. Washington was not leaning too hard on China, one may suspect, given how much U.S. public debt was owned by China. One may suspect, too, that Beijing was not leaning too hard on Khartoum because of China's reliance on Sudan's oil. This tangled tale made the U.S. president's involvement in awarding the Dalai Lama the Congressional Gold Medal somewhat curious. One may wonder about the calculations the White House was making regarding longer-term relations with China.

The foreign policy analyst looking for a research problem would find the previous paragraph packed with possibilities. For the purposes of this chapter, let's consider the state players named in the tale—China or Beijing, the United States or Washington, Sudan or Khartoum. It is common in the popular media and academic writings to switch the names of countries for the names of capitals and even for the names of current leaders. This usage implies that states speak with one voice in international affairs. This usage also portrays states almost as individuals making decisions that take into account how other states/individuals will react and calculating how to leverage long-term advantage from other states. This is the "stuff" of our first individual-level approach to studying foreign policy—the rational actor model.

Before going further, it is important to indicate what our point of reference is here. That this is the first of three chapters on the individual level of analysis tells us that our focus is on individual leaders who make decisions on behalf of their countries. In this chapter, though, we explore a model that intentionally ignores the particular characteristics of individuals in favor of the study of national leaders pursuing national interests. (Alternatively, the following two chapters intentionally focus on the characteristics of individuals in leadership roles.) What is meant by the term "leader?" The easiest definition is the chief executive of the country: Sudanese president Omar al-Bashir, Chinese president Hu Jintao, U.S. president George W. Bush. The slightly broader term "leadership" refers to the group of top decision makers—a cabinet, an administration, a junta, or some other central decision-making body.

In this and the next two chapters, we will focus on national leaders (whether as individuals or not) and not on individuals who do not represent states. Thus it would be appropriate to examine George W. Bush (Bush 2) here but not Osama bin Laden, although the two became irrevocably linked by the events of September 11, 2001. Bin Laden is not a national decision maker, and so he is placed in the category of "nonstate" actors. In chapter 10, we explore the impact of nonstate actors—such as bin Laden and the al Qaeda terrorist network—on the foreign policies of states.

Another concept used interchangeably with "leadership" is "regime." "Regime" is defined as "the group that controls the central political structures of a national government."[1] The concept of a regime is flexible in that it is used to incorporate single leaders as well as different configurations of leadership groups. Sometimes the word regime is used to denote some kind of authoritarian leadership or "bad" government, but this use of the word is not definitional. It is commonplace for the leaders of country A who dislike the leaders of country B to call B's leadership a regime and imply that it is thus somehow illegitimate. However, democratically elected leadership also can be referred to as a regime if we stick with the objective definition of the term.

THE RATIONAL ACTOR MODEL

The rational actor approach to studying individuals in foreign policy making actually is not about studying individuals at all. This approach derives directly from the realist worldview that conceptualizes a state as a unitary actor. In international politics, by this view, states are only distinguishable by the relative power they hold, and not by their internal characteristics. Thus government type, history, economics, and the qualities of the individuals holding political leadership positions hold no importance in and of themselves to the analyst. The decisions taken by the leaders of the state are seen as the decisions of the state. This conflating of leader and state is possible because of a key assumption that realists make about leaders: any and all leaders act in ways consistent with the long-term and persistent national interests of the country. Since the national interests do not change, changes in leadership have little consequence.

The clearest statement regarding leaders and national interest and the study of foreign policy comes from Hans Morgenthau, one of the most significant post–World War II international scholars in the realist tradition. In the statement below, note how the assumption binding leaders and national interests creates a simple model for the analyst to employ:

> We assume that statesmen think and act in terms of interest defined as power, and the evidence of history bears that assumption out. That assumption

allows us to retrace and anticipate, as it were, the steps a statesman—past, present or future—has taken or will take on the political scene. We look over his shoulder when he writes his dispatches; we listen in on his conversation with other statesmen; we read and anticipate his very thoughts. Thinking in terms of interest defined as power, we think as he does, and as disinterested observers, we understand his thoughts and actions perhaps better than he, the actor on the political scene, does himself.

The concept of national interest defined as power imposes intellectual discipline upon the observer, infuses rational order into the subject matter of politics, and thus makes the theoretical understanding of politics possible. On the side of the actor, it provides for rational discipline in action and creates that astounding continuity in foreign policy which makes American, British, or Russian foreign policy appear as an intelligible, rational continuum, by and large consistent with itself, regardless of the different motives, preferences, and intellectual and moral qualities of successive statesmen. A realist theory of international politics, then, will guard against two popular fallacies: the concern with motives and the concern with ideological preferences.[2]

The "concern for motives" or "ideological preferences" entails examining the characteristics of individuals or groups of individuals, or even examining the political dynamics within a country, pursuits that have no merit in the realist, rational choice view. Morgenthau does allow that, in rare cases, psychological disorders in an individual or the emotions of mass democratic politics may cause leaders to make decisions that are out of line with national interests. Morgenthau might warn that when studying most foreign policy decisions, follow the old advice given to fledgling doctors in medical school: When you hear hoof beats, think horses, not zebras. When you see a foreign policy decision, think rational decision making and national interests, not idiosyncrasy. The standard expectation is the one upon which to base your diagnosis or explanation.

How can rational choice theorists make the assumption that individual differences are insignificant when studying foreign policy decision making? Michael McGinnis is a rational choice adherent who eschews the use of the word "individual" in favor of "regime" precisely because "regime" takes our focus away from personalities. McGinnis explains:

Any individual who attains a position of major foreign policy responsibility will have been socialized through education and processes of political selection to pursue some set of common goals. Individuals differ in their perception of the national interest but role expectations reinforce a sense of common interests.[3]

For McGinnis, political culture and socialization matter, but not in a way that requires the study of such. Instead, culture and socialization produce regularities among the individuals who rise to national office, eliminating individual differences and any need to study those differences. Further, McGinnis's working assumption is that

> changes in foreign policy goals attributed to changes in individual leaders or ruling coalitions can be interpreted as random (but not necessarily insignificant) fluctuations around a common "regime interest," which is based on domestic support structures and geopolitical concerns which act as the primary sources of continuity in foreign policy interests.[4]

"Regime interest" can be read here as "national interests" (although at the end of this chapter, this claim will be revisited). The term "national interests" can be and has been used expansively by leaders seeking to justify various policies, but in the realist framework national interests refer to persistent, long-term values associated with the entire country and identifiable over the course of the country's history. These interests do not change, although the means for pursuing them may. George Kennan, the former U.S. diplomat who famously warned about Soviet expansionism, explained that long-term national interests include ensuring the "military security" of the country, the "integrity of its political life, and the well-being of its people."[5]

In promoting and protecting the national interests, the regime or leadership operates as a rational actor. The rational actor model has its roots in basic decision-making theory. Decision making is defined as the "act of choosing among available alternatives about which uncertainty exists."[6] One of the first systematic discussions of the decision-making model was offered by Richard Snyder, H. W. Bruck, and Burton Sapin in 1954.[7] In their "general decision-making model," they set out the following details: Since states are unitary actors, the decisions and actions of the ultimate decision makers can be considered the same as the decisions and actions of the state. Since all states are said to pursue national interests, all states make decisions in the same way. State decision making can be portrayed as a process in which the ultimate decision makers examine the internal and external environments, define the situation at hand, consider alternate courses of action, and then select the course of action that is best suited to the pursuit of national interests. The actions are considered "planful," that is, the result of strategic problem solving and are embedded in an action-reaction interaction.

This decision-making model has often been imagined as a "black box." We cannot see inside the box and have no need to, since all black boxes (countries/regimes/leaders) work the same way. "In modern decision theory, the rational decision problem is reduced to a simple matter of selecting among a set of given alternatives, each of which has a given set of consequences: the agent selects the alternative whose consequences are preferred in terms of the agent's utility function which ranks each set of consequences in order of preference."[8] In other words, information about the problem at hand, possible courses of action, possible reactions, and estimates of success for the different courses of action are fed into the box. Inside the box, a basic economic utility calculation is made: which choice of action best maximizes national goals and minimizes costs? A decision then results—or comes out of the box. The environment reacts to the decision/action, and the reaction becomes part of a new set of factors that are fed into the box again.

Of course, decision makers do not live in a perfect world and so do not have before them all the relevant information upon which to make the best decision. Given the imperfect nature of the available information, leaders make the best possible choice or even select the first option that satisfies the minimal requirements of a good choice. The rational actor model does not require perfect information, but recognizes instead that "rationality refers to consistent, value-maximizing choice within specific constraints."[9] Herbert Simon called this "bounded rationality," or rational decision making within human limitations.[10]

In terms of the daily affairs of state, "bounded rationality" may not be a major detriment to solid decision making since leaders have a chance to reconsider their choices in light of the steady flow of feedback. This feedback qualifies the next choices to be made—feedback or the reaction of other actors can even be anticipated and possible reactions planned in advance of events. The interactive nature of decision making (where country A's choices are dependent on country B's choices and vice versa) is explored in game theory, an issue we'll take up shortly.

Rationality is not just bounded by the limitations of humans as decision makers but by the environment in which multiple other actors are present and acting. How does the decision maker anticipate what other actors might do? This realist foundation of the rational actor model contains assumptions about the environment and other actors that help decision makers keep their focus. As already noted, realists assume that all states are unitary actors who make cost-benefit calculations about alternative courses of action. *All* states make such calculations and *all* states are motivated to promote and secure their interests through the acquisition and use of power. States act, furthermore, in an international environment characterized by anarchy, or the lack of an overarching legal authority. Although some realists conceptualize states as power-driven and aggressive, others explain that it is the anarchic nature of international politics that requires states to make choices that are power-driven. Graham Allison and Philip Zelikow say that this is the basic difference between classical realists and neorealists.[11]

Whether one starts with the view that all states are motivated to arm themselves and acquire more power (classical realism) or that states must arm themselves because the international environment requires it (neorealism), all realists see states locked in an unavoidable situation called a security dilemma. Glenn Snyder explains the security dilemma in this way:

> The term is generally used to denote the self-defeating aspect of the quest for security in an anarchic system. The theory says that even when no state has any desire to attack others, none can be sure that others' intentions are peaceful, or will remain so; hence each must accumulate power for defense. Since no state can know that the power accumulation of others is defensively motivated only, each must assume that it might be intended for attack. Consequently, each party's power increments are matched by the others, and all wind up with no more security than when the vicious cycle began, along with the costs incurred in having acquired and having to maintain their power.[12]

Because of anarchy, states are motivated to amass power and rely upon only themselves for protection. Because all states are so motivated and thus are locked into action-reaction cycles, conflict is the distinguishing characteristic of international politics. The rational actor constantly seeks to increase its power in reaction to these "realities." Because the rational actor is engaged in a game of many iterations (or steps), the rational actor may seek short-term gains through risky foreign policy behavior in order to secure long-term goals and power. For many realists, no state should be content with the status quo given the dynamics of international politics. But discontent with the status quo drives states into unending security dilemmas that can only be "won" through short-term gains. Decision making in such circumstances can be understood as choosing between less-than-optimal alternatives and settling for the best of the worst, rather than the best of the best as envisioned by the rational actor model. This will be taken up again when we discuss nuclear deterrence and the prisoners' dilemma.

An example is in order here to demonstrate the kind of analysis produced by reliance on the rational actor model. Ben Mor sets out to understand the strategic calculations made by Egyptian president Gamal Abdel Nasser that resulted in the critical 1967 war with Israel—a war that Nasser had wanted to avoid.[13] Gamal Abdel Nasser was president of Egypt from 1954 to 1970. Egypt had been a primary enemy of Israel since it became a state in 1948. Nasser—portrayed by Mor as a rational actor and strategic thinker—had two primary goals: establish Egypt as the clear leader of the Arab states, and restore the displaced Palestinians to lands taken over by Zionists (i.e., Israel). In 1956, the Egyptian leader sought to nationalize the Suez Canal for purposes of prestige and economic power. The canal, opened in 1865, had been built by the British and operated by the British and French. It became the principal maritime route between the Mediterranean Sea and Indian Ocean, via the Red Sea. Nasser did succeed in nationalizing the Suez Canal, but only after a war with Israel in which Israel—with the collusion of the British and French—managed to quickly capture the Sinai Peninsula. The end of the 1956 war saw the placement of the first official United Nations peacekeeping operation, the United Nations Emergency Force (UNEF). The purpose of UNEF was to keep peace in the Sinai by maintaining a cease-fire between Egypt and Israel while maintaining the prewar borders of each state. Despite the recovery of the Suez Canal, the quick Egyptian losses and the agreement to allow foreign (UN) troops to be stationed on Egyptian soil were great humiliations to Nasser and Egypt.[14]

According to Mor, Nasser wanted to undo the humiliations of 1956 and regain Egyptian leadership in the Arab world especially vis-à-vis the Israeli problem without having to engage Israel in a war. Toward these goals, Nasser undertook a series of steps in May 1967—steps that could be interpreted as clearly power-seeking and thus provocative. First, Nasser ordered the Egyptian army into the Sinai Peninsula. Second, he ordered UNEF to withdraw from the Sinai.[15] Third, he ordered the blockading of the Straits of Tiran. The Straits of Tiran sit at the end of the Sinai Peninsula where the Gulf of Aqaba meets the Red Sea, roughly parallel to the Gulf of Suez. Blocking the Straits of Tiran effectively cut Israel off from direct access to the Red Sea via the Gulf of Aqaba. Israeli leaders—famous for their use of "red lines" establishing permissible ranges of action by their enemies—already had stated that any closing or attempted closing of the Straits would be considered an act of war. When Nasser ordered the blockade, Israel did nothing in immediate response. Nasser then signed a defense pact with Jordan on May 30. Having seen enough and with its own security and power on the line, Israel launched an attack on Egypt on June 6, beginning the Six Days' War.

Mor's interest, as stated above, was to understand why Nasser appeared to take steps that provoked Israel into war with Egypt, when war was the one thing that Nasser wanted to avoid the most. Using a rational choice model, Mor details the calculations Nasser made along the way, some of which will be explored below. These calculations need to be understood in the context of some key assumptions that Mor ascribes to Nasser. The first assumption was that Israel was a status quo country—that is, Israel benefited from the status quo and would not take steps to undo it. Second, and related to the first, Nasser assumed that Israel would not engage in a war in which it would be perceived as the initiator by the international community.

With these two starting assumptions, Nasser calculated that he had considerable room for movement vis-à-vis Israel. Nasser employed an escalation-de-escalation strategy involving a series of moves; Nasser would make a move and then await the Israelis' reaction. As long as the Israelis made no countermove such as issuing a warning, initiating diplomatic discussions, or mobilizing troops, Nasser was free to continue with the next step. As soon as the Israelis signaled that Egypt had approached a "red line," Nasser would order a de-escalation.

Mor concludes that Nasser's decision making was rational, given the limits of information available to him. This follows Simon's idea of bounded rationality. Critical to Mor's rational actor analysis, the external environment—Israel and other interested international actors—failed to provide Nasser with the feedback necessary for sound decision making. Nasser approached and crossed a "red line" but did not know this until Egypt was under military attack. The failure, then, according to Mor, was not that Nasser's decision making itself was faulty but that he lacked important information on which to calculate his next move.[16] Of course, one could argue that Nasser failed as a rational actor to account for the possibility that it was not in Israel's interests to provide feedback in the expected form, but Mor does not address this possibility. Nor can the rational actor analysis Mor employs—which only seems to take into account a two-player game—accommodate the fact that other players were active in this game. When Egypt blocked the Straits of Tiran, the Israeli policy makers were inclined to give an immediate response, but U.S. president Lyndon Johnson asked them to wait forty-eight hours while Johnson explored an international response to Nasser's activities.[17]

Although Mor tells us that Nasser's provocations were calculated moves that were not intended to lead Egypt to war with Israel, war is not necessarily seen as a negative point along the calculated path of the rational actor. Media analyses of international events tend to privilege accounts in which conflict is seen as an acceptable short-term position on the road to larger relative gains. For example, in a *New York Times* report over failing peace talks between the Israelis and Palestinians in September 2000, Deborah Sontag considers why Palestinian leader Yasser Arafat would take an unyielding negotiating stance on the disposition of Haram al Sharif (the Temple Mount to Israelis). Such an unrelenting stance gave Israeli prime minister Ehud Barak little room to maneuver, virtually guaranteeing continued conflict between the two sides. Arafat was willing to take this risk, suggests Sontag, because it served longer-term Palestinian interests. "Some Palestinian experts say Mr. Arafat thinks it less risky to protract the conflict than to seal a deal that would be perceived as selling out not just Palestinian, but also Arab and Muslim rights."[18] By this account, protracted conflict between Israelis and Palestinians was an acceptable cost on the way to obtaining a goal more important to Arafat than peace with Israel.

Similarly, in a news report with the curious title, "Attack on Iraq May Be Outcome Hussein Wants," Robin Wright considers the calculations of Iraqi leader Saddam Hussein in January 1998. According to Wright,

> After seven years of diplomatic battles with the United States, Iraqi President Saddam Hussein may actually welcome a major military assault, say analysts in the US and diplomats from allied countries.
>
> The Iraqi leader, they say, apparently sees a military showdown as a catalyst for settling a critical question: whether international sanctions, which have cost Baghdad $100 billion in lost oil revenues since 1990, will be lifted as long as he remains in power.[19]

Wright reports that the Iraqi leader might have been willing to incur military strikes in the short term on the assumption that such strikes by the United States would lead to international condemnation of America and international sympathy for Iraq. Ultimately, the United States would look like a bully and the sanctions on Iraq would be lifted, while Hussein stayed in power. Although the wisdom of such a calculation can be (and has been) debated, what is important for us is the clear presence of the rational choice model in these reports by political analysts. Whenever you read that conflict "serves" a purpose, try to discern the calculations that surround the steps in pursuit of that interest.

Returning briefly to the "Tangled Tale of Tibet" discussed in chapter 1, note that both the Bush 1 and Clinton administrations drew criticism for not linking issues of human rights to issues of trade in their China policies. Ultimately, the defense each administration gave for its China policy was one that suggested many calculated moves on the way to a long-term goal. Engagement with China would not only promote the short-term interests of American business and farm groups but also would integrate China into the world community. As this integration occurred, and as American business interests penetrated China, China would move toward greater opening both in terms of its relations with foreign partners and at home. Ultimately, down the road several years, the human rights situation in China would improve as China started to conform to the behavioral expectations of the United States and the international community. That is, the United States could gain power over China in the long run in economic and political terms, as American interests penetrated the Chinese market and American political ideas penetrated the Chinese polity. China would be bound by its economic interdependence with the world economy, and it would have to curb its internal and external negative behaviors or risk considerable economic loss. These calculations by two American presidents of different political parties demonstrate the realist proposition that particular leadership does not matter; what matters is the long-term, persistent, rational pursuit of national interests.

RATIONALITY, DETERRENCE, AND "IRRATIONALITY"

Realism, with its emphasis on rational choice, was the dominant grand theory of international relations throughout much of the twentieth century. Its dominance was at its peak at the close of World War II and the start of the Cold War. Realism dictated that the United States needed to pursue greater military might than the Soviet Union—indeed, the United States needed to pursue global domination—lest the world be dominated by the Soviet Union.

As the Cold War deepened and both the Americans and Soviets developed massive nuclear weapons capabilities, the Americans and Soviets achieved a balance of nuclear power that former British prime minister Winston Churchill called a "balance of terror." This balance was struck on the assumption that the nuclear arsenals of both sides were sufficient to ensure that an attack by either would be met with an unacceptable nuclear response. Thus, policy makers and some realist scholars began to reassess the role nuclear weapons played in the pursuit of power and security in international anarchy. The rational choice of any leader confronting a nuclear foe was to avoid any action that might be punishable with a nuclear reaction/retaliation.

In situations where both parties to a conflict held nuclear weapons, both were said to understand that aggression by either would likely result in unacceptable costs for both. Each side, then, was deterred and the situation was one of mutual, "mature," or stable nuclear deterrence. Taken further, when both sides held sufficient nuclear weapons that a nuclear attack initiated by either side could be absorbed by the target and then matched with an equally punishing counterattack (that is, both sides possessed what is called second strike capability), the awareness of the likelihood of mutual assured destruction (MAD) would deter both from provocative, directly confrontational acts toward the other.

Given the understood costs of a nuclear war (in terms of immediate destruction and the long-term aftermath), rational leaders would not entertain the idea of using nuclear weapons in a conflict. Realists proposed that nuclear weapons were not for fighting a war, but for deterring a war. Indeed, Kenneth Waltz declared that a world of nuclear armed states would be a more stable and peaceful one given nuclear deterrence.[20] However, recent history provides us with at least one example of a leader who was willing to think the unthinkable—use nuclear weapons—in the name of protecting national interests (a realist pursuit). Former U.S. president Ronald Reagan was a committed realist in his approach to foreign affairs, yet Reagan was also committed to the development of a strategy and capability for fighting and winning a nuclear war. He was not convinced that a nuclear "holocaust" was inevitable if either side in the Cold War initiated war with the other. Instead, Reagan urged his military strategists to think about what the United States needed in order to engage the Soviet Union in nuclear war and win. The strategic defense initiative was seen as one tool to use for potentially winning a nuclear war. There is no way to understand the Reagan desire for a winnable nuclear war fighting strategy outside a realist framework. Yet, nuclear deterrence—a concept that requires *rational* leaders to understand that the cost of using nuclear weapons is greater than any expected gains from such use—is a concept that comes straight from the realist framework as well.

For Reagan, "winning" the ultimate game between the United States and Soviet Union meant considering how to use nuclear weapons not as threats, but as weapons. This is but one contradiction in the realist/rational choice framework. There are other paths by which we can encounter problems inherent to the rational actor model and nuclear deterrence, paths that also derive from realism. We will examine two of these. The first involves the use of game theory to demonstrate that "rational decisions" are made by humans who may choose very destructive courses of action. The second takes us back to an old realist assumption: states will seek to dominate if at all possible.

The assumption that actors are rational decision makers is critical to a line of realist-based research called game theory. Game theory borrows from mathematical reasoning and the formal study of logic in order to develop mathematical models of the strategies adopted in the "games" of foreign policy, such as crisis and noncrisis negotiations, alliance formation, and arms racing. In the following explanation of game theory from James Dougherty and Robert Pfaltzgraff, we can see the rational actor model inserted into an interactive relationship:

> Game theorists say . . . : If people in a certain situation wish to win—that is, to accomplish an objective that the other party seeks to deny them—we can sort out the intellectual processes by which they calculate or reach decisions concerning what kind of action is most likely to be advantageous to them, assuming they believe their opponents also to be rational calculators like themselves, equally interested in second-guessing and trying to outwit the opponent.[21]

All games contain common features: every player seeks to "win," certain rules govern the behavior of players in the game (with the primary rules privileging cost-benefit analyses and self-interest), players perceive that different moves are associated with different rewards or pay-offs, and all the choices made in the game are interactive. Some games are said to be zero-sum in that when one player wins, the other loses. Zero-sum games reflect the most distilled version of realism: when your country increases its power, it is only because my country has lost power. In other games, the results are non-zero sum, or mixed, in that players can register relative wins or gains over other players, reflecting the more sophisticated recent discussions of realism.

One of the most frequently discussed mixed-motives games is that of the prisoners' dilemma. In this game, players attempt to "win," but the interactive choices they make leave each in a position of achieving only the best of the worst situation, rather than the best possible situation. It is important to note here that all the basic realist assumptions are in place: actors are self-interested or selfish, actors have no reason to trust other actors because there is no ultimate authority to enforce justice, and actors are presented choices that involve limited information on different alternatives and their consequences. Karen Mingst describes the standard setup of this game:

> The prisoners' dilemma is the story of two prisoners, each being interrogated separately for an alleged crime. The interrogator tells each prisoner that if one of them confesses and the other does not, the one who confessed will go free and the one who kept silent will get a long prison term. If both confess, both will get somewhat reduced prison terms. If neither confesses, both will receive short prison terms based on lack of evidence.[22]

Faced with this dilemma, and working on realist assumptions, both prisoners confess. Or, to put it another way, both confess because each assumes that the other—acting in self-interest only—will confess. Although neither "wins" by being set completely free, neither "loses" to the other by drawing the harsher penalty. The prisoners don't achieve the best solution—no jail time—but they achieve the best of the worst—a shorter sentence and parity. Parity—ending up in the same bad situation with one's opponent, even in terms of mutual punishment—is preferred over sacrifice in a realist, self-help system.

The prisoners' dilemma illustrates the most fundamental realist problem: because no action is made in a vacuum but instead is part of a series of interactions with other actors, actors rarely can obtain ultimate security or freedom or superiority or whatever they seek to achieve over other actors. Instead, actors can only hope to obtain relative security or freedom or superiority, and so forth. In the realist model, actors acknowledge this reality but still make choices that would, only under ideal circumstances, earn them the best possible result.

This dilemma can be taken further with far worse results. Akin to the prisoners' dilemma is the realist security dilemma. As we've seen, the security dilemma is the result of choices a state makes to secure itself against usually unspecified but predictable outside threats. Although the initial step is only taken in self-defense, other states perceive it with suspicion and fear, and, due to the logic of anarchy, they must react to it. A cycle of action-reaction results. Ultimately, the states caught in this cycle find their environment to be more dangerous and more threatening than ever. To return to the first actor, the initial moves it made to increase its security have served only to lessen its overall security—and the security of others as well—thus the state is trapped in a dilemma. Realists acknowledge that this dilemma is real and unfortunate but also as inevitable as conflict in the international system.

We can use the prisoners' dilemma framework to consider the use of nuclear weapons. Nuclear deterrence tells us that each side recognizes that it is more rational not to initiate an attack with nuclear weapons because of the expected result—a counter nuclear attack. But in competitive relationships (as always exist in the realist world), "winning" (dominating the opponent) is the best possible result and "losing" is the worst. In between is "breaking even" with one's competitor. Using the basic prisoners' dilemma setup, the rational choice of either side is to attack the other side first. If you attack first and your opponent does nothing, you win. But, since your opponent is also a rational actor (as all states are) it also has decided to pursue a "win" and it attacks. Both sides attack and both sides suffer nuclear war, but break even with the other. The best possible solution is not possible; the best of the worst—mutual war, even mutual nuclear war—is both possible and rational.

Robert Jervis, one of the leading early scholars in the cognitive school to which we turn in chapter 3, proposes that deterrence theory is dangerous because decision makers and scholars misperceive the "rationality" of others. Jervis authored a number of articles and books in which he presents a number of important misperceptions made by decision makers. For example, Jervis hypothesizes that "actors tend to overlook the fact that evidence consistent with their theories may also be consistent with other views."[23] One "partner" in a relationship premised on stable nuclear deterrence might accept the "fact" of mutual assured destruction (MAD), and may assume that the other "partner" also accepts this rational "fact." But what if the second partner believes, as Ronald Reagan did, that MAD was not inevitable and that a nuclear war could possibly be won? The actor who believes that MAD is incontrovertible and who bases decisions on this could be confused and alarmed by the "inconsistent" behaviors of the other partner—or, at the very worst, this actor could be destroyed by the opponent who was looking at the "facts" and drawing very different conclusions all along.

As another example, Jervis hypothesizes that it may be very difficult for an actor to understand that the other actor is "playing an entirely different game."[24] During the Cold War, the Soviet Union and the United States seemed at times to be "playing" the nuclear "game" with very different rules. The Soviets had a policy of "no first use" of nuclear weapons. Soviet leaders announced that they would not be the first to introduce nuclear weapons into any conflict, but once such weapons were introduced by others, the Soviets would use them to the fullest and maximum extent. American leaders refused to make a pledge of no first use. Instead, American leaders retained the right to use nuclear weapons as needed, but they pledged to use those weapons in a limited, rational manner, deescalating to conventional weapons as the situation allowed. Both sides assumed that the other would appreciate and conform to the other's expectations and rules—but what guarantees were there that this would happen? Who would yield to the other's rules? When? There was within the view of each side a certain rationality, yet on a battlefield the failure to understand that two different rationalities were at play could have resulted in nuclear holocaust.

POLIHEURISTIC THEORY:
A BRIDGE TO THE NEXT CHAPTER?

The systematic study of perceptions and misperceptions is part of the cognitive approach to understanding why individuals decide what they decide. This approach is the topic of the next chapter. Typically, foreign policy scholars explain that the rational actor model and the cognitive model are incompatible approaches. This is the position taken in this book. Some scholars have argued that the approaches are not necessarily incompatible, but only focus on different subjects. As Jerel Rosati explains, "Those who emphasize rationality tend to focus on 'preferences' and 'outcomes,' while cognitive perspectives tend to focus on 'beliefs' and 'process,' as well as where 'preferences come from' and 'how preferences are established' among policymakers."[25] Of course, the reason why rational actor scholars focus on "preferences" and "outcomes" is because they believe they understand the "process" in decision making: inputs, cost-benefit calculation, outputs, feedback, and so on. To return to the ideas of Morgenthau presented at the start of this chapter: when you see a foreign policy decision, think rational choice. The decision to focus on outcomes versus process results from a bias that says process is not important.

A relatively new approach to studying foreign policy at the individual level also contends that the rational actor and cognitive approaches are not incompatible and takes the position that process is important. This approach, one that is firmly at home in the rational actor school, is called the "poliheuristic theory" (PH). A "heuristic" is a guide or a method or a problem-solving technique. Another way to think about a heuristic is to consider it an approach to understanding a subject matter. Thus, rational choice is an approach or heuristic; cognition is an approach or a heuristic. The PH theory proposes that a better way to understand decision making is to use both rational choice and cognition (thus the "poli" and the "heuristic").

Scholars who use the PH theory explain that all decisions involve a two-step decision process. In the first step, leaders "simplify the decision problem by the use of cognitive short-cuts." These shortcuts involve discarding some alternatives outright.[26] What helps decision makers discard some alternatives in this first step? Alex Mintz, David Brulé, and others in this research program explain that domestic political survival is always the guiding principle. Thus, faced with a foreign policy problem, leaders rule out any course of action that might have bad consequences for them in domestic politics.[27] Then, the remaining alternatives are evaluated in the second step of the decision process by using the "analytical calculations" of rational choice.[28] PH scholars contend that this process describes the decision making of leaders "regardless of their nationality or ideological position" and regardless of the type of government they lead.[29]

As we will see in the next chapter, this use of the term "cognitive short-cuts" is not in line with standard usage. Indeed, rather than combine rational choice and cognition in a two-step process, the PH scholars just change our focus from national interests to regime interests and borrow the idea of "shortcuts" from cognitive scholars (the next chapter explains the idea of cognitive shortcuts). That is, the PH theory says that instead of selecting among alternative foreign policy actions that serve the national interests, decision makers select among foreign policy actions that serve their own domestic political needs, or that help them survive. The promotion and protection of interests is still what drives decision makers in this theory whether in the first step or the second. Rational calculations about domestic political survival drive the first step (the discarding of unacceptable courses of action), and then rational calculations are made in the second step.

The PH theory does not bridge the gap between theories of the rational actor and individual cognition, but it does provide an example of how scholarship works to continually refine our understandings of our subject matter.

CHAPTER REVIEW

- The rational actor model is derived from the realist worldview.

- The rational actor model assumes that all leaders are motivated to preserve the long-term national interests, thus individual differences between leaders are insignificant.

- The rational actor model assumes that all state-level differences are insignificant as well.

- Rational decision making is understood to be bound by limited information and time.

- Rational choice assumptions underscore the notion of stable nuclear deterrence.

- The poliheuristic theory posits that decision making is a two-step process involving "cognitive shortcuts" and rational choice.

3

Cognitive Misers and Distrusting Leaders

IN THIS CHAPTER

- The Definition of "Leaders," Part Two
- Cognition: A Different View of Rationality
- Belief Sets and Cognitive Structure
- Operational Code
- Personality
- Chapter Review

Cases Featured in This Chapter

- The worldviews of British prime ministers Neville Chamberlain and Tony Blair and how these contributed to each man's view of alliances and wars.
- Mikhail Gorbachev's decision to view the breakup of the Soviet bloc as a nonthreatening event.
- Israeli prime minister Ariel Sharon's use of the Munich analogy in the events leading up to the 2003 U.S.-led invasion of Iraq.
- Egyptian president Anwar Sadat's operational code and its implications for the 1973 Arab-Israeli War and the 1978 peace accord with Israel.

THE DEFINITION OF "LEADERS," PART TWO

Former British prime minister Tony Blair was a committed partner to the U.S. president in the lead-up to the invasion of Iraq in March 2003. Although the United Kingdom and the United States have what is called a "special relationship" or partnership, Blair's ardent support for the Iraq war was not seen as an outcome of this relationship but instead a product of Blair's personal worldview. "Reflecting upon the decision to attack Iraq, a senior British cabinet minister commented that 'had anyone else been leader, we would not have fought alongside Bush.'"[1] Stephen Dyson recounts that Blair had opportunities to step away from Bush's war plans, especially in the face of growing public opposition to the war in Britain, but Blair remained steadfast. Dyson concludes that Britain's participation in the Iraq war can be understood by assessing Blair's personality traits, traits that predisposed him to take Britain firmly and resolutely into the war.[2]

An earlier, much-maligned British prime minister has become synonymous with the word "appeaser," but Neville Chamberlain's position in history perhaps should be recast to highlight how his strong negative beliefs about the Soviet Union took Britain to war without the help of a potentially powerful ally. In the months before the United Kingdom declared war on Germany, British and Soviet officials had been involved in negotiations about forming a military alliance against Germany. Politicians from across the British political spectrum, including Winston Churchill, put aside their own "political and ideological hatred" toward the Soviet Union to urge Chamberlain to make an alliance for the sake of British national security interests.[3] Yet, as Louise Grace Shaw describes, Chamberlain was never willing to put aside his ideological animosity and political suspicion of the Soviet Union. Indeed, he deliberately tried to prevent ministers from putting aside their own hostility toward Moscow by withholding important information. Finally, he devised a plan to ensure Britain would not be wholly committed to the Soviet Union in the event of war and by doing so he destroyed the last chance for a mutually acceptable peace.[4]

Both of these examples—Tony Blair predisposed to go to war, Neville Chamberlain willing to go to war without a key ally because of his strong negative beliefs about that potential ally—suggest that "rational" cost-benefit calculations were not at play. According to one insider in the Bush 2 administration, no cost-benefit calculation about the 2003 Iraq invasion and war occurred there, either. Richard Haas, the former director of planning in the State Department, said that the decision to go to war "was an accretion, a tipping point. . . . A decision was not made—a decision happened, and you can't say when or how."[5] To understand why these leaders made the choices they did (or the choices they fell into), we need to examine Blair, Chamberlain, and key members of the Bush administration as individuals with particular beliefs and traits. In this chapter, we explore two approaches to understanding individual decision makers: the cognitive approach and the personality approach. All through this chapter the working assumption is that leaders or individuals matter.

For example, consider the case of the last leader of the Soviet Union. Mikhail S. Gorbachev made active, determined policy choices affecting the internal and external environments of the Soviet Union that led to its peaceful dissolution and contributed to the end of communist single-party states throughout Central and Eastern Europe. When the people of the countries of the former Soviet bloc took hold of their national destinies and undid communism, Gorbachev could have chosen to react with pleas, promises, threats, coercion, and even military force to hold the bloc together under Soviet control. The leader of the weakening superpower might not have been able to hold off the tide for long; but he could have tried, making the transition period fraught with tension and even bloodshed. Instead, Mikhail Gorbachev decided to let the Eastern bloc go—peacefully, gracefully. The decision credited to this single leader no doubt saved many lives and prevented much pain and destruction.

Gorbachev saw the Soviet Union and the world in which it operated as changing in fundamental ways. Had Gorbachev been an older man with different life-shaping experiences, he might have decided to hold on to the Eastern bloc and the former Soviet republics at all costs. Margaret Hermann and Joe Hagan explain Gorbachev's role and the importance of all leaders in this way:

> Leaders define states' international and domestic constraints. Based on their perceptions and interpretations, they build expectations, plan strategies, and urge actions on their governments that conform with their judgments about what is possible and likely to maintain them in their positions. Such perceptions help frame governments' orientations to international affairs. Leaders' interpretations arise out of their experiences, goals, beliefs about the world, and sensitivity to the political context.[6]

Leaders—even single, supreme leaders—do not work alone, cannot just consider their own judgments and concerns, and cannot afford to pay attention to just one context (domestic or foreign). As noted in chapter 1, leaders are engaged in a two-level game between domestic and foreign interests. This two-level game is interpreted by and filtered through the orientation of leaders. In this way of thinking, leaders can be considered the nexus of the domestic and international political systems.

Hermann and Hagan take this a step further. After surveying the research on leadership, they conclude:

> The lesson learned so far is that international constraints only have policy implications when they are perceived as such by the leaders whose positions count in dealing with a particular problem. Whether and how such leaders judge themselves constrained depends on the nature of the

domestic challenges to their leadership, how the leaders are organized, and what they are like as people.[7]

Gorbachev scanned the international environment and concluded that the old security threats that had made the Eastern bloc so critical to the Soviet Union had changed in fundamental ways. Further, he could see that Soviet restraint in the face of the self-opening of Eastern and Central Europe could earn the Soviet Union more international credibility and friendship, thereby allowing the Soviet leaders to turn inward to the serious crises proliferating in the domestic realm. Thus Gorbachev decided to view the tide of anticommunism rising in the Eastern bloc as a welcome and nonthreatening phenomenon.

How leaders define situations that confront them has much to do with their personal characteristics, including social and educational background, previous experiences, ambitions, and worldview. In September 1970, air reconnaissance photos of southern Cuba convinced U.S. national security adviser Henry Kissinger that the Soviet Union was building a naval facility at Cienfuegos.[8] Kissinger's worldview and personal experience convinced him that the only way to protect national interests was to stand up to totalitarianism and confront the threat directly, promptly, and with force. Kissinger felt deceived by previous commitments made by the Soviet leadership to stay out of Cuba. Kissinger's boss, President Richard Nixon, had a much different interpretation of the nature of the situation and a different interpretation of national interests. To Nixon, the situation was less a crisis than an example of "adventurism" that should be handled quietly through diplomatic circles.[9] Nixon believed that the Cuban Missile Crisis of 1962 had been mishandled by President John F. Kennedy (who had beat Nixon in his first run for the White House in 1960), and he was determined to demonstrate better leadership.

Whose interpretation of the problem in Cienfuegos won? Kissinger was able to orchestrate a campaign of information "leaks" to the media in order to build the situation into a crisis in the minds of American political elites and public. By doing this, Kissinger forced Nixon into taking a strong and public stance against the Soviet action, rather than the quieter diplomatic approach Nixon preferred, in order to avoid appearing soft on U.S. national security. This example is interesting in the way it demonstrates both the importance of how leaders define and interpret the international (and domestic) environment, and the ways key individuals within a single administration (or regime) can and do differ in their interpretations. The ultimate decision maker—in this case, the U.S. president—is not always the person whose interpretation wins. For every policy decision, there may be different individuals with a stake in how a problem is defined and a policy response is built and executed (this will be discussed in the next chapter).

COGNITION: A DIFFERENT VIEW OF RATIONALITY

As the preceding discussion makes clear, not every analyst has been satisfied thinking about leaders as decision-making "boxes," utility-maximizers, or rational actors (based on a single notion of rationality). Scholars have long studied great leaders as well as notorious ones in order to understand their motivations, thoughts, and actions. But, in the post–World War II era, political biographies of leaders were regarded by mainstream political scientists as too unscientific for the nascent field of foreign policy analysis. The study of individuals needed to take on the same rigor as the competing study of rational decision making.

The move toward incorporating a more thorough, scientific investigation of individuals into the study of foreign policy took off in the 1950s. In the aftermath of World War II, behavioral scientists and psychologists had begun to examine issues such as whether aggression was inherent to humans or a learned (socialized) behavior that could be unlearned. Kenneth Waltz and Jerel Rosati—writing in different time periods and with very different orientations—credit the peace researchers of the 1950s with bringing the insights of psychology into the study of foreign policy.[10] The motivation of peace researchers was simple: if humans learn to make war, then they can learn to make peace. If, instead, aggression is part of human nature, perhaps aggression could be channeled into nonviolent pursuits. Behavioral scientists and psychologists were studying cognition—which the American Heritage Dictionary defines as "the mental process or faculty of knowing, including aspects such as awareness, perception, reasoning, and judgment." Peace researchers believed that the insights from the study of cognition could be used to shape peaceful leaders and peaceful countries.

A key starting assumption for the study of cognition is that humans do not necessarily think "rationally," or, more to the point, that "rationality" itself is context-driven. Individual differences can and do have a huge impact on foreign policy decision making, but it is possible to systematize our understanding of basic human thinking, developing constructs that have utility in a variety of settings.

In his important early work on misperception, Jervis offers this starting point for understanding the focus of cognitive foreign policy study:

> In determining how he will behave, an actor must try to predict how others will act and how their actions will affect his values. The actor must therefore

develop an image of others and of their intentions. This image, may, however, turn out to be an inaccurate one; the actor may for a number of reasons
misperceive both others' actions and their intentions.[11]

Why might actors misperceive? What are the processes that cause this to
happen?

> The evidence from both psychology and history overwhelmingly supports
> the view . . . that decision makers tend to fit incoming information into their
> existing theories and images. Indeed, their theories and images play a large
> part in determining what they notice. In other words, actors tend to perceive
> what they expect. Furthermore, . . . a theory will have greater impact on an
> actor's interpretation of data (a) the greater the ambiguity of the data and (b)
> the higher the degree of confidence with which the actor holds the theory.[12]

Is the process that Jervis proposes an example of irrational thinking?
Jervis says that it is not, or, rather, that we need to rethink "rationality" in
terms of the logic of the actor's existing beliefs and images. Borrowing
from others, Jervis asserts there is a "psycho-logic" that structures each individual's cognitive processes. To combine this notion with one of Jervis's
hypotheses on misperception stated above, we might say that I have a
logical structure to my beliefs that makes it difficult for me to understand
why you look at the same world I do and draw very different conclusions.
Indeed, I may not even be able to comprehend that you draw different
conclusions. Miscommunications and antagonistic foreign policy behaviors can easily result from the clash of different, often unknowable, yet internally rational belief sets.

Another important early contributor to the study of cognition is Irving
Janis. Janis proposes that that in every situation there is a "decisional conflict" that distorts decision making.[13] A decisional conflict refers to the situation in which opposing tendencies within an individual interfere with
what realists would call "rational" decision making.

A quick example is in order. Imagine a group of top foreign policy decision makers meeting in a cabinet session. Present at the meeting is a new
appointee, a young "rising star." This new member might have several
personal and professional goals wrapped up in the meeting. She might
want to be well liked and well respected by all the others in the cabinet,
and to have an impact on the group's process and final decision. During
that meeting, another cabinet member—older and very influential—begins to make an argument in favor of one particular course of action. As
the youngest member listens to the older member explain his reasoning,
the youngest member begins to feel rising alarm. She believes the speaker
is fundamentally wrong and potentially could take the group and the
country down the wrong path. But, as she looks around the room and no-

tices other key cabinet members nodding in agreement, she begins to doubt her own view about what is right. Wanting to be part of the group, wanting to be respected and accepted, the younger member feels conflicted about speaking out—it would be correct to speak out, but it would jeopardize her standing in the group if so many others agree with the older speaker.

During the Lyndon Johnson administration, a similar sort of self-censorship was exercised by some conflicted members of the president's Vietnam War decision-making circle. This self-censorship was encouraged by the fairly ruthless exclusionary practice exercised by President Johnson in his so-called Tuesday lunch group. People who spoke out against the direction favored by the group were told pointedly not to return for the next group meeting. Those who wanted to stay in the group silenced their own concerns. From the many books written by former insiders of the Bush 2 administration, it appears that similar self-policing and self-censoring for fear of retribution took place.[14]

Adopting a realist view, we might conceptualize the opposing tendencies that most people feel in any given social interaction as "distortions" in "rational" decision making. These distortions might be imagined as screens or filters that keep altering the direction in which thoughts are processed. Still assuming a realist view, we might conclude that the presence of these filters limits the range, creativity, and responsiveness of the decision maker. As Jerel Rosati suggests:

> Where the rational actor perspective assumes individual open-mindedness and adaptability to changes in the environment, a cognitive approach posits that individuals tend to be much more closed-minded due to their beliefs and the way they process information—thus, they tend to resist adapting to changes in the environment.[15]

Leaving the realist view, we find a different view:

> A cognitive approach assumes a complex, and realistic, psychology about human reasoning and decisionmaking. It does not assume individual awareness, open-mindedness, and adaptability relative to an "objective" environment, but assumes individuals are likely to view their environment differently and operate within their own "psychological environment."[16]

BELIEF SETS AND COGNITIVE STRUCTURE

Cognitive scholars have tried to elucidate the various kinds of screens or filters that produce what some may term "nonrational" decisions. A number of concepts are foundational to this work, starting with the rather simple notion of belief sets. A belief set is a more or less integrated set of images held by an individual about a particular universe. This set of images acts as a screen, letting in information that fits the belief set and keeping out information that does not.

One illustration of a belief set is the enemy image. Images of other international actors can be categorized according to stereotyped views of the motivations of the subject and the behaviors that result from such.[17] The "enemy" is imagined as evil by nature, with unlimited potential for committing evil acts. The enemy is also imagined as a strategic thinker and consummate chess master—establishing and carrying out a plan bent on destroying its enemies and their way of life. When a foreign policy maker holds a fairly strong enemy image of an opponent, only those images that confirm the inherently evil and cunning nature of the opponent are stored and remembered. Images that suggest a more complicated nature in the opponent, or that suggest less capability by the opponent are screened out. Arguably, the inability of the U.S. leadership and intelligence community to predict the sudden and terminal collapse of the Eastern bloc and the Soviet Union can be attributed to a firmly entrenched enemy image that failed to take note of signs of a rapidly deteriorating Soviet empire and a differently oriented Soviet leadership under Gorbachev. In the present era, George W. Bush's active use of the idea that the enemy is always plotting and planning to attack innocent people derives from this same basic assumption that the evil enemy may be more organized and proactive than the good guys. Enemy images may do more than cause an actor to miss signs of change or weakness in the enemy; the presence of strong enemy images may sustain international conflict over time, a prophetic conclusion drawn by Ole Holsti in the 1960s regarding American decision makers' images of Soviet leaders.[18]

A belief set is a fairly simple idea the elements of which can often be depicted in simple metaphors. When a leader is described as a "dove," the image of a dove of peace is evoked, suggesting the leader is inclined to interpret international events in an optimistic way and to act cooperatively with others. When a leader is described as a "hawk," the image of a bird of prey is evoked. Predator birds must be constantly alert to threats and opportunities in the environment, and they never turn away from the use of force when such use can further self-interest. In recent American political debate, a new metaphor is often used of the "chicken hawk." The "chicken hawk" is someone who wants the country to engage as a first resort in muscular diplomacy and war although this person has never experienced war because he or she is a "chicken" or afraid of personal harm.

A related concept is cognitive consistency. This is the idea that the images contained in a belief set must be logically connected and consistent. Cognitive theorists claim that when an individual holds conflicting be-

liefs, the individual experiences an anxiety known as cognitive dissonance. Individuals strive to avoid this dissonance and the anxiety it produces by actively managing the information they encounter and store in
their belief sets. This active management is not as energetic as it sounds.
Individuals are assumed to be *limited* information managers—or cognitive misers—who rely on cognitive shortcuts to understand new information. The shortcuts are images in their belief sets that look like some idea
they already hold. Individuals use existing beliefs to not only screen out
dissonant information, but to interpret new information. The new information is "recognized" as similar to an existing belief and so is stored as
the same. Great distortion can occur in this act of interpreting and storing,
but the distortion is necessary because it is quicker and easier, and it helps
individuals avoid dealing with new and potentially dissonant information.

The Bush 2 administration will long be studied for the examples it provides of cognitive misers who were closed to new information or who
sought information that already conformed to their accepted worldview.
For example, Richard Clarke, the former counterterrorism expert in the
Clinton and Bush 2 administrations, writes that Bush looked for "the simple solution, the bumper sticker description of the problem." Further,
"Bush and his inner circle had no real interest in complicated analyses; on
the issues that they cared about, they already knew the answers."[19] The
administration knew what it knew and then looked for information that
fit its conclusions. Seymour Hersh describes an intelligence operation set
up in the Pentagon as an alternative to the CIA as a channel through
which confirming information—on Saddam Hussein's ties to al Qaeda
and his weapons of mass destruction arsenal—could be "found."[20]

It is important to note here that the idea of the individual as a cognitive
manager actively attempting to avoid dissonant information does not
necessarily mean that individuals cannot learn something new. Scholars
who study learning among foreign policy makers study the "development of new beliefs, skills, or procedures as a result of the observation and
interpretation of experience."[21] Learning is possible and belief sets can
change.

Janice Gross Stein's study of Mikhail Gorbachev provides an interesting
example of how cognitive scholars explain the conditions under which
beliefs can change. Stein argues that learning—a change in held beliefs—
occurs easiest with problems that are "ill-structured" in the mind of the
individual. An ill-structured problem is akin to an incomplete belief set.
Gorbachev's primary interests within the Central Committee and, after
1980, within the Politburo, centered on the domestic economy of the Soviet Union. On topics of external security, Stein asserts, including the
United States, Gorbachev held few preexisting beliefs. According to Stein,

"learning is the construction of new representations of the problem"; new representations of a problem occur most easily when there is an underdeveloped existing representation of the problem in the mind of the individual.[22] Gorbachev was unconstrained by well-structured existing beliefs about Soviet external security, and so he was "free" to learn. Stein argues that Gorbachev was prompted to learn new ideas about Soviet security and about the United States by the failure of Soviet policy in Afghanistan. Learning, then, requires two elements: the lack of strongly established beliefs and some "unanticipated failures that challenge old ways of representing problems."[23] Learning requires some prompt and some need.

However, beliefs that are firmly held and supported by one's society and culture are more rigid and unlikely to change. Matthew Hirshberg provides a demonstration of the rigidity of preexisting beliefs and the reconstruction of information to make it resemble preexisting beliefs. Hirshberg presented fictional news stories to three groups of college students to test two hypotheses. His first hypothesis was that "the stereotype of a prodemocratic America serves to maintain its own cultural dominance by filtering out information that does not fit it, making it difficult for Americans to test the validity of their preconceptions."[24] The fictional news accounts portrayed the United States intervening in three different ways: (1) on the side of a democratic government besieged by rebels, (2) on the side of an unspecified type of government besieged by communist rebels, and (3) on the side of an unspecified type of government besieged by democratic rebels. When asked to recall the events depicted in the particular story read, most students recalled that the United States had intervened in support of democracy.[25] The students' strongly held belief that the United States always supported democracy and freedom caused them to re-create the information in the news account to fit what they believed.

Hirshberg tested a second hypothesis on what is called attribution bias. An attribution bias or error is triggered by information that is inconsistent with preexisting beliefs and cannot be re-created to fit those beliefs. The attribution bias involves both the enemy image discussed above and another perceptual move called the mirror image. The starting belief is that we are a people who are inherently good and well-intentioned. Our opponent, on the other hand, is evil and has malevolent intentions—the opposite or mirror image of us. In an attribution error, the individual goes a step further in order to explain behavior, especially behavior that does not fit one's beliefs about one's own country as good and well-intentioned. When our evil opponent does bad things—like using military force or coercing another country into a one-sided trade arrangement—it is because such bad behavior is in our opponent's nature. Conversely, we are by nature good and so only do good things. When we do bad things, it is because we have been forced to do so by external events. When an individual must explain a behavior that is inconsistent with preexisting foundational beliefs, cognitive scholars say the individuals attribute the inconsistent behavior to outside circumstances.

Hirshberg's second hypothesis was tested with fictional news accounts that either depicted the United States dropping "tons of incendiary bombs," causing "panic" and "horror" among villagers, or depicted it dropping "tons of relief supplies," causing "joy" and "glee" among villagers.[26] After having his subjects read one version of the fictional accounts, he had them answer questionnaires on the "nature of the United States" and why it acted as reported. Hirshberg found that 70 percent of those reading about the dropping of relief supplies agreed that it was American nature to do so (an internal attribution bias). However, he did not find significant statistical support for the external attribution bias— that the United States dropped bombs because it was forced to do so by external events.

The public surveyed by Hirshberg may have been less likely to demonstrate an external attribution bias than U.S. national leaders. Consider the Bush 2 administration explanations for why the United States went to war in Iraq. In May 2004, the president said:

> We did not seek this war on terror, but this is the world as we find it. We must keep our focus. We must do our duty. History is moving, and it will tend toward hope, or tend toward tragedy. Our terrorist enemies have a vision that guides and explains all their varied acts of murder. . . .[27]

Note in this quote the use of an image of the enemy as determined and cunning (it has a vision that guides its actions). In a similar address in November 2005, the president explained, "We didn't ask for this global struggle, but we're answering history's call with confidence, and with a comprehensive strategy."[28] And in January 2006, the president said "You know, no President ever wants to be President during war. But this war came to us, not as a result of actions we took, it came to us as a result of actions an enemy took on September the 11th, 2001."[29]

When preexisting beliefs are used to interpret, re-create, or explain away behavior, cognitive scholars say that the individual is acting as a cognitive miser, using shortcuts to deal with the new information. The name given by some scholars to these cognitive shortcuts is a schema. A schema is a shortcut like a menu that is more or less particular to place and event. When scholars study schemas, they are interested in identifying the nature or internal structure of schemas and the policy decisions that might result from different schemas.

For example, it is well known that individuals use analogies to understand a new situation and to determine a course of action. An analogy is a comparison made to similar events or phenomena. For instance, if a leader uses the "Munich analogy" to determine a course of action, he or she has decided that events at hand resemble the events of 1938 when the British prime minister Neville Chamberlain "appeased" Adolph Hitler. In the Munich Treaty—which essentially amounted to a green light for Germany to move east into Czechoslovakia, thereby sparing countries to the west—Chamberlain proclaimed that he had bought "peace in our time." But the Munich Treaty did not satisfy Hitler's aggression; he ultimately brought war to countries in all directions. When a leader says that a new situation brings to mind the "Munich analogy," he or she is saying that it does no good to try to appease an aggressive leader; instead, the aggressor must be met with immediate and decisive force. Keith Shimko writes that when individuals use a schema to understand a new problem, they "fill in the blanks of current events with knowledge accumulated from past experiences."[30] Once a leader decides a new situation resembles the effort to appease Hitler, the leader need not seek out detailed information about the new situation in order to know what policy is necessary.

Policy makers can cause problems for themselves in their use of analogies. We can see this in a diplomatic tussle that resulted from remarks made by the Israeli prime minister in the immediate aftermath of the September 11, 2001, terrorist attacks on the United States. In pursuit of Arab support for its campaign against international terrorism, the Bush 2 administration announced in early October that it was in favor of a longstanding demand of the Arab world—Palestinian statehood. This announcement prompted a speech by Israeli prime minister Ariel Sharon in which he made use of the famous analogy discussed above:

> I call on the Western democracies and primarily the leader of the free world, the United States: Do not repeat the dreadful mistake of 1938 when enlightened European democracies decided to sacrifice Czechoslovakia for a convenient temporary solution. Do not try to appease the Arabs at our expense. This is unacceptable to us. Israel will not be Czechoslovakia. Israel will fight terrorism.[31]

The Israeli prime minister's use of the Munich analogy provoked a public rebuke from the White House press secretary: "The president believes that these remarks are unacceptable. Israel can have no better or stronger friend than the United States."[32] Opposition party members from within Israel also condemned Sharon's remark, pointing out that Israel and the United States shared the same interests in eliminating international terrorism. Sharon subsequently retracted the remark—in part—agreeing that the United States was a good friend of Israel's.

Besides prompting an angry U.S. retort, Sharon's use of the Munich analogy telegraphed a new course of action—an abandonment of the most recent cease-fire between Israel and the Palestinian National Authority (this conflict is explained in more detail in chapter 6). Within a few hours of his use of the Munich analogy, Sharon ordered Israeli tanks, infantry, helicopter gunships, and armored bulldozers into parts of Palestinian-controlled Hebron. Analogies can signal leaders' intentions to embark on certain courses of action. Rather than allow Israel to be sacrificed by the United States in order to curry Arab favor, Sharon demonstrated that he was prepared to take Israeli security into his own hands, setting his own policy direction. Abandoning the cease-fire was a clear statement to this effect, especially in the face of U.S. pressure on Israel to be more accommodating with the Palestinians in order to help along the Bush 2 administration's new war on terrorism.

Finally, some scholars have been interested in mapping out the cognitive complexity or simplicity of decision makers. Allison Astorino-Courtois explains, "The cognitive complexity-simplicity construct reflects the degree to which individuals both differentiate and integrate various sources of information in considering a decision problem."[33] Peter Suedfeld and colleagues elaborate: "Integrative complexity is an attribute of information processing that generally indicates the extent to which decision makers search for and monitor information, try to predict outcomes and reactions, flexibly weigh their own and other parties' options, and consider multiple potential strategies."[34]

The study of integrative complexity involves an examination of the public utterances of leaders. The utterances, or statements, are scored as to whether they demonstrate simple information processing, more complicated contingency-based reasoning, or highly complex, multicausal information processing. Scholars have found that leaders demonstrating higher levels of complexity tend to be more cooperative in their international initiatives than those demonstrating lower levels.[35] However, in situations of prolonged stress, such as the 1962 Cuban Missile Crisis or the months leading up to the 1991 Persian Gulf War, the measured integrative complexity decreases for all decision makers as they begin to feel that their time and options are running out.

In many respects, these scholars equate cognitive complexity with rational decision making, and cognitive simplicity with decision making through the use of preexisting beliefs:

> At the lower end of the complexity scale, the amount of information used in cognitive processing is limited . . . decision makers often rely on analogs or stereotyped images, and discrepant information is either ignored or discounted. . . . Complex thinking, on the other hand, involves a broader search

and use of varied information sources concerning the decision problem. Discrepant information is integrated most thoroughly at higher levels of cognitive complexity, and more flexible consideration is given to the complete set of options and outcomes relevant to a decision situation.[36]

By equating high levels of complexity with the tasks typically associated with rational decision making, this line of research attempts to bridge the differences between rational choice and cognitive studies. It should be noted as well that scholars in this tradition link more "rational," high levels of complexity with liberalism and good behavior like cooperation, while lower cognitive complexity is associated with the less-desirable use of cognitive shortcuts and belligerency.

OPERATIONAL CODE

When a leader makes use of an analogy, it is possible to make a safe guess about the kind of behaviors that follow. Once a leader identifies an opponent as another Hitler and therefore the lessons of Munich must apply, we can safely predict that the leader thinks that some kind of forceful reply to the new Hitler is in order. Once a leader declares that his or her country will not be abandoned in the same way that Czechoslovakia was abandoned, we can safely predict that the leader will demonstrate his or her willingness and capability to go it alone. If we as analysts can map out the operating beliefs of a leader we are studying, looking for the analogies and other pronouncements that demonstrate the leader's worldview, we can use this "map" to explain why certain policies were made and certain actions taken. A cognitive map that details both the normative beliefs held by an individual and his or her behavioral beliefs is called an operational code. "Operational code analysis provides a means of testing a leader's fundamental predispositions toward political action."[37]

Alexander George is the scholar who brought the discussion of operational codes to the forefront in foreign policy study in the late 1960s. George defines the operational code as a "political leader's beliefs about the nature of politics and political conflict, his views regarding the extent to which historical developments can be shaped, and his notions of correct strategy and tactics."[38] Delineating a leader's operational code involves a two-step process, as described by Stephen Walker and colleagues:

First, what are the leader's philosophical beliefs about the dynamics of world politics? Is the leader's image of the political universe a diagnosis marked by cooperation or conflict? What are the prospects for the realization of fundamental political values? What is the predictability of others, the degree of control over historical development and the role of chance? Second, what are the leader's instrumental beliefs that indicate choice and shift propensities in the management of conflict? What is the leader's general approach to strategy and tactics and the utility of different means? How does the leader calculate, control, and manage the risks and timing of political action?[39]

Operational code studies typically depend on an examination of the writings and statements of a leader from which philosophical beliefs can be extracted. Scott Crichlow explains that

> Although it may be altered (e.g., by learning) or modified in specific situational environments, the operational code of a leader rests on a core set of predispositions, such that the taking of actions that contradict it is by definition out of the norm. Therefore, it is expected that such patterns of preferences in a leader's political statements are indeed largely accurate illustrations of his or her basic predispositions regarding the nature and conduct of politics.[40]

By way of example, consider Ibrahim Karawan's efforts to elaborate the operational code of Egyptian president Anwar Sadat to explain Sadat's decision to make peace with Israel in the 1979 Camp David Accords.[41] Anwar Sadat assumed the presidency of Egypt in 1970 upon the death of Gamal Abdel Nasser. Recall that in the last chapter we explored the rational choices made by Nasser in the events leading up to the 1967 war between Egypt and Israel. The losses incurred by Egypt and the Arab states collectively in the 1967 war—the Old City of Jerusalem, the Sinai peninsula, the Gaza Strip, the West Bank, and Golan Heights—caused Nasser to lose his leadership position in the Arab world. Although Nasser attempted to resign from the presidency after the 1967 defeat, his popularity among Egyptians remained high and he remained as president until he had a heart attack and died in 1970. The political ramifications of the Six Days' War continue to reverberate to this day in the Middle East.

According to Karawan, Sadat took over the Egyptian presidency committed to setting Egypt on a different foreign policy course than that pursued by Nasser. Rather than follow Nasser's pan-Arab policy, Sadat embarked on an "Egypt first" policy course. Karawan contends that Sadat's writings and speeches indicate that "Egypt first" was the driving philosophical belief of Sadat's operational code.[42] The instrumental belief that follows is that Sadat would negotiate Egypt's future without regard for the opinions and interests of the other Arab states. To illustrate Sadat's "Egypt first" operational code, Karawan points to Sadat's speeches and actions at several key junctures in the 1970s.

For instance, in 1973, Egypt and Syria launched a concerted two-prong attack on Israel. Egyptian forces managed to reclaim a small part of the Sinai peninsula in this attack, a victory Sadat attributed to the power of Egyptian nationalism. This was the first time an Arab leader made battlefield gains against Israel. Following his "Egypt first" philosophy and despite the fact

that he had engaged in the war alongside ally Syria, Sadat declared a unilateral cease-fire and negotiated a subsequent disengagement without consulting or even informing ally Syria. Similarly, Sadat pursued peace with Israel in the 1978 Camp David Talks, which led to the 1979 peace treaty
between Egypt and Israel, in order to pursue Egypt's national interests. Sadat's decision to engage in peace talks with Israel and his agreement to the
terms of the Camp David Accords occurred in the absence of any consultation with or consideration of the other Arab states. Sadat's pursuit of Egyptian national interests vis-à-vis Israel constituted the behavioral manifestation of his driving philosophical belief.

Sadat's pursuit of his "Egypt first" philosophy caused the other Arab
states to turn their backs on Egypt. His decision to negotiate peace and
normal relations with Israel ultimately gave incentive to some Egyptian
Islamic fundamentalists to assassinate Sadat in 1981. But his actions in the
1970s flowed directly from his primary beliefs. The elaboration of Sadat's
operational code explains the foreign policy he followed; that is, the elaboration of Sadat's cognitive map points out the direction of the course he
set for Egypt.

PERSONALITY

When operational code scholars propose that a leader's core set of philosophical beliefs make it unlikely that the leader will act in ways inconsistent with this norm, these scholars link operational code to cognitive studies. When operational code scholars explain that they ultimately are
establishing a leader's fundamental behavioral predisposition they link
operational code to the study of personality and affect.

The American Heritage Dictionary defines personality as "(1) The quality or condition of being a person. (2) The totality of qualities and traits,
as of character or behavior, that are peculiar to a specific person. (3) The
pattern of collective character, behavioral, temperamental, emotional and
mental traits of a person." The study of personality in foreign policy
analysis involves the study of affect—or emotions or feelings—that represent enduring character traits. Psychologist Roger Knudson tells us that
character traits are stable behavioral dispositions.[43] Thus, when foreign
policy scholars study personality traits, they attempt to discern which foreign policy behaviors are associated with which traits.

Margaret Hermann is the pioneering scholar in this study. Hermann's
research reveals that six personality traits are related to specific foreign
policy behaviors. These traits are: the need for power, the need for affiliation, the level of cognitive complexity, the degree of trust in others, nationalism, and the belief that one has some control over events.[44] Other

studies have added an additional trait: task orientation.[45] Two basic leadership types and expected foreign policy behaviors arise out of certain configurations of these traits:

> If we examine the dynamics of the traits associated with the aggressive leader, we find a need to manipulate and control others, little ability to consider a range of alternatives, suspiciousness of others' motives, a high interest in maintaining national identity and sovereignty, and a distinct willingness to initiate action. . . . [Such leaders] urge their governments to be suspicious of the motives of leaders of other nations. When interaction is necessary, they expect it to be on their nation's terms.[46]

> The personal characteristics of the conciliatory leader indicate a need to establish and maintain friendly relationships with others, an ability to consider a wide range of alternatives, little suspiciousness of others' motives, no overriding concern with the maintenance of national identity and sovereignty, and little interest in initiating action. These dynamics suggest a more participatory foreign policy. . . . [Conciliatory leaders] will probably keep attuned to what is going on in international relations, being sensitive and responsive to this environment.[47]

Based on her research and that of many others, Hermann developed a Leadership Trait Analysis (LTA) system. One illustration of the use of the LTA system comes from a study by Vaughn Shannon and Jonathan Keller on the inner circle of the Bush 2 administration. Shannon and Keller's specific concern is whether the personality traits evidenced in the Bush 2 inner circle made the administration more or less likely to invade Iraq, thereby violating the international norm against the use of force except for self-defense. With some slight exceptions, they found that Bush administration officials did demonstrate traits that made them more likely to engage in aggressive behavior. Their conclusion was that a "belief in ability to control events, need for power, ingroup bias, and especially distrust may be particularly important predictors of one's willingness to violate international norms."[48] Shannon and Keller note that in 1999 Hermann drew conclusions from her LTA work that aptly describe the Bush administration's foreign policy. For leaders who are high in distrust and ingroup bias, "International politics is centered around a set of adversaries that are viewed as 'evil' and intent on spreading their ideology or extending their power at the expense of others; leaders perceive that they have a moral imperative to confront these adversaries; as a result, they are likely to take risks and to engage in highly aggressive and assertive behavior."[49]

Another recent study of the Iraq war makes use of Hermann's LTA system. Stephen Dyson used the LTA to compare Tony Blair to fifty-one other world leaders and to twelve previous British prime ministers.[50] Using

Blair's answers to parliamentary questions from 1997 to the day that the Iraqi invasion began, Dyson concludes that Blair scored far above the average on his belief in his ability to control events, well below the average on cognitive complexity, and far above the average on the need for power.[51] That is, Dyson finds that Blair fits Hermann's depiction of an aggressive leader. Putting these two studies together, we might conclude that there was a "perfect storm" forming for war with Iraq because the leaders of both the United States and the United Kingdom were predisposed to see other actors in the world as suspicious (particularly the regime of Saddam Hussein) and to see themselves as having high ability to control world events, and were generally insensitive to international norms, views, or information that would have moderated their actions.

The issues of a leader's orientations to the world—how the leader views his or her state in the world—and the sensitivity of leaders to advice and information must be understood in terms of the context in which the leader makes decisions. In the next chapter, we continue to discuss the individual in foreign policy making, but we start to contrast the single leader with other leadership groups. Scholars contend that different types of decision units can impact foreign policy in various ways. Next we consider decision units in a chapter that begins with individuals but serves as a bridge to the study of state-level factors shaping foreign policy.

CHAPTER REVIEW

- Individual differences matter—individual leaders perceive international and domestic constraints differently based on their worldviews and beliefs.

- The study of cognition is the study of how individuals perceive, reason, and judge issues before them.

- Belief sets act as rigid screens, letting in information that fits established views and re-creating or keeping out information that is contradictory.

- Individuals are assumed to be cognitive misers who use shortcuts in decision making.

- Operational codes describe individuals' philosophical and operational beliefs.

- Leadership trait analysis examines how leaders' emotional traits predispose them to certain kinds of action.

4

✛

Decision Units, Small Groups, and Bureaucratic Politics

Cases Featured in This Chapter

- The decision rules and key members of Iran's top decision unit involved in formulating Iran's position on nuclear negotiations with the International Atomic Energy Agency and the West.
- The decision rules and decision units involved in Turkey's 1974 decision to intervene militarily in Cyprus.

THE DECISION UNITS FRAMEWORK

Who speaks for Iran? Who made the decisions that put Iran on a course of confrontation with other states over its possible acquisition of nuclear weapons? Which voice coming from Iran counted the most when leaders and analysts in other countries tried to predict what Iranian motivations and intentions were on the nuclear issue? Realists would answer that there are persistent Iranian national interests—say, to become a great power—and that individual persons sitting in particular positions in the Iranian government are all committed to the national interests. Cognitive scholars might want to use the speeches and actions of Iranian president Mahmoud Ahmadinejad to construct an operational code that would help outsiders understand Iran's pursuit of nuclear technology. These same scholars might want to take into account the operational codes of others in the government as well; for instance, it would be useful to understand the worldview of Supreme Leader Ayatollah Ali Khamenei. Ahmadinejad and Khamenei might have the same basic objective to make Iran a great power, but they might hold different opinions about how best to achieve that objective. Can the analyst conclude that the supreme leader's opinion is the one that matters? What if Khamenei stayed silent on certain foreign policy issues, deferring to known as well as behind-the-scenes politicians to make policies?

If the foreign analyst hears different voices and opinions coming from the Iranian leadership, using the rational actor approach will not help to capture these differences. Similarly, the cognitive approach is also limited, because it does not help identify to whom we should listen when different voices are heard on any given issue. What we hope to identify is the ultimate decision maker. As Margaret Hermann and Charles Hermann explain,

> [recognizing] that numerous domestic and international factors can and do influence foreign policy behavior, these influences must be channeled through the political structure of a government that identifies, decides, and implements foreign policy. Within this structure is a set of authorities with the ability to commit the resources of the society and, with respect to a particular problem, the authority to make a decision that cannot be readily reversed. We call this set of authorities the "ultimate decision unit," even though in reality the unit may consist of multiple separate bodies rather than a single entity. It is our contention that the configuration and dynamics of such an ultimate decision unit help shape the substance of foreign policy behavior.[1]

Who speaks for Iran? Who is the ultimate decision unit? U.S. president George W. Bush has tended to attribute all Iranian foreign policy decisions to Ahmadinejad. Neoconservative supporters of the president have called for "regime change" that would take Ahmadinejad out of power and put in someone else. But regime change that is limited to Ahmadinejad and his advisers or even to the presidency and the parliament would not change ultimate decision making in Iran. Power in Iran is split between different leadership roles and different elected and non-elected groups. The power structure and, therefore, the identity of the ultimate decision unit in Iran is complicated and opaque. Understanding who speaks for Iran means understanding the configuration of the ultimate decision unit and the decision-making rules governing conflict within that unit.

The decision units framework goes beyond who may sit in the foreign policy decision-making circle. Indeed, this framework tells us that different entities may exist for different foreign policy decisions. The most important part of the decision unit approach is its emphasis on understanding the dynamics or the processes by which decisions are made given the different configurations possible for the ultimate decision unit. Many of the expectations about the dynamics at play derive from the cognitive and personality studies of leadership. There are three basic decision units, according to Hermann and Hermann and others who have elaborated upon the approach: the single, predominant leader; the single group; and the group that is comprised of multiple autonomous units.

PREDOMINANT LEADER

The predominant leader is a "single individual [who] has the power to make the choice and to stifle opposition."[2] Not all single, predominant leaders are the same, however; and so it is important to know whether "a leader's orientation to foreign affairs leads him [or her] to be relatively sensitive or insensitive to information from the political environment."[3] A sensitive predominant leader is likely to use diplomacy and cooperation, taking an incremental approach to action in order to stay tuned to feedback from the environment. An insensitive leader is not open to external influence and so knowledge of his or her personality or operational code is important. Drawing upon cognitive studies, Hermann and Hermann explain that "If a leader's orientation suggests that he has a strongly held view of the world and uses his view as a lens through which to select and interpret incoming information, the leader is likely to be looking only for cues that confirm his beliefs when making foreign policy decisions. As a result, he will be relatively insensitive to discrepant advice and data."[4] More on this topic was discussed in the previous chapter.

SINGLE GROUPS AND THE GROUPTHINK SYNDROME

The single group is a "set of individuals, all of whom are members of a single body, [that] collectively select a course of action in face-to-face interaction."[5] This group may be as small as two people or "as large as a parliament of hundreds, so long as there is a collective, interactive decision process in which all the members who are needed to make authoritative commitments participate."[6] The individuals in this single group must be able to "form or change their positions on a problem without outside consultation," that is, the members of the single group are not bound by decisions made elsewhere and do not need to defend those decisions made elsewhere.[7] For instance, the group may be assembled from heads of departments, but for the particular problem at hand the group members do not represent their departments and do not need to answer to their departments for the decision made.

Although members do not represent departments, members of the single group may be open to external influences, especially information that is relevant to the group's decision. But the single group may also be self-contained (not open to outside information) and quick to reach consensus. Crucial to understanding decision making in the single group is understanding the "techniques used for managing conflict in the group" and the degree to which group loyalty is required.[8] Closed single groups that privilege group loyalty and suppress dissent are associated with the notion of groupthink.

Groupthink is a process described by Irving Janis.[9] The small group locked in such a process puts the maintenance of the group and the loyalty of its members at the center of its purpose as a group, rather than focusing on the problem to be solved. The group self-monitors or self-polices to suppress nonconforming views from within and discounts information from outside sources that might challenge the group's judgment and inherent morality. Janis offers a list of ten antecedents that might suggest a situation of groupthink, but of these ten, Janis says, "[o]nly when a group of policymakers is moderately or highly cohesive can we expect the groupthink syndrome to emerge."[10] Groupthink typically is associated with policy failure because the decision-making group fails to critically assess all the relevant information on the problem at hand, settling on the policy preference of the dominant leader in the group. Hermann, Stein, Sundelius, and Walker explain groupthink less as a "syndrome" (with negative implications) than as "premature closure around an initially advocated course of action."[11] "A group experiences premature closure when it accepts the option prominently presented, usually by an authoritative member, early in its deliberations without engaging in a serious evaluation of its potential limitations or understanding a careful comparison of it with any other possible alternatives."[12] The classic case of groupthink in American foreign policy study is the failed decision making around the Bay of Pigs fiasco.

Group cohesiveness also was found to be one of the critical antecedents to groupthink in a study by Mark Schafer and Scott Crichlow. Schafer and Crichlow contend that leadership style and the traditional group procedures and patterns of group behavior that privilege group cohesiveness are the most damaging preconditions for group decision making. But, they warn, the key to better decision making is to focus on eliminating the adverse antecedents *prior* to the time the group meets because "by the time the group engages in information processing, it is generally too late to avoid faulty decision making."[13]

Hermann, Stein, Sundelius, and Walker see groupthink as one dynamic that produces a tendency to avoid group conflict and moves the group to quick concurrence. Some small-group processes, however, do not lead to concurrence but instead lead to unanimity (resolution of group conflict), or to plurality (acceptance of group conflict). Group identity, rather than group cohesiveness, is the crucial variable for this research team in their study of small groups. Members of the small group are assumed to have different identities. The primary issue is whether group members have their primary identities in the small group or in their "home" departments or agencies. Ultimately, Hermann, Stein, Sundelius, and Walker create a decision tree that takes the researcher through different branches exploring the role of leaders and group decision-making norms. These branches lead to four possible decision types: the adoption of the dominant solution, a deadlocked solution, an integrative solution, and a subset solution. This decision tree is presented in figure 4.1.

The first point in this decision tree is to ask whether the members' primary identity lies with the group.[14] If yes, then the second question is whether the leader suppresses dissent. If the answer is yes, the next question is whether the group norms reinforce the leader's suppression of dissent. If the answer is yes, then it is very likely that the dominant solution advocated by the leader will be selected. Alternatively, the answer to the second question—does the leader suppress dissent—could be no. Then, the researcher asks whether group norms discourage dissent. If the answer is no, then the question is does the group evaluate multiple options regarding the problem at hand? If no, then the dominant solution advocated by the leader is very likely to be chosen. If the group does evaluate multiple options, then it is likely that the group will choose an integrative solution that is "agreed to by all involving some shift from initial preferences."[15]

If the answer to the first question is no—the members' primary identities are not with the group—then we take different branches in the tree. Following figure 4.1, the next question to ask is do all members have the same initial preferences? If no, then do the decision rules require that all members agree? If no, is the group expected to meet again on other issues and continue as a group? If the answer is no, then is there a respected minority within the group that expresses intense preferences? If no, then it is likely that the solution will be one that reflects a subset of the group members' preferences.

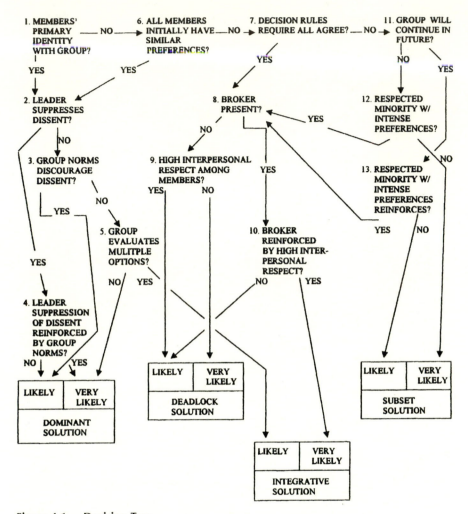

Figure 4.1.   Decision Tree
Source: This figure originally appeared as Figure 2 in Charles F. Hermann, Janice Gross Stein, Bengt Sundelius, and Stephen Walker, "Resolve, Accept, or Avoid: Effects of Group Conflict on Foreign Policy Decisions," *International Studies Review* 3, no. 2 (Summer 2001), 146. Used with permission of Wiley-Blackwell Publishers.

   This tree has a lot of branches and perhaps some leaves might help us evaluate its usefulness in case analysis. Hermann, Stein, Sundelius, and Walker provide three case studies, but let's continue with the problem posed at the start of this chapter: Who speaks for Iran? We'll rephrase this inquiry to ask who makes foreign policy decisions for Iran and how. The specific problem will be how to understand Iranian negotiations with the West on matters of nuclear technology.

Who Makes Foreign Policy Decisions for Iran?

The International Atomic Energy Agency (IAEA) is the U.N. agency responsible for ensuring countries' compliance with the Treaty on the Non-Proliferation of Nuclear Weapons (NPT). The NPT essentially says that countries with nuclear weapons technology agree not to transfer that technology and countries without nuclear weapons technology agree not to acquire it. Iran is a signatory to the NPT and so has obligations under it. In 1983, the IAEA acknowledged that Iran had a right to acquire nuclear technology for civilian energy use; and Iran agreed to suspend its enrichment of uranium and allow IAEA verification inspections.[16] The Bush administration, however, was convinced that Iran was pursuing nuclear weapons technology; and in the international commotion over the issue, Iran removed IAEA seals from its research plants. In 2006, Iranian leaders claimed Iran had succeeded in enriching uranium; and the Iranian president stated that Iran had an "inalienable right" to produce nuclear weapons.

In response, the U.N. Security Council passed two resolutions in 2006 calling on Iran to stop its enrichment activities and return to compliance with IAEA agreements. Limited sanctions were imposed to back the resolutions. Iranian negotiators had continued to talk with European Union (EU) negotiators during these tense years, but mutually acceptable agreements proved elusive.[17] Despite the sanctions, Iranian leaders were prepared to compromise with the IAEA and the West until summer 2006. Gareth Smyth concludes that changes in the international environment at this time caused Iranian officials to be less willing to compromise on the issue of enrichment. These changes included a reluctance by China and Russia to support harsher sanctions, the overextension of the United States in the wars in Iraq and Afghanistan, Israel's apparent defeat by Hizbollah (a nonstate actor based in Lebanon and supported in part by Iran) in the July–August war in Lebanon, and then the loss of the U.S. Congress by the Republicans in the fall 2006 elections.[18] Although negotiations with the European Union continued, Iran's bargaining position had hardened considerably. Although it took longer than the Bush administration might have wanted, the Security Council passed another resolution in March 2007 (1747) condemning Iran for its noncompliance with earlier resolutions and placing economic and other sanctions on Iran. By fall 2007, an apparent shake-up occurred in the top Iranian leadership, including the resignation of the lead nuclear negotiator. Meanwhile, the Bush administration kept beating the drum of war against Iran for its nuclear weapons ambitions and for its alleged support for insurgents in Iraq.

Did the hardening of the Iranian negotiating position signal changes in leadership? Can we even begin to understand what might be happening at the highest decision-making levels with only news accounts and a couple of expert analyses? We can try! Let's begin with a quick primer on the structure of and the personalities in the Iranian government.

According to the constitution, there are elected and nonelected institutions in the Iranian government. The most powerful post is the unelected position of supreme leader. The supreme leader is chosen by the Assembly of Experts, an elected body composed of eighty-six religious officials. The Assembly of Experts has the power to monitor the supreme leader's performance, but generally the position is held for life. As of the fall of 2007, the supreme leader was Ayatollah Ali Khameini. The supreme leader controls the armed forces and all decision making on security, defense, and major foreign policy issues. The supreme leader also appoints half of the unelected Guardian Council, a body that must approve all legislation and must approve all candidates for the presidency and parliament. Khameini was a hard-line conservative who completely supported President Mahmoud Ahmadinejad, but Khameini had also appointed opponents of Ahmadinejad to critical posts (more on this later). The International Crisis Group, a nongovernmental organization that monitors conflict in the world, calls Khameini a balancer among different factions in the leadership.[19] Ray Takeyh, writing in *Foreign Affairs*, takes a different view that Khameini was indecisive, with weak religious credentials that made him dependent on reactionaries like Ahmadinejad for support.[20]

The second most important position in Iran is the elected Presidency. Since 2005, the president was Mahmoud Ahmadinejad, a former mayor of Tehran, noncleric, and hard-line conservative. Ahmadinejad was known for his threatening rhetoric, especially against Israel. Inside Iran, Ahmadinejad appeared to be close to Khameini and the ultraconservative chair of the Guardian Council, Ayatollah Ahmad Janati. Additionally, Ahmadinejad had the support of the Islamic Revolutionary Guard Corps and awarded lucrative government contracts and positions to its officers. In terms of the nuclear issue, Ahmadinejad had never supported compromise with the IAEA or the EU negotiator. In December 2006, elections for municipal councils and the Assembly of Experts went against Ahmadinejad's faction in favor of the faction headed by the man who ran against Ahmadinejad for president in 2005 (more on this man soon).

The unelected institutions—the supreme leader, Armed Forces, Judiciary, Expediency Council, and Guardian Council—would seem to have more power than the elected institutions—the Presidency, Cabinet, and Parliament. The exception is the elected body of the Assembly of Experts. In September 2007, the Assembly of Experts elected as its chair former Iranian president Ali Akhbar Hashemi Rafsanjani, the man who lost the 2005 presidential elections to Ahmadinejad. Right after the 2005 elections, Khameini had appointed Rafsanjani as the chair of the Expediency Council to check Ahmadinejad's power.[21] When Rafsanjani was president of

Iran, he had favored more cooperative negotiations with the West on the nuclear issue. He and his chief negotiator, Hassan Rowhani, were vocal critics of Ahmadinejad's uncompromising position regarding the West.[22] The position of chair of the Assembly of Experts is an extremely influential post, since the Assembly chooses the supreme leader. A key ally of Rafsanjani and a protégé of Khameini was Ali Larijani, the head of the Supreme National Security Council and outspoken opponent of Ahmadinejad. Until October 2007, Larijani was the chief nuclear negotiator for Iran but resigned and was replaced with a hard-line, relatively unknown supporter of Ahmadinejad's. Interestingly, Larijani was considered one of the hard-liners most responsible for undercutting the democratic reforms attempted under the previous presidency.[23]

In this discussion so far, some of the key members of the Khameini's inner circle (presumably the decision-making circle) have been named: Ahmadinejad, Janati, Rafsanjani, Larijani. Using open-source news reports, we might also include Ali Akbar Velayati, Khameini's adviser on foreign affairs, who had made it clear that Ahmadinejad's rhetoric did not always represent the official government view. We might also include in the inner circle former nuclear negotiator Rowhani; General Mohammed Ali Jafari, the newly named head of the Revolutionary Guard (in September 2007); and Kamal Kharrazi, the foreign minister under the previous reformist president who served as chair of the relatively new Strategic Committee for Foreign Policy in late 2007.

For the most part, this list merely reflects news reports that mention key office holders and advisers rather than any authoritative list. But the top Iranian leadership is an opaque body. This allows us as analysts to make interesting speculations on how the top leadership interacts and makes decisions. A critical point to make is that analysts agree that the top leaders are in strong agreement on critical Iranian national interests but that they differ on how best to pursue these interests. Takeyh explains that Iranian politics is dominated by the young of the "new right."[24] The new right is split between two primary factions, the hard-line conservative radicals represented by Ahmadinejad, and the pragmatic conservatives represented by Rafsanjani and Larijani. The new right is in agreement that Iran is destined to be a great power while the United States is a declining great power. The new right is split over how best to facilitate Iran's rise— through a hard-line approach to the failing United States and West or through compromise and coexistence. The new right also is split in terms of the hardliners' adherence to Islamic identity and the pragmatists' adherence to Iranian nationalism.[25] These two factions of the new right were inside Khameini's inner decision-making circle.

Where did that inner decision-making circle stand on the issue of nuclear negotiations with the IAEA and West? If all we had to base our guess

on was the October 2007 resignation of Larijani from the role as chief negotiator, we might conclude that the pragmatists had fallen out of favor
and the hard-liners controlled the policy. But the election of Rafsanjani to
the chair of the Assembly of Experts suggests that the pragmatists were in
an excellent power position, especially with Khameini reported to be in
such poor health. Perhaps the resignation of the pragmatist negotiator
Larijani was Khameini's way to give Ahmadinejad enough rope to hang
himself (as the expression goes) since previously Ahmadinejad blamed
Larijani for failed negotiations.[26] Thus the hard-liners may have been out
of favor. Alternatively, the situation might continue in a kind of stalemate.
As Takeyh concludes: "The supreme leader, who is generally prone to in-
decision, now seems disinclined to settle the internal debates in Tehran in
a conclusive manner."[27] The West might be perceiving a hard-line Iranian
regime, but it might be more accurate to see the regime as deadlocked.
Hermann, Stein, Sundelius, and Walker's decision tree can be a very useful tool for examining this situation as of late 2007.

Using the decision tree in figure 4.1, we start our analysis with question
1: Do all the members of the small inner circle have their primary identity
with the group? Although they all are conservatives, they are conservatives with very different views about how best to pursue Iranian national
interests. Thus, the answer is "no." This takes us to question 6: Do all
members initially have similar preferences on how to conduct nuclear negotiations? The answer is emphatically "no." Question 7 then asks do the
decision rules of the group require that they all agree? From the speculations above, we would be safe to conclude that there are not rules that require unanimity. Indeed, if Khameini has seen himself as a balancer
among different factions (and he has acted as such with his appointments)
then it would make no sense to have unanimity rules. The answer to question 7 is "no." This takes us to question 11: Will the group continue into
the future? There appear to be significant power shifts in the top leadership and with some important reshuffling at the next highest level of leadership in different institutions. It seems likely that this particular group
may not continue into the future. This takes us to question 12: Is there a
respected minority with intense preferences in the group? Although close
to Khameini, Ahmadinejad's position is closer to a minority in the changing inner group. Smyth notes that when in 2006 the inner circle was willing to make greater compromises on the nuclear negotiations, Ahmadinejad already was in a minority position among the top leaders.[28] The
municipal losses and the rise of Rafsanjani also point to Ahmadinejad's
minority position. Yet, his preferences regarding negotiating with the
West are well known and he still has the "respect" that comes with powerful allies elsewhere in the government (such as the Revolutionary
Guard). The answer to question 12 would be "yes," taking us to question

8. Is there a broker present who can mediate between views? On this question, a "yes" is just as plausible as a "no" answer. And either answer will eventually take us to the same place. Following the "yes" branch, we can say that Khameini serves as a broker. This takes us to question 10: Is the broker reinforced by high interpersonal respect? The answer here is "no," since key members of the top decision-making circle have publicly criticized each other's stances. A "no" here means that a deadlock solution is likely. Going back to question 8, which could be answered "yes" or "no," let's follow the "no" branch—"no," there is no broker because Khameini has been unable to balance the interests of the main factions. This takes us to question 9 that asks again whether there is high interpersonal respect among members of the group and the answer here remains "no." This leads to the conclusion that deadlock is very likely.

Using what we have learned about the Iranian highest decision-making group, the facts surrounding Iran's negotiations with the West on its nuclear program, and the small-group decision tree in figure 4.1, we arrive at the conclusion that many analysts have made: the top Iranian decision makers were deadlocked on how to proceed with the nuclear negotiations. From the outside, this looked like defiance and to some states a cause for war. But a more judicious reading of this situation might be to understand the deadlock that Khameini set in place. Further, the West, especially the United States, could modify its own stance, in Takeyh's view, and strengthen the pragmatists by offering relief from sanctions in order to reward the view that compromise and coexistence are the best foreign policy paths to follow.[29] Our experiment with Hermann, Stein, Sundelius, and Walker's decision tree may not be dead-on accurate, but the finding of deadlock seems to match the Iranian situation in late 2007.

MULTIPLE AUTONOMOUS ACTORS AND BUREAUCRATIC POLITICS

The third decision unit in the framework proposed by Hermann and Hermann is that of a coalition of multiple autonomous actors. In this unit, the "necessary actors are separate individuals, groups, or coalitions which, if some or all concur, can act for the government, but no one of which has the ability to decide and force compliance on the others; moreover, *no overarching authoritative body* exists in which all the necessary parties are members."[30] As always, the analyst must determine the rules for interaction in the group, especially those governing conflict and whether the group must form a unanimous or plurality decision.

Complicating interactions within this decision unit is the problem that members of the coalition are "representatives of multiple autonomous

actors [and thus] have no authority except as agents of their respective entities."[31] To understand this decision unit, we need to understand that the
members are motivated to protect the interests of the groups they represent. Thus we must understand some of the basic assumptions of what is
called the bureaucratic politics model. This model is also called the organizational politics model, particularly in the work of Graham Allison. Allison and Philip Zelikow explain the basics of the model in this way:

> The nature of foreign policy problems permits fundamental disagreement
> among reasonable people about how to solve them. Because most players
> participate in policymaking by virtue of their role, for example as secretary
> of the Treasury or the ambassador to the United Nations, it is quite natural
> that each feels special responsibility to call attention to the ramifications of an
> issue for his or her domain. . . . Because their preferences and beliefs are re-
> lated to the different organizations they represent, their analyses yield con-
> flicting recommendations.[32]

In such a system dominated by parochial interests, "government decisions and actions result from a political process."[33] The political process is
dominated, as always, by a competition for resources. The competition for
resources can be "won" by being the actor/group that dominates discussion of the policy choices. This means that "the domestic objectives of bu-
reaucrats may be more significant than the international objectives of governments."[34] For the chief executive who awaits policy recommendations
from different relevant bureaucracies, he or she may find that the recommendations are limited and skewed because they are the result of compromises that were reached among competing agencies to suit their own
bureaucratic needs.

In the multiple autonomous decision-making unit, the chief executive
is one of many actors involved in the bargaining process that eventually
results in a decision. Drawing from the single-group discussion above, we
know that chief executives and others may play the role of broker among
different interests in order to try to put together an integrative or subset
solution. But, of course, at times the process may also tend to stalemate
and deadlock.

An example of how this works would be useful here. Esra Çuhadar-
Gürkaynak and Binnur Özkeçeci-Taner have used the decision unit
framework to analyze two foreign policy problems confronting Turkey.[35]
The first case demonstrates how the multiple autonomous unit makes decisions. Some background is necessary. Cyprus is a country that contains
people of Turkish and Greek origin. When Cyprus became an independent country in 1960, a Treaty of Guarantee was signed between the interested parties of Great Britain, Turkey, and Greece, giving one or all the
right to intervene should the independence of Cyprus be threatened by

anyone. Former Greek nationalists who had fought Great Britain for Cypriot independence turned their attention to Turkish Cypriots upon independence. Intercommunal violence broke out, and eventually a U.N. peacekeeping force was deployed to Cyprus in late 1964 to establish a buffer zone. Nationalist Greek Cypriots, encouraged by Greece, continued to push for Cypriot unification (*Enosis*) with Greece. In 1975, those committed to *Enosis* conducted a coup against the Cypriot power-sharing government and claimed that they would proceed to unification. Turkish authorities were faced with the problem of the coup, the threat to unite Cyprus with Turkey's enemy Greece, and the fate of the Turkish Cypriots if this unification occurred.

Çuhadar-Gürkaynak and Özkeçeci-Taner explain that three choices confronted the Turkish leadership: (1) unilateral military intervention to stop the coup under the authority of the Treaty of Guarantee; (2) bilateral military intervention with the British under the Treaty of Guarantee; or (3) no military action out of concern for Greek or American reaction.[36] What was the nature of the decision unit grappling with this problem? Çuhadar-Gürkaynak and Özkeçeci-Taner rule out the single predominant leader. Prime Minister Bülent Ecevit "had neither the sole authority to commit the resources of the government during any occasion for decision, except at the implementation stage, nor were his decisions irreversible by another entity within the Turkish political system."[37] Further, no single group qualified as the authoritative decision unit since any decision to use the military had to be formally approved by the Turkish Senate, and agreed to by the National Security Council and the military. Thus, the decision unit was a coalition of multiple autonomous actors.[38]

Having identified the decision unit, the analyst must determine the decision rules within the unit. By the Turkish Constitution in place in 1974 and by established rules and practice, the governing rule allowed for a majority decision, rather than unanimity.[39] Members of the coalition held different views about the proper response to the Cypriot coup. Yet, Prime Minister Ecevit had a strong preference for bilateral military intervention working with Great Britain. If Britain would not act, then Ecevit preferred unilateral intervention. Çuhadar-Gürkaynak and Özkeçeci-Taner conclude that Ecevit convinced the military and other members of the coalition that a military response could be successful, thereby brokering a majority of actors in favor of intervention. In the coalition, there may be several actors engaging in the broker role; in this case the foreign minister also worked to create a majority in favor of Ecevit's preferences. Ultimately Britain would not intervene, and so Turkey intervened unilaterally. This caused the Cypriot coup to fail. Turkish forces remained in Cyprus, in time assisting in the creation of a Turkish Republic that no state recognized except Turkey. That is another story for another time!

The multiple autonomous coalition framework might be useful for puzzling through a foreign policy problem facing Turkey in 2007 and into 2008. Turkey had long had a problem with a Kurdish separatist group called the Kurdistan Workers' Party or PKK. The PKK operated within Turkey, but it also took up positions in Kurdish-controlled northern Iraq, at least as far back as the 1991 Gulf War. In 2007, the PKK in Iraq started attacking Turkish positions across the border. Turkey warned the United States, as the occupying power in Iraq, to end the attacks or Turkey would do so itself. The American forces and the troubled Iraqi government had different views on the issue, but ultimately the Iraqi government agreed to work with Turkey to limit the cross-border attacks. When nothing happened to satisfy Turkish concerns, Turkish Prime Minister Recep Tayyip Erdogan sought the permission of Parliament to use military force against the PKK in northern Iraq. By a vote of 507–19, permission was granted. In October 2007 the military assembled 60,000 soldiers, armor, and attack helicopters on the border and conducted air strikes against suspected PKK sites.[40] Four months later, on the evening of February 21, 2008, Turkish troops launched an invasion into Northern Iraq. The invasion force consisted of between 500 and 2,000 troops, a number whose uncertainty resulted from the lack of outside access to the area. After eight days of fighting, the Turkish troops withdrew. The number of fatalities, too, was contested, with the PKK claiming that it had killed 120 Turkish soldiers and only had suffered ten deaths of its own, while the Turkish government claimed it had killed more than 230 PKK fighters and only had lost 24 Turkish soldiers.[41]

When more information is available on this episode, foreign policy scholars might try to map out the internal Turkish politicking that led the prime minister to ask and receive parliamentary approval for military action. It can be assumed that Erdogan already had a policy coalition behind the decision to threaten and use military force before formal approval was asked of parliament. Thus, the key decision making period to examine is in the fall before the October vote. Scholars might ask who was in the coalition that supported the use of military force, whether the members of the coalition acted on primary loyalties outside or within the coalition, whether there was high interpersonal respect within the coalition, whether key individuals played the broker role, whether group norms favored open discussion of dissenting views, and, finally, whether decision rules required a unanimous or plurality decision. This last issue would need to be revisited (despite the earlier case discussion) because of Turkish constitutional changes that have occurred in the last decade. The framework examined in this chapter might help us understand how the Turkish government embarked upon a risky foreign policy action in the winter of 2008.

CHAPTER REVIEW

- The ultimate decision unit is the authority or set of authorities with the ability to commit the resources of the state.

- The ultimate decision unit may be composed of a single predominant leader, a single group, or multiple autonomous groups in a coalition.

- Groupthink is a dynamic in which members of a single group attempt to avoid group conflict before all else.

- In decision unit analysis, a key issue is whether the group's norms discourage dissent or open discussion.

- In decision unit analysis, individuals may play the role of broker to forge a compromise solution.

5

National Self-Image, Culture, and Domestic Institutions

IN THIS CHAPTER

- Similar Countries but Different Foreign Policies?
- Rosenau's Ideal Nation-Types
- National Self-Image
- Culture and Institutions of Governance
- Culture, Institutions, and the Democratic Peace
- Chapter Review

Cases Featured in This Chapter

- The similar characteristics but different foreign policies of Denmark and the Netherlands.
- Canada's self-image as helpful fixer and premier peacekeeper.
- Israeli and Serbian siege mentality and how this national characteristic leads to expectations about preemptive foreign policy behavior.
- Japan's antimilitaristic political culture and Peace Constitution and the nationalist challenges to these.

SIMILAR COUNTRIES BUT DIFFERENT FOREIGN POLICIES?

Denmark and the Netherlands are two small European countries situated on the northwestern coast of the continent. Both have approximately the same amount of territory—43,094 square kilometers for Denmark and

41,526 square kilometers for Netherlands—although the Netherlands has three times the population of Denmark—almost sixteen million people for the Netherlands, and just over five million people for Denmark. Both are founding members of the United Nations and the North Atlantic Treaty Organization (NATO), and both are members of the European Union (EU). Finally, both are parliamentary democracies.

Despite their similarities, there is a difference between the two countries that some scholars have attributed to a difference in national self-image. For example, in a cross-national study that includes Denmark, Ulf Hedetoft depicts the Danes as being "peaceful nationalists"[1] who are somewhat disdainful of countries whose nationalism led them to war—especially war against Denmark:

> Political defeats in war(like) situations have regularly been used to boost the country's cultural nationalism and the reputed "homogeneity" between state and people. This anomaly is based on three distinctive criteria: Denmark is small; Denmark is not the aggressor; Denmark has survived.[2]

Hedetoft writes that, in sport as in war, the Danes hold a different view of themselves when compared to others: "The UK has its violent, racist 'hooligans'; [Germany] has its often intimidating 'Schlachtenbummler' (soccer rowdies); but Denmark takes pride in its 'roligans,' i.e., 'peaceful supporters,' and laps up the international praise it can collect on that account."[3]

Internationally, the Danes contribute substantially to U.N. peacekeeping, in line with the notion of "peaceful supporters," but as a people they tend to be reluctant to cooperate too quickly with others. The Danes are famous for the "no" vote they cast on the Maastricht Treaty on European Union in June 1992. The Maastricht Treaty is the plan for the broadening of the European Community into the European Union—a monetary and economic union that gives citizens of each member state European citizenship and ushered in the single European currency, the euro, among other things. In order for the union to go forward, voters in each of the member states needed to approve it. When the Danes took a vote on union, they voted "no," demonstrating their reluctance to jump onto any bandwagon, no matter how carefully planned. In May 1993, the Danes took another vote and this time agreed to the union on the promise that Denmark would be exempted from certain expectations in the new European Union.

The Dutch could also be considered "peaceful supporters" of the international system, but there is no reluctance on their part to participate. The Netherlands is a country that takes the lead in the writing and promotion of international law. The Hague has been the long-standing home of the

International Court of Justice and, since 1993, has been the site of the International Criminal Tribunal for the former Yugoslavia (ICTY). The Hague is also home to the International Criminal Court (ICC), established formally in July 2002. What is especially remarkable is that the Dutch people have paid most of the costs of the ICTY since its inception.

Peter Baehr asserts that the Netherlands is a country unusually committed to the rule of law internationally, and to human rights law particularly, because of the combination of system-level factors and national self-image. On the system level, the Netherlands always has been dependent on international trade, and the development of international law was crucial to protecting the interests of a trading state. In terms of national self-image, the Dutch as a people believe they must "do some good" in the world, a belief that derives from their religious heritage.[4] This combination of national interest and national self-image creates an interesting domestic political arena where all four major political parties stand committed to an activist human rights policy. Because of this widespread agreement, the details of such policy are left to the Foreign Ministry. By law and practice, Foreign Ministry officials work side by side with human rights nongovernmental organizations (NGOs) to plan and execute Dutch human rights foreign policy.

To understand how the Netherlands came to be called the "international legal capital of the world" by former U.N. secretary-general Boutros Boutros-Ghali, or to understand why Denmark voted "no" on Maastricht, we need to go "inside" each country to explore the dynamics at play within each. A more complete understanding of these phenomena would require us also to examine where each country "sits" in the world (in terms of the power hierarchy of states) and its relations with other countries (i.e., system-level factors), but an examination of the inner workings of each country can yield interesting insights into how and why these countries follow the distinct foreign policies that they do.

Foreign policy study that proceeds from the state level of analysis involves examining different features of a country to see which of those factors shape its foreign policy. At this level of analysis, we include leaders and leadership as important factors, but we add into the mix the country-specific context. This level of analysis is the one that most directly borrows from the insights of comparative politics and regional area specialists. The focus here is what goes on *within* states that ultimately has an impact on what goes on *between* states.

There are two broad categories of factors that we examine at the state level: governmental and societal. Governmental factors include the type of political system, the type of regime that sits atop the government, the division of powers and authority between government institutions, bureaucratic in-fighting among government agencies, and the size and institutionalization of bureaucracies. Societal factors include the type of economic system; the history of the people(s) in the country; the ethnic, racial, and religious mix of the people; the number and activities of interest groups and political parties; and the role of the media in setting the public agenda. These two categories are not exclusive; for instance, it would prove informative in some cases to study state–society relations, the lobbying of government officeholders by interest groups, and the mobilization of public opinion by national leaders.

ROSENAU'S IDEAL NATION-TYPES

There have been some serious efforts to develop midrange theories of foreign policy at the state level of analysis, and some of these go back to the "founding" of the field. In his foundational work (known as the "pre-theories" article), James Rosenau hypothesized that three state-level factors influence foreign policy choice and behavior: size (large or small by population), economic system (developed or underdeveloped as determined by gross national product), and political system (open or closed as determined by whether the country is democratic or not). Rosenau proposed that these factors could be grouped into eight configurations or "ideal nation-types."[5]

Rosenau's primary focus was to develop a typology for ranking variables from five levels of analysis according to the relative importance of each in the foreign policy-making process of the eight nation-types. The following is a list of Rosenau's eight nation-types, his examples of each, and a list ranking the levels of analysis by relative importance for the given nation-type. Keep in mind that Rosenau was writing in the mid-1960s, so some of his examples would not work any longer; for instance, there is no Soviet Union or Czechoslovakia, and India and China have booming economies in 2007 (economies that would no longer fit his "underdeveloped" category).

1. Large, developed, open; example: United States; key levels of analysis: role, societal, governmental, systemic, individual
2. Large, developed, closed; example: Soviet Union; key levels of analysis: role, individual, governmental, systemic, societal
3. Large, underdeveloped, open; example: India; key levels of analysis: individual, role, societal, systemic, governmental
4. Large, underdeveloped, closed; example: China; key levels of analysis: individual, role, governmental, systemic, societal
5. Small, developed, open; example: Netherlands; key levels of analysis: role, systemic, societal, governmental, individual

6. Small, developed, closed; example: Czechoslovakia; key levels of analysis: role, systemic, individual, governmental, societal
7. Small, underdeveloped, open; example: Kenya; key levels of analysis: individual, systemic, role, societal, governmental
8. Small, underdeveloped, closed; example: Ghana; key levels of analysis: individual, systemic, role, governmental, societal

The purpose of the "pre-theories" article was to sound a call to action (research) for foreign policy scholars. With Rosenau's musings as launching pads, scholars could begin a systematic search for pieces of knowledge that could be used both for grounding future research as well as for building generalized theory around which the scientific study of comparative foreign policy could coalesce.

> The concept of nation-type [made] it unnecessary to examine individual nations in considering the certain types of foreign policy activity. To this extent, [scholars could] move away from analysis of discrete objects and concentrate on classes of objects and the different patterns of foreign policy associated with each.[6]

Thus, ideal nation-types were conceived as tools for facilitating the development of general statements linking state type and foreign policy behavior.

Upon Rosenau's call, other researchers started searching for statistical evidence to support the proposition that physical size, economic development, and political orientation were significant in explaining the variation in states' foreign policy behaviors. One research effort in this vein was conducted by Maurice East and Charles Hermann. East and Hermann used the Comparative Research on the Events of Nations (CREON) data set to test twenty-seven bivariate hypotheses linking size, economic development, and political accountability with nine foreign policy behaviors. Of the single indicators, East and Hermann concluded that physical size best accounted for behavior. The next most important indicator was political accountability, especially when combined with economic development.[7] On the other hand, they were unable to find much support for Rosenau's ideal nation-types. That is, "large, developed, open" states did not engage in foreign policy behaviors that were distinctive from, say, the behaviors of "small, developed, open" or "small, underdeveloped, closed" states.

Although Rosenau's ideal nation-types were not shown by research efforts to be linked to specific foreign policy behaviors, the idea that particular kinds of states engaged in particular foreign policies was not put to rest. Similar research attempts to rank states on combinations of indicators that suggest something, for example, about the degree to which states are penetrated by and successful at globalization,[8] are failing or have failed to function as states,[9] or create and sustain peace.[10] A recent ranking of states is illustrative here. The First Global Peace Index was constructed by the *Economist* Intelligence Unit in early 2007.[11] This index was intended as a measure of states' peacefulness based on twenty-four indicators, including local "ease of access to 'weapons of minor destruction' (guns, small explosives), military expenditure, local corruption, and the level of respect for human rights." The results were reviewed and approved by "an international panel of the world's leading peace experts."[12] The top ten countries on the Peace Index were, in order: Norway, New Zealand, Denmark, Ireland, Japan, Finland, Sweden, Canada, Portugal, and Austria. The United Kingdom ranked forty-ninth on the list, and the United States ranked ninety-sixth. Also "at the wrong end of the scale"[13] were Russia (118th), Israel (119th), Sudan (120th), and finally Iraq (last at 121st).

Despite the poor rankings of the United States and United Kingdom (democracies both, but bellicose countries of late), one of the more enduring research lines linking state type and foreign policy behavior is the "pacific democracies" or democratic peace research that will be discussed at the end of this chapter (and in the next chapter). The democratic peace theory says that a democratic country's culture and the resulting political institutions make it more likely than not to engage in peaceful foreign policy behaviors, especially toward other democratic countries. To get to this theory, we first need to consider the impact of a country's culture and self-image on its foreign policy.

NATIONAL SELF-IMAGE

National self-images "consist, at least in part, of idealized stereotypes of the 'in-nation' which are culturally shared and perpetuated."[14] The Dutch view that their country should "do some good" in the world is a manifestation of aspects of the Dutch self-image that comes out of a common sense of history, religious imperative, and social obligation. As suggested earlier, Baehr attributes the substantial strength and depth of Dutch commitment to an international legal system, particularly on human rights issues, in part to this Dutch national self-image.

National self-image, like its close sibling nationalism, can have a good face and a bad face. Historically, the good face of nationalism is linked to the demand for self-government, and often democracy. Similarly, a positive national self-image can contribute to stable governance. As Matthew Hirshberg writes,

The maintenance of a positive national self-image is crucial to continued public acquiescence and support for government, and thus to the smooth, on-going functioning of the state. . . . This allows government to go about its business, safe from significant internal dissension, and to expect a healthy level of public support in times of crisis.[15]

Like the Netherlands, with its national self-image constructed on the notion of doing some good in the world, Canada has a similar national self-image—that of the "helpful fixer" and "peacekeeper par excellence."[16] Canadian self-image, like Dutch self-image, is attributed in part to religious heritage. J. L. Granatstein writes,

Probably the idea [of the helpful fixer and peacekeeper par excellence] emerged out of the missionary strain in Canadian Protestantism and Roman Catholicism that saw Canadian men and women go abroad in substantial numbers in the nineteenth and twentieth centuries to bring the word of God to India, Africa, and China . . . the "do-good" impulse that they represented was a powerful one, and it had its strong resonances in the Department of External Affairs.[17]

Granatstein goes on to explain that many members of the early Canadian diplomatic corps (in the interwar period) were the children of missionaries or clergy and had been born abroad.

The self-image of Canada as the peacekeeper par excellence is backed with substantial evidence: Canadian U.N. ambassador Lester Pearson won the Nobel Peace Prize in 1957, along with U.N. secretary-general Dag Hammarskjöld, for developing the idea of neutral peacekeeping. Canada has been a leading participant in nearly all of the U.N. peacekeeping operations. Extending the notion of "keeping the peace" into other political dimensions, Canada has been one of the leading countries in accepting refugees from war-torn areas. Further, Canada's foreign policy since the end of the Cold War has been reoriented to addressing a wider notion of "human security," a concept that requires attention to the problems of civilians in war zones, the use of children as combatants, and rebuilding war-torn societies.[18] In 1997, Canada was a leading state in the International Campaign to Ban Land Mines, a campaign involving for the first time concerted efforts by states and NGOs (in fact, the NGOs led the way). On March 1, 1999, the Convention on the Prohibition of the Use, Stockpiling, Production, and Transfer of Antipersonnel Mines and on Their Destruction—also known as the Ottawa Treaty—came into force with ninety-four states as signatories, a product of Canada's strong commitment to peace and security in the world.

Paradoxically, positive national self-image also can have a negative effect on a country's foreign policy. For example, Matthew Hirshberg tested the hypothesis that a positive, patriotic self-image interferes with Americans' ability to keep watch over the government's foreign policy behaviors. Hirshberg's subjects were only able to recall details of fictional news stories that featured the United States doing stereotypically good things, and his subjects re-created the details of news stories that featured the United States doing bad things (such as supporting nondemocratic governments against prodemocracy dissenters) in order to select out the negative information about the United States. Hirshberg claims that his findings show that "Americans rarely interpret or remember things in . . . ways that threaten their patriotic self-image." As a result, he concludes:

> even if American news consisted equally of information consistent and inconsistent with this [patriotic American] stereotype, Americans would, at least in the short term, tend to find its confirmation in the news. The stereotype interferes with information otherwise capable of cuing alternative perspectives. This increases popular support for military interventions that are or can be viewed as instances of a benevolent America protecting freedom and democracy from a perceived threat, such as communism. It also allows politicians and officials to elicit such support by promoting the application of the stereotype to specific conflicts.[19]

The danger in this is that "in the end, citizens' abilities to critically monitor and evaluate American foreign policy is [sic] impaired, and the ability of government to pursue unsavory policies with impunity is enhanced."[20]

Alastair Johnston sees a dynamic at play between positive self-image and a negative stance toward out-groups: "The creation of and intensification of group identities . . . positively correlates with the degree of competitiveness with the out-group."[21] Johnston contends that government efforts to promote active nationalism and group identity have a direct impact on relations between states:

> Identity construction, and its intensity, determine anarchy and how much fear and competition results. Applied to international relations, then, the literature would suggest that changing intensities of in-group identity affect the degree of outwardly directed realpolitik behavior, regardless of changes in structural environment.[22]

At issue for Johnston is Chinese government policy aimed at constructing a Chinese ethno-identity and nationalism. By Johnston's argument, we can expect such a policy—if successful—to correlate with an increasingly self-interested, aggressive, and competitive foreign policy, even in the absence of external threats to China.

National self-image contains a message (implicit or explicit) about those outside the nation—our nation is good, therefore other nations are not (as) good. This mirror image may even suggest that vigilance must be the constant order of the day or the good nation will be at risk. Studies of siege mentality, such as Daniel Bar-Tal and Dikla Antebi's study of Israeli siege mentality, suggest that governments are given permission to conduct aggressive, preemptive foreign policies in order to protect the good nation from the actions of evil nations. Bar-Tal and Antebi define siege mentality as "a mental state in which members of a group hold a central belief that the rest of the world has highly negative *behavioral* intentions toward them." This culturally shared and perpetuated belief is complemented by the belief that the group is alone in the world, that it cannot expect help in times of crisis from anyone, and therefore "all means are justified for group defense."[23] Siege mentality is more than a group-shared paranoia; paranoia is an unfounded fear of others, whereas an historical, evidentiary basis exists for siege mentality.

Yugoslavia in the postcommunist era is an excellent example of a country manifesting strong elements of siege mentality. The former Yugoslavian president Slobodan Milosevic manipulated historical examples of Croatian and "Turkish" or Muslim attacks on the Serbian nation to foster a strong and particularly aggressive modern Serbian nationalism. Milosevic used this nationalism to wage war on Croatia and then Bosnia in the early 1990s toward the goal of creating a greater Serbia. When Milosevic turned Serbian nationalism on the ethnic Albanian people of the Yugoslavian province of Kosovo in early 1998, his Serbian forces managed to displace or kill a third of the total population in a matter of weeks. This prompted nearly two months of NATO air strikes against Serbia, which only reinforced Serbian siege mentality and nationalism. These air strikes came on the heels of nearly a decade of international economic sanctions against Yugoslavia for its involvement in the Bosnian war. Ultimately Milosevic was forced from power through elections and a "people's revolution," but the new Serbian leaders demonstrated the same suspicion of the intentions of the outside world. Countries exhibiting high degrees of siege mentality require careful handling by the outside world in order not to cue automatic distrust and noncooperation. Bringing Yugoslavia back into the community of states will take time and patience given the intensity of Serbian nationalism and siege mentality during the 1990s.

The leaders of the former Soviet Union displayed siege mentality when they viewed their country as a "besieged fortress" in the 1950s. There was clear cause for suspicion about the intentions of other countries. By 1955, the United States had managed to form military alliances with a series of countries that, taken altogether, nearly encircled the Soviet Union and communist China. Present-day, post-Soviet Russia appears to have retained this suspicion about the outside world, even as it struggles with an age-old identity conflict over whether it is essentially a Western country or a unique Slavic country. A conflicted national self-image results in a conflicted, sometimes contradictory foreign policy as competing tendencies vie for control over who and what defines the nation.

CULTURE AND INSTITUTIONS OF GOVERNANCE

A culturally maintained national self-image does more than just influence the broad notions and directions of a country's foreign policy. National self-image and the culture that supports it also influence the types of institutions constructed within a state and the foreign policy decision-making authority allotted to those institutions.

It should go without saying that a people's culture will influence the shape and type of its political structures when that people is self-governing. For example, once we have found that a country exhibits high degrees of siege mentality, it should come as no surprise to find mandatory, universal military conscription. The urgent need to protect the in-group results in the practical need for a strong and ready military. The need for a strong military necessitates conscription. In Israel, all Jews and Druse must serve in the military—men for thirty-six months and women for twenty-one months. Switzerland's well-known image as a neutral country contains the same elements of distrust of out-groups. Swiss men between nineteen and twenty years of age must perform fifteen weeks of active military duty, followed by ten three-week reservist training periods over the subsequent twenty-two years.

Consider the case of Japan. After its defeat in World War II, Japan reconstructed itself into a antimilitaristic country, as signified by its Peace Constitution. Chapter II, Article 9 of the Japanese Peace Constitution reads:

> Aspiring sincerely to an international peace based on justice and order, the Japanese people forever renounce war as a sovereign right of the nation and the threat or use of force as means of settling international disputes.
>
> In order to accomplish the aim of the preceding paragraph, land, sea, and air forces, as well as other war potential, will never be maintained. The right of belligerency of the state will not be recognized.

Japanese nationalism since 1945 until the present has been channeled into the pursuit of economic security, especially the goal of reducing reliance on imported raw materials through the development of "technological autonomy."[24] Two dominant cultural norms—antimilitarism and economic nationalism—informed and reinforced the institutions of governance as well as defined what the Japanese perceived as appropriate foreign policy behavior. For instance, on the issue of human rights, the Japanese believed that they were in no position to preach to others given their militaristic past, opting instead to pursue straightforward, nonpolitical economic goals in bilateral relations, especially in Asia.[25]

As might be expected, the Japanese government agencies in charge of pursuing economic security were given more real power and authority than those tasked with military defense. What is surprising is the degree to which this has been true, as elaborated by Peter Katzenstein and Nobuo Okawara. The three most powerful state institutions—and the ones with essential control of national security policy—are the Ministries of Foreign Affairs, Finance, and International Trade and Industry.[26] Conversely, the Japanese Defense Agency (JDA) did not have cabinet-level status until 2007. The civilian staff of the JDA was "colonized" by civil servants from other ministries, and the JDA lacked a mobilization plan, an emergency civil defense system, and rules for engaging the enemy.[27] Military ambitions were kept in check by cultural norms that structured institutional constraints.

Japanese military defense in the post–World War II era has rested on three pillars: the Peace Constitution, the Japanese-American Security Treaty, and the Charter of the United Nations. In the new millennium, American pressure on Japan to commit greater resources toward its defense, along with international pressure on Japan to play a more significant role in global affairs (especially U.N. peacekeeping) have run headlong into Japanese cultural and institutional rigidity. But of late there are signs of divisions among the Japanese that could indicate that the dominant pacifist culture is under challenge from a more nationalist subculture. Two recent prime ministers, Junichiro Koizumi and Shinzo Abe (both of the Liberal Democratic Party or LDP), were known for their more open nationalism and for their vision of a more assertive Japan in the world. Koizumi was noted for his trips to the Yasukuni Shrine honoring Japan's war dead. Koizumi even committed Japanese naval vessels to assist in the U.S.-led war on terrorism and sent Japanese military personnel into Iraq in noncombat roles. Abe went further by supporting a revised history of Japan that would eliminate references to Japanese wartime human rights abuses, such as those committed against so-called "comfort women." And, in late 2006, Abe pushed two laws through the Japanese parliament that were intended to be the start of the rewriting of the Peace Constitution.[28]

In December 2006, on Abe's urging, the Japanese parliament "broke two postwar taboos" by passing legislation that upgraded the status of the JDF to ministry level and required schools to teach patriotism.[29] The new Defense Ministry does not have the range of powers of other ministries, but the upgrade sets the military on a course that could be accelerated by more vocal Japanese nationalism. More Japanese nationalism is the goal of the second piece of legislation. Schools are one of the most effective transmitters of patriotic and nationalistic values in any country, as any government knows. The new education requirements were supported by school boards but strongly opposed by Japanese teachers as too reminiscent of Japan's war-era education system that encouraged support for imperialism and the military.[30]

The governing party's nationalist turn and its inability to overcome leadership failures and serious economic problems led to the LDP's electoral loss of the upper house of parliament in July 2007. The Democratic Party won the upper house by focusing on domestic issues, although its opposition to Abe's nationalist goals and the deployment of troops to Iraq were well known.[31] The Democratic Party flexed its muscle by refusing to reauthorize the refueling of American and allied warships by Japanese tankers. The Democratic Party contended the refueling mission violated the pacifist constitution.[32] With the lower house in the hands of the LDP and the upper house in the hands of the Democratic Party, parliamentary paralysis resulted. This paralysis ultimately contributed to the resignation of Abe, and haunted the new LDP prime minister, Yasuo Fukuda, as well. The lower house finally reauthorized the refueling mission (knowing the upper house would resist) within days of a mid-November 2007 White House visit by Fukuda. Still, Fukuda met the U.S. president for the first time against the backdrop of more delay by the upper house as Japanese tankers headed home.[33] Ultimately, the refueling mission was restarted. The full impact of this crisis on the Japanese pacifist culture is yet to be seen.

CULTURE, INSTITUTIONS, AND THE DEMOCRATIC PEACE

The greatest concentration of scholarly activity on the impact of culture and institutions on foreign policy has been on the idea of the democratic peace. This research finds its intellectual roots in philosopher Immanuel Kant's proposition that democracies are peace-loving countries.[34] In the first modern variation on this idea, it was asserted that democracies are less likely to go to war than nondemocratic states. In a later version, the idea was refined to the proposition that democracies do not fight wars with other democracies. If true, a world of democracies would be a world freed from war. When national leaders, such as former U.S. president Bill Clinton, speak about "enlarging the circle of market democracies," they speak (and sometimes act) on the assumption that the idea of the democratic peace is more than an idea, it is an operating reality.

There are two explanations of why democracies are or should be more peaceful than nondemocracies—the first explanation emphasizes the culture of democracies and the second emphasizes domestic institutional structures. The cultural explanation proposes that "liberal democracies are more peace loving than other states because of the norms regarding appropriate methods of conflict resolution that develop within society."[35] Further, "leaders choose to employ the standards and rules of conduct which have been successful and acceptable at home in their international interaction."[36] Leaders of democracies are not constrained by peaceful standards when dealing with nondemocracies, since nondemocracies cannot be expected to be similarly constrained. The second explanation stresses the constraining role of democratic institutions on foreign policy decision makers. The division of and checks on power within democratic governments and the ultimate restraint of officeholders having to face voters in regular elections prohibit violent (and costly) foreign policy behaviors.[37]

The idea of the democratic peace has generated much excitement and much criticism. Critics point out a number of weaknesses in the proposition: that interstate war is rare; that the number of democracies at any given point in history has been small; that, for the bulk of the second half of the twentieth century, most democracies were primarily Western states bound together in military alliances against the Soviet bloc; and that these same democracies were also the world's richest states bound together by class-based interests. The democratic peace idea also has been accused of being another justification for Western imperialism.[38] This criticism is that Western states claim moral cause to impose their political and economic structures on other peoples in the name of creating a more peaceful world. During the Cold War, these same states claimed the need to defend democracy against communism as their justification for neoimperial policies in the developing world. Other criticisms of the democratic peace literature focus on the methodology or the manner in which democratic peace research is conducted.

Despite the criticism, proponents declare that the proposition of the democratic peace is so robust that it amounts to the only "law" in the study of international relations.[39] The criticisms have not deterred research programs intent on fleshing out the nuances of the proposition. It may well be, however, that the democratic peace idea has had a setback with the more militaristic foreign policies of the U.S. Bush administration and the British Blair government. Bruce Russett, one of the leading theorists on the democratic peace, writes that the Bush administration grossly distorted the theory in order to justify war against Iraq post hoc.

Many advocates of the democratic peace may now feel rather like many atomic scientists did in 1945. They had created something intended to prevent conquest by Nazi Germany, but only after Germany was defeated was the bomb tested and then used—against Japanese civilians whose government was already near defeat. Our creation too has been perverted.[40]

CHAPTER REVIEW

- Efforts to link state type with particular foreign policy behaviors go back to the founding of foreign policy analysis and the "pre-theories" work of James Rosenau.

- Except for the contested theory that democracies do not go to war with other democracies, there is little evidence that state type is linked to particular foreign policy behavior.

- National self-image helps build a loyal population that will not evaluate leaders' decisions too critically.

- National self-image is like nationalism; both have positive and negative sides.

- The political institutions of a self-governing people should reflect the dominant political culture of that people.

6

Domestic Politics

IN THIS CHAPTER

- Considering Government Type and Process
- Domestic Politics: The Critical Side of the Nested Game
  Accommodate, Insulate, or Mobilize
  Democratization and War
- Chapter Review

Cases Featured in This Chapter

- How the governing United Progressive Alliance coalition of India almost let a nuclear treaty with the United States slip away in order to keep the coalition together and in power.
- The nested game and domestic political problems confronted by Palestinian leader Yasser Arafat and Israeli leader Ehud Barak that stopped them from concluding a significant accord regarding Palestinian sovereignty.
- The unruly domestic political situation that encouraged Russian leaders Boris Yeltsin and Vladimir Putin to adopt neoimperial, belligerent policies, sending Russian democracy off-course.

CONSIDERING GOVERNMENT TYPE AND PROCESS

In 2004, the Indian National Congress Party, led by Sonia Gandhi, formed an alliance with four communist parties to govern India. The coalition

95

was called the United Progressive Alliance (UPA). Manmohan Singh was selected by the Congress Party leadership to be the prime minister. In August 2007, the leader of the largest communist party threatened to bring down the coalition government on a critical foreign policy agreement with the United States. As these things go, the main opposition party, the Bharatiya Janata Party (BJP), also opposed this agreement and might have benefited if the communists pulled their support from the UPA and caused the government to collapse. The agreement at issue did not require parliament's approval, but the Congress Party–dominated UPA needed the communist parties to stay in the coalition in order to get any of its legislation passed.[1]

The Singh government found itself in a near-paralyzing and potentially embarrassing foreign policy situation because of Indian domestic politics. Such a nested game problem should remind the readers of this book of the situation confronted by the Japanese prime minister when his party lost the upper house of parliament to an opposition party that refused to reauthorize Japan's military refueling mission to the U.S.-led war on terror, which was recounted in chapter 5. That particular Japanese prime minister ultimately resigned, leaving the domestic political fray (and the resulting fissures in Japanese-U.S. relations) to a new prime minister. Although the Indian prime minister did not offer to resign over the intracoalitional dispute, he almost let the agreement with the United States collapse in order to keep the communists in the UPA and thereby keep the UPA in power.[2] This was no standard-issue agreement for India, yet Singh and the Congress Party apparently were willing to see it die rather than lose political power.

The agreement at issue was a nuclear treaty signed between India and the United States in 2005. As quick background: India has never signed the Nuclear Non-Proliferation Treaty (NPT). Indian leaders have stated that until the world is nuclear weapons-free, India will retain its sovereign right to arm and defend itself in whatever way it can. In 1974, India successfully tested a nuclear weapon. Since then, India has been prohibited by the United States and other countries from buying civilian nuclear fuel and technology. Despite this ban, India's nuclear weapons program continued; and, in 1998, India and enemy Pakistan engaged in tit-for-tat nuclear weapons tests. The following year, India and Pakistan fought a war in India's Kargil region.[3] Additional U.S. sanctions were put in place against both countries in response to these tests, but these sanctions were eventually altered after the 9/11 terrorist attacks on the United States and the start of the U.S. global war on terror.

According to the terms of the 2005 treaty, India would still not sign the NPT, but it would be given the right to buy civilian nuclear fuel and technology. In return, India would allow inspections of its civilian nuclear facilities by the International Atomic Energy Agency (IAEA). Its military nuclear facilities would be separated from its civilian facilities and *not* subject to IAEA (or any other) inspection. India also bargained for and won the right to reprocess nuclear fuel for energy generation. For India, the treaty validated its position as a nuclear weapons power and would help its booming, "energy-hungry" economy.[4] For the United States, the treaty would open the door to the Indian economy for U.S. manufacturers and put U.S.-India relations on a different footing. Before the treaty could become fully operational, India would ask for "India-specific" exemptions and safeguards from the IAEA and then seek the approval of the Nuclear Suppliers Group (a coalition of forty-five countries that export nuclear material but only to coalition-approved countries). Ultimately, the U.S. Congress needed to approve the treaty in its final form.

The Indian communist parties—coalition partners in the same government that negotiated the treaty—objected to the treaty because it would tighten the relationship between India and the United States. In August 2007, the communist parties threatened to leave the government unless the Congress party rewrote the treaty before the Indian government went before the IAEA.[5] If the communists withdrew from the coalition, early elections would be called with no guarantee that the Congress Party could win enough seats and coalition partners to retain control of the government. In mid-October, the prime minister and party head indicated that they would not risk a general election for the sake of the treaty. That is, holding onto power at home was more important than consolidating a treaty that was a win-win situation for India, diplomatically, militarily, and economically.

Political fortunes change, however, and the strength of coalition members can also change. A few weeks after Congress capitulated to the communist parties, the communist parties removed their objections to the treaty process. "Communist leaders finally relented after they apparently saw their own political standing diminish after weeks of criticism over their response to violent farmers outraged over land rights issues in West Bengal," a state controlled by the largest communist party.[6] In mid-November, the Indian government began its negotiations with the IAEA for the "India-specific" safeguards. Attempting to reassert their position, the communist parties warned that all they had agreed to were negotiations, not a final deal.

The leaders of the UPA coalition in India found themselves in a classic nested game. On the other side of the deal, the Bush administration had had to move the treaty through a less-than-enthusiastic U.S. Congress in late 2006 and early 2007, and would need to take the treaty back through congress in 2008 right before national elections in the fall. For the Bush administration, however, the dual game was less threatening since Bush was prohibited from seeking a third term in office. Singh, Gandhi, and the Congress Party were not term-limited and apparently would scuttle a significant international agreement rather than lose their grip on power.

The dual or nested game, as discussed in chapter 1, is one in which national leaders (however leadership may be configured) find themselves working between domestic and international politics, generally putting domestic goals ahead of international. As Peter Trumbore and Mark Boyer explain, "At the national level, domestic groups pressure the government to adopt policies they favor, while politicians seek power by building coalitions among these constituents." Meanwhile, at "the international level, governments seek to satisfy domestic pressures while limiting the harmful impact of foreign developments."[7] The critical point is that the domestic political game is primary for any government, regardless of government type. "[N]o leader, no matter how autocratic, is completely immune from domestic pressure, whether that takes the form of rival political parties seeking partisan advantage, as in a democratic setting, or rival factions jockeying for influence and power in a bureaucratic-authoritarian system."[8]

DOMESTIC POLITICS:
THE CRITICAL SIDE OF THE NESTED GAME

Government type is important in that it tells us which political actors and resources are legitimate and the processes by which policy decisions are made. But regardless of government or regime type, what is important to the analyst is identifying the domestic political process by which winners and losers are determined on any given foreign policy issue. The process involves some interaction between members of the governing regime and other critical actors, interaction that is characterized by formal (generally written) and informal rules. The motivation of the actors, in the most basic terms, is to retain or gain political power within these rules (and sometimes despite these rules when their aims are revolutionary). Political power is not necessarily the end point, as the actors also have policy agendas they want enacted. Thus, the actors are also motivated to build and maintain policy coalitions.[9] How actors attempt to manage the domestic political game—to bargain with opponents and/or supporters or not, to attempt to make decisions as if they are not bargaining when they are, to push through a dominant solution or attempt to strike a compromise position, to take actions that lock all the actors into a stalemate or deadlock—has consequences in both the immediate and longer term.

Two scholarly frameworks can help us understand the impact of the domestic political game on foreign policy choices and behaviors. The second of these frameworks is offered as an explanation for why certain kinds of countries might engage in risky foreign policy behaviors, specifically the use of force or war. But with some minor modifications, the basic dynamics of both of these frames can help us understand why the Singh-Gandhi government would be willing to put a decidedly good-for-India treaty with the United States on the chopping block.

Accommodate, Insulate, or Mobilize

Building and maintaining policy coalitions and retaining political power are particularly difficult in highly politicized contexts in which a large and vocal opposition exists. When the issue at hand is a foreign policy matter and it becomes linked to questions about the legitimacy of the leadership, Joe Hagan proposes that leaders resort to three different political strategies to manage the challenge posed by the domestic opposition: (1) accommodation, (2) insulation, and (3) mobilization.[10] Each of these represents a single dynamic at play in a larger, complex political environment in which choices made on one issue can confound and restrain a government's choices on other issues.

The accommodation strategy involves bargaining with the opposition and controversy avoidance. Here "leaders seek to contain opposition, and thus retain political power, by avoiding publicly disputed policies and actions that make the country appear weak in international affairs or are closely associated with a widely acknowledged adversary."[11] Restraint in foreign policy is the expected result of an accommodation strategy, but at times efforts intended to avoid controversy can result in foreign policy deadlock. In the insulation strategy, the leadership attempts to deflect attention from foreign policy issues through suppressing or overriding the opposition, or, if all else fails, through neutralizing the opposition with favors and promises. The goal is to maintain a chosen foreign policy course by reducing the domestic constraints.[12] Finally, a mobilization strategy involves the manipulation of foreign policy to one's own political advantage usually through greater risk taking. Leaders assert their legitimacy by confronting the opposition through appeals to nationalism, imperialism, or by "scapegoating" foreigners. Leaders claim that they—and not their domestic opponents—have a "special capacity" to maintain the country's security and status abroad. When successful, this strategy works by "diverting attention from divisive domestic problems."[13]

Another case study can illustrate these strategies and how each has implications for foreign policy choices. In 1996, Yasser Arafat was elected president of the Palestinian National Authority (shortened here to the Palestinian Authority, or PA), the governing body of the Palestinian people living in the West Bank and Gaza. Arafat was also the leader of Fatah, one of several Palestinian organizations that joined together under the umbrella framework known as the Palestine Liberation Organization (PLO). Arafat served as chairman of the PLO in its long struggle to reclaim territory subsumed by the state of Israel in its 1948 unilateral declaration of independence and in subsequent wars with Arab states. The West Bank and Gaza were captured by Israel in the 1967 war from Jordan and Egypt, respectively.

The government of Israel and the PLO signed a peace treaty in 1993. This treaty set in place mechanisms for future negotiations regarding the transfer of authority and land in the West Bank and Gaza to the PA. The amount of territory to be transferred to the PA, the enumeration of details regarding whether the PA was to be partially or fully independent of Israel, the rights of displaced Palestinians, and the resolution of competing claims to Jerusalem were left to subsequent negotiations.

In 1996, Benjamin Netanyahu was elected prime minister of Israel in a landslide election, defeating sitting Labor prime minister Shimon Peres. Although a hard-liner by reputation and the leader of the conservative Likud Party, Netanyahu began the transfer of some territory to the PA as part of the continuing peace process. But after a series of deadly suicide attacks against Israelis, Netanyahu stopped some troop withdrawals from, and lifted a freeze on Jewish settlements in, the disputed territory in contravention of the peace process. Then, in October 1998, more negotiations between the Israelis and Palestinians resulted in a three-stage agreement for the transfer of more lands. Netanyahu completed the first stage of this transfer and then was defeated in Israeli elections by Ehud Barak in 1999.

Barak led a coalition called One Israel to a landslide victory over Netanyahu and Likud. One Israel was a fragile coalition of divergent parties, including Barak's own Labor Party. In a demonstration of the fragility of Barak's coalition and hold on power, the Knesset (the Israeli parliament) elected to the powerful role of speaker a Likud party leader. Barak and Yasser Arafat signed the Wye River Agreement under the mediation of U.S. president Bill Clinton in September 1999. Barak transferred land and released two hundred political prisoners in the second part of the three-stage peace process. In July 2000, President Clinton sponsored another series of talks at Camp David in order to initiate the third stage of the peace process. These talks failed to produce an agreement, and both Barak and Arafat indicated that the position of their respective sides had hardened. Arafat announced that the PA would make a unilateral declaration of independence in September absent further agreement with the Israeli government.

Although Arafat postponed the unilateral declaration, events in late September 2000 brought the peace process to a deadly halt. Ariel Sharon, one of the leaders of the opposition Likud Party, and a group of followers and Israeli troops went to a disputed site in the Old City of Jerusalem, a place the Jews call the Temple Mount and the Muslims call Haram al-Sharif (Noble Sanctuary). Sharon's goal was to demonstrate Israeli commitment to maintaining full access to the Old City. His very public display on a Friday, a day of special religious observation for Muslims, prompted a Palestinian crowd to form in protest. Rocks were thrown and bullets were fired—the rocks from the Palestinian side, the bullets from the Israel side—and months of active low-intensity conflict began. In this conflict (which in some ways is still simmering as of mid-2008), the death toll was taken disproportionately on the Palestinian side.

The Hagan framework can be used to explore responses to this conflict on both the Palestinian and Israeli sides. On the Palestinian side, Arafat governed with the assistance of a small council of appointees from his political party Fatah. Arafat had a major domestic opponent in the person of Sheikh Ahmed Yassin, the spiritual leader of Hamas. Hamas was formed in 1987 at the start of the intifada, or Palestinian uprising, in Gaza and the West Bank. Hamas could be termed an indigenous organization as opposed to Fatah and the PLO who spent decades outside of the disputed territories and thus outside of Israeli occupation. Hamas's purpose was twofold—to provide humanitarian assistance to Palestinians in Israeli-occupied territory and to coordinate military/terrorist activities aimed at the Israelis. Sheikh Ahmed Yassin spent eight years in Israeli prison until released in 1997 in a deal made between Israel and Jordan. Yassin had declared that Israel was attempting to destroy Islam and because of this loyal Muslims had a religious obligation to destroy Israel. Arafat and the PLO also had been committed to the violent elimination of the state of Israel, but this position was reversed in 1989 (the same year that Yassin was imprisoned by Israel). It should go without saying that Yassin and Hamas opposed the agreements made between Arafat and the Israeli government.

In the first week of fighting after the Sharon visit to Haram al-Sharif, seventy Palestinians were killed in the streets while confronting Israeli security forces. During that week, the Israeli government demanded that Arafat reestablish order in the West Bank. Arafat's reply was to express outrage, but he made no move to deploy an effective Palestinian police presence to quell the uprising. As Israeli leaders continued to demand that Arafat assert control and the Israeli defense forces were deployed, Arafat's leadership began to be called into question. Either Arafat could not control the uprising, or he did not want to control it; the former suggested that the political balance had shifted in favor of a dangerous element in the Palestinian community, the latter suggested that Arafat condoned the use of violence to force Israeli concessions in negotiations. Neither explanation implied good things for the peace process.

One explanation of Arafat's lack of effective police response is that political power had shifted in the Palestinian community, putting into doubt

Arafat's ability to retain political control, much less retain a strong coalition in support of further agreements with the Israelis. After the first week of conflict, Hamas declared that the following Friday would be a "day of rage" against Israeli rule—the first of many to come. The first "day of rage" call was answered by a mass outpouring in the West Bank and Gaza with the end story being ten Palestinians killed and dozens injured. Significantly, Arafat's Fatah issued support for the "day of rage" after it was clearly under way.[14]

Once begun, the street uprising and violence continued. International efforts to broker a cease-fire were met at times with obstinacy from both Arafat and Barak and, at other times, with agreements that subsequently were broken. Arafat kept insisting that the Palestinian people were only defending themselves against the Israeli military and that a multinational investigation should be conducted into the causes of the violence.

Arafat's hard line toward Israel had started months before at the Camp David talks. Arafat's approach to Camp David and his later threat to unilaterally declare the independence of Palestine might have been manifestations of his decision to employ a mobilization strategy (as per Hagan's model). Perhaps Arafat calculated that in the face of growing opposition by Hamas and his own worsening public opinion standing he needed to assert a hard face toward the Israelis. This hard line would demonstrate his continued commitment to the Palestinian people and his special capacity to lead them to statehood. Taking a tough negotiating stance with the Israelis might slow down the peace process in the short term, but reinvigorating his regime against domestic opposition and retaining political power were Arafat's priorities. Arafat's initial refusal to order an effective Palestinian police presence to stem the riots might be seen as the continuation of this risky behavior. There was a symbolic Palestinian police presence in the streets, but Arafat insisted that the uprising was a spontaneous response of the people which would stop when the Israelis stopped using violence and conceded to a multinational investigation.

Unfortunately, Arafat's mobilization strategy worked to the advantage of Hamas. Until Fatah announced its support for the first "day of rage," Arafat's regime had said nothing publicly to encourage violence against Israelis. Hamas forced Arafat's hand in calling for the "day of rage," forcing him to adopt a violent pose or risk being seen as unsupportive of the people's right to defend themselves against Israeli aggression.

On the other side of this particular dual game, Arafat's support for the second intifada provided evidence to Israeli hard-liners of Arafat's true intentions and untrustworthiness. This, in turn, would create strong domestic opposition to Barak's government. Barak's fragile One Israel coalition was all but gone by the time of the Camp David talks. By late November, after two months of violence in the West Bank and Gaza, Barak was forced to call for early elections in the face of mounting domestic political attacks on his government. Before Barak made the call for new elections, he had issued ultimatums to Arafat, approved significant escalations in the use of military force, and desperately courted Ariel Sharon to join a new emergency government. Barak's bid to woo Sharon failed, while peace with the Palestinians—still Barak's long-term foreign policy goal—seemed more remote with each passing day.

Applying the Hagan concepts, we can say that Barak's use of military force against the Palestinians was a manifestation of a mobilization strategy. Barak was demonstrating that he and his government were willing and able to defend the state of Israel against all threats, implying by comparison that his political opponents possessed no special capacity to do so. Barak's subsequent efforts to bring Ariel Sharon into an emergency government can be seen as an accommodating, co-opting move, signaling Barak's desire to preserve some maneuvering room for his long-term foreign policy agenda. Significantly, Barak maintained throughout the crisis that the peace process was not dead and could be recommenced.

The Barak government did not survive the crisis despite efforts to co-opt or neutralize Sharon. Early elections in February 2001 brought Ariel Sharon to power. Sharon served as Israeli prime minister until he was debilitated by a stroke in January 2006. His successor, Ehud Olmert, facing his own difficulties retaining political power and maintaining a policy coalition, brought Labor back into his cabinet. In mid-2007, Barak returned to the cabinet as defense minister and head of Labor, threatening to pull Labor out of the coalition if Olmert and Likud did not comply with Labor's demands regarding an investigation into Israel's 2006 war with Hizbollah in Lebanon.

Democratization and War

The Hamas-Fatah political struggle continued in the Palestinian territories, sometimes eclipsing the Israeli-Palestinian conflict. There were some indications that the Palestinian territories were moving to incorporate democratic institutions by 2005 and 2006. In January 2005, Mahmoud Abbas of Fatah was elected to the presidency in an election that Hamas supporters boycotted. The next year, Hamas ran in and won parliamentary elections in which participation was widespread and competition was unfettered. Would these elections change the dynamics of the Palestinian-Israeli relationship? Would democratic Israel and an apparently democratizing Palestine move into a "democratic peace" relationship? Events on the ground made this contemplation moot as Fatah and Hamas soon engaged in open civil war. Further, Hamas kidnapped an Israeli soldier in 2006, initiating a series of events—including punishing Israeli military operations against Gaza—that ultimately led to a war between Israel and Hizbollah in Lebanon. At the same time, evidence from other scholarship would tell us that countries undergoing democratic transitions are *more* bellicose than countries that are fully autocratic or fully democratic. A democratizing Palestine, if such were the case, would not necessarily seek peaceful solutions to common problems with Israel.

The last chapter ended with a consideration of the "law" of international relations that democracies do not engage in war with other democracies—the democratic peace theory. This theory is based on an expectation of a strong relationship between stable democratic norms or culture and stable democratic institutions. Getting to this point, however, may involve a difficult transition in which changing norms, expectations, and institutions combined with threatened old elites and rising new elites create dynamics that lead to war. The transition to democracy may be a period in which a state is *more* likely, not less likely, to go to war with other states, regardless of whether the targeted state is a democracy or not. The dynamics in this offer both a note of caution to the democratic peace idea and an elaboration on the domestic political processes at issue in this chapter.

The definitive research on the dangers of the democratic transition comes from Edward Mansfield and Jack Snyder. Building on the work of other scholars, they conceptualize democratization as a process in which societies move toward open, competitive, and well-regulated political competition; open competition and recruitment for the position of chief executive; and constitutional constraints on the exercise of power by the chief executive. Analyzing data often used to support the democratic peace theory, they find that "an increase in the openness of the selection process for the chief executive doubled the likelihood of war"; "increasing the competitiveness of political participation" increased the chances of war by 90 percent; and "increasing the constraints on a country's chief executive" increased chances of war 35 percent. States moving from full autocracy to full democracy "were on average about two-thirds more likely to become involved in any type of war."[15]

Transitions involve phases, and countries may get stuck in a phase; or the process may even get reversed as the country returns to autocracy. Mansfield and Snyder conclude that states "stuck" in the first phase of democratization "during which elites threatened by the transition are often still powerful and the institutions needed to regulate mass political participation tend to be very weak" are especially bellicose.[16]

What accounts for these findings? Mansfield and Snyder suggest that the dynamics of democratization combine to form an unstable mix of "social change, institutional weakness, and threatened interests."[17] As citizens are freed to participate in politics through political party and interest group activities, they begin to make demands on the central government. These demands must be met or quelled, even as the central government's power is being intentionally diminished by constitutional design. The government, then, must build and maintain a policy coalition among diverse and vocal interests—some old actors in the system, some new actors in the system—while hanging on to its crumbling power and authority. Mansfield and Snyder conclude that "one of the simplest but riskiest strategies for a hard-pressed regime in a democratizing country is to shore up its prestige at home by seeking victories abroad."[18]

Let's put this into the context of culture or norms and institutions. Democratization is a period in which a society must acquire liberal norms and identity. At the same time, the society experiences institutional change including the "establishment of stable institutions guaranteeing the rule of law, civil rights, a free and effective press, and representative government."[19] The relationship between democratic culture and institutions is of course weak in this period, but each is critical to the deepening of the other. The transition can be completed—democratic norms and institutions can be consolidated—without war. But sometimes the transition period (and the still-to-come democracy) so threatens the position of elites that they attempt to retain control by substituting populist or nationalist norms for liberal democratic norms in order to win the support of mass publics and stay atop the political game. To the extent that elites can get mass publics to buy into a populist and/or nationalist ideology, they may be able to suspend the process toward fuller democratization.[20]

How does this lead to international military disputes? Mansfield and Snyder offer three "related mechanisms" that are similar in process and result to Hagan's strategies discussed above. First, Mansfield and Snyder say that elites may engage in "nationalist outbidding: both old and new elites may bid for popular favor by advancing bold proposals to deal forcefully with threats to the nation, claiming their domestic political opponents will not vigorously defend the national interests."[21] This should sound similar to Hagan's mobilization strategy in which elites attempt to stay in power by claiming a special ability to defend the national interests. Second, Mansfield and Snyder offer a second mechanism they call "blowback from nationalist ideology: nationalists may find themselves trapped by rhetoric that emphasizes combating threats to the national interest because both the politicians and their supporters have internalized this worldview."[22] This blowback is similar to what happens in Hagan's accommodation strategy when elites attempt to accommodate the nationalist rhetoric of opponents only to become trapped into limited policy choices by their own talk. Finally, Mansfield and Snyder say that elites may engage in "logrolling." In this, various elites form a nationalist coalition weakly held together by a protracted external problem, usually military engagement abroad. Here, we might consider Hagan's insulation strategy with a twist: a coalition of elites can agree that they wish to stay on top but the only way they can do so is if they create an external situation that diverts attention from them, insulating them from critical domestic opponents and popular demands. Protracted military conflict becomes the method by which elites "logroll" and put off further steps toward the consolidation of true democratic change.

Mansfield and Snyder use historical and recent examples to illustrate their statistical findings. One example is particularly compelling—post-Soviet Russia. This example demonstrates how elites may be tempted to use force abroad and at home to deal with the threat and chaos of democratization.

Fifteen countries were formed at the collapse of the Soviet Union, but there might have been at least one more. One month before the collapse of the Soviet Union, Chechen nationalist leaders declared the independence of Chechnya. Chechnya, one of twenty-one Russian republics (administrative units), sits in southwestern Russia, along the northern border of the former Soviet Republic of Georgia (now an independent country). The Chechen people are Sunni Muslims, and their land contains considerable oil reserves.

Russia did not recognize the Chechen unilateral declaration of independence, but it also made no move to do anything about the "breakaway" republic until late 1994. In December 1994, the Russian government launched a massive military invasion of Chechnya. Most of the Russian fire power was concentrated on the capital city of Grozny, the home of almost half of the republic's population. Grozny was nearly flattened by the Russians, yet it did not fall to them for almost two months. Fighting in the first Chechen war raged on until 1996, despite the overwhelming force employed by the Russians against the Chechen guerrillas.

Why did Russian leaders delay responding to the Chechens in 1991? Why was there no response even when Russian troops were expelled from Chechnya a short time after the unilateral declaration of independence? It is safe to argue that the Russian leadership was too preoccupied with managing all the other changes in Russia—as well as those in some of the former Soviet republics—to give Chechnya much notice. When the Russian leaders did move to reestablish control of Chechnya, it was probably to reestablish control in all of Russia and its "near abroad," not just in Chechnya.

What kinds of challenges were confronting the government at this time? Those that spring from democratization. Fourteen months before the Russian troops launched the invasion of Chechnya, Russian troops were ordered to fire upon the Russian Duma (parliament). Russian president Boris Yeltsin had been feuding with the Duma over constitutional changes he wanted. The Duma was full of various and sundry parties and factions, many of whom were left over from the Soviet days and opposed to Yeltsin's overall political agenda, especially his economic reforms. Fed up with the Duma, Yeltsin called in the troops and launched a two-day shelling of the White House where the Duma sits. The action killed as many as 150 people but was fairly popular among the Russian public and went without much official notice by foreign governments. Yeltsin did get the constitutional changes he wanted, but the reconstituted Duma remained fairly defiant and argumentative. Such was the difficult domestic political context facing the Yeltsin government.

Recall Mansfield and Snyder's warning: "One of the simplest but riskiest strategies for a hard-pressed regime in a democratizing country is to shore up its prestige at home by seeking victories abroad." When Yeltsin decided to send troops into Chechnya in December 1994, it was in the context of a volatile Russia and unwieldy democratization. Mansfield and Snyder write that,

> One interpretation of Yeltsin's decision to use force in Chechnya is that he felt it necessary to show that he could act decisively to prevent the unraveling of central authority, with respect not only to ethnic separatists but also to other ungovernable groups in a democratizing society. Chechnya, it was hoped, would allow Yeltsin to demonstrate his ability to coerce Russian society while at the same time exploiting a potentially popular issue.[23]

Of course, Chechnya was an internal security problem for Russia, not a foreign policy issue. But the same forces that propelled Russian leaders to use force in Chechnya were apparent in Russian relations with the other former Soviet republics in this same time period. Neil MacFarlane points out the degree to which Russia was engaging in aggressive foreign policy behavior:

> Elements of the Russian military assiduously manipulated the civil conflicts in the [Transcaucasus] region (notably the Nagorno-Karabakh conflict between Azerbaijan and Armenia and the conflicts between Ossets and Abkhaz on the one hand and Georgians on the other in the Republic of Georgia) in order to return the governments of the region to a position of subservience. . . . Azerbaijan is the only country in the Transcaucasian region with no Russian forces within its border, but it has been under significant Russian pressure to allow a return of the Russian military, coordination of air defense systems, and joint border control. Many have interpreted Russian support of the Armenian side in the Nagorno-Karabakh dispute as a means of bringing Azerbaijan to heel.[24]

Rajan Menon, in an article that appeared in print the summer before the Russians launched their invasion of Chechnya, gave this same basic domestic politics calculation for determining whether Russia would assert its neoimperial face in the former Soviet Central Asian Republics.[25] The likelihood of neoimperialism—a "risky" foreign policy behavior using Hagan's term—depended upon the strength of proimperial coalitions versus the "democratic reformers" led by Yeltsin. The proimperial coalition was composed of groups nostalgic for different reasons for the old Soviet empire. This same coalition was part of the problematic Duma that Yeltsin shelled in October 1993. Shelling the Duma might be considered an insulation strategy as described by Hagan (an effort to neutralize the Duma), but it might be difficult to maintain the guise of democratic reformer if one uses military force against one's own parliament too often!

Instead, Menon proposed that Yeltsin engaged in an accommodation strategy to deal with the proimperial groups:

> More important than the existence of such coalitions is the extent to which Russia's governing democratic elites feel compelled by their weakness to engage in appeasement and accommodation toward these coalitions. They have done so to avoid being outflanked by ultra-nationalists, who have successfully manipulated the symbolic appeal of a virile defense of Russian interests and ethnic Russians in the former Soviet republics.[26]

Unable or unwilling to neutralize the opposition, Yeltsin switched strategies and co-opted the powerful symbols of the opposition in order to assert his own regime's special capacity to preserve the security and prestige of Russia. Yeltsin's strategic policy spoke of the former Soviet republics as the "near abroad" in which Russia had special rights, "obligations," and "responsibilities." And democratic reformers noted that Russia had a security interest in "our own foreign countries," that sometimes would require the use of Russian "peacekeepers" therein.[27]

Menon warned that, in adopting an accommodation strategy, "forces within the state capable of countering neoimperial elites and offering alternative paradigms of statecraft have been weakened."[28] The reformers became trapped by co-opting neoimperial rhetoric, increasing the possibility of neoimperial behavior. Menon worried about the Central Asian republics, but he might have looked within Russia to see where Yeltsin would turn next to legitimize his power.

Yeltsin's military campaign in Chechnya in 1994–1996 did not play out the way he had hoped. Domestic and international opposition to the campaign arose quickly. Indeed, Yeltsin could blame the new climate of democratization with its requisite political openness and mass participation in politics for the failure of his Chechnya policy, at least in part. Russian journalists quickly exposed the campaign for its barbarity, stupidity, and costliness. Other actors in the newly created Russian civil society actively opposed the war. One group, the Committee of Soldiers' Mothers of Russia (CSMR), was a particularly vocal opponent, organizing demonstrations and the March of Mothers' Compassion from Moscow to Grozny in spring 1996. As reported by the Inter Press Service, "Hundreds of mothers went to Chechnya to take their sons away from the battlefront. Some carried out negotiations themselves with the Chechen army to secure the release of sons held as prisoners of war."[29] Once the protests began, they did not end until a cease-fire was arranged in August 1996.

However, in 1999, Yeltsin restarted the military campaign in Chechnya after a number of unsolved "terrorist" bombings of civilian apartment buildings and public spaces in Russia. By this time, Yeltsin had instituted political change that made his office into a super-presidency, rather than a restrained chief executive. Perhaps because the economic and social fabric of Russia was still so unstable and perhaps because the government successfully scapegoated the Chechen rebels for the bombings, the public rallied behind the military campaign. At the start of 2000, Yeltsin's hand-picked acting president and soon-to-be-elected successor Vladimir Putin also enjoyed considerable public support for his own military campaign in Chechnya. In one campaign stunt designed to take advantage of popular support for the new nationalist war in Chechnya, Putin visited troops in Grozny aboard a two-seat Sukhoi-27 fighter bomber.[30] In time, Putin would do even more than Yeltsin to reverse course and return Russia to near-autocracy.

CHAPTER REVIEW

- National leaders play a two-level or nested game between international and domestic politics.

- National leaders in any type of political system are motivated by two similar goals: retain political power and build and maintain policy coalitions.

- Leaders will sometimes engage in risky foreign policy behaviors in order to undercut the nationalist rhetoric of opposition elites and prove their own government's legitimacy.

- Democratization is a transitional phase that can get stuck or reversed when threatened elites use nationalist mobilization strategies to stop the erosion of their power.

7

Public Opinion and Media

IN THIS CHAPTER

- Public Opinion Matters—But How?
- Different Views on the Public
- Public Opinion in Nondemocracies and Democracies
- Public Opinion and the "CNN Effect"
- A Complicated Relationship: Government, Elite, Media, and the Public
- Chapter Review

Cases Featured in This Chapter

- Chinese public protests in 2005 against the possibility of U.N. Security Council permanent membership for Japan and the role of the Chinese government in the protests.
- The relationship between public opinion and regime legitimacy in nondemocratic Arab countries.
- How integration into the mainstream culture increases the power of ethnic interest groups in the United States.
- British government efforts post–World War II to shape a single media portrayal of the Soviet Union.
- How the Reagan administration's successful framings of the shootdowns of a Korean Air Lines flight by the Soviet Union and an Iran Air flight by the U.S. Navy stopped the opposition and media from producing alternative explanations for the events.

PUBLIC OPINION MATTERS—BUT HOW?

In chapter 5 we discussed how the dominant Japanese pacifist political culture was being challenged by a nationalist subculture. This potential change in political culture had an impact on public opinion in China in 2005, as will be discussed shortly. That nationalist challenge in Japan resulted in the election of ardent nationalist leadership in the governing Liberal Democratic Party (LDP). In early 2005 the LDP leadership issued new history texts to remove the more unsavory events in Japanese military history during the first half of the twentieth century. Two years later, the government passed legislation requiring the teaching of patriotism in Japanese schools.

In the same time period that the history texts were revised, Japan was making its case internationally for a permanent seat on the U.N. Security Council. The Security Council has five permanent seats (held by the United States, United Kingdom, France, Russia, and China) and ten rotating seats. Japan's bid for a permanent seat rested largely on the strength of its financial contributions to the United Nations. U.N. membership dues are calculated by the size of national economies. Japan makes the second-highest financial contribution to the United Nations after the United States. Using 2005 figures, Japan's assessment was 19.47 percent ($279.6 million) and the United States's was 22 percent ($362.7 million). The American assessment should have been higher, but the American government insisted on a lower rate cap of 22 percent. Of the other permanent members, the United Kingdom was ranked fourth in assessments at 6.13 percent, France was fifth at 6.03 percent, and China was ninth at 2.05 percent. Russia did not rank among the top ten U.N. financial contributors in 2005. If assessments were considered in terms of per capita income, the top ten contributors in 2005 were, in order, Luxembourg, Switzerland, Japan, Liechtenstein, Norway, Denmark, Iceland, Qatar, Austria, and the Netherlands.[1] This list contains not a single member of the permanent five. Japan's view was clear: if it paid so much to maintain the U.N. system, it should have a voice commensurate with its contributions. That voice meant permanent membership, since the real power of the United Nations lies there.

Japan was pushing its candidacy in 2005 because of a World Summit scheduled for September that was to consider the issue of reforming the United Nations. Adding permanent member seats to the Security Council was one critical issue under debate. As the Japanese began their public relations campaign in early 2005, a different campaign opposed to Japan's bid took form in China. Many popular Chinese websites began a petition campaign in February against the Japanese. By the beginning of April, the websites claimed they had gathered twenty-two million signatures that they would present to the U.N. secretary general as proof that world (but mostly Chinese) opinion was against a permanent seat for Japan. The primary reason given for this was Japan's lack of serious remorse and retribution for its wartime atrocities.

China was not known (and still is not known) for its unrestricted Internet. Large Internet providers engage in self-censorship in order to avoid Chinese government sanctions. Thus, the online campaign was seen as facilitated by the government to serve its own purposes. "By allowing millions of people to sign their names to a petition against Japan, Beijing's new leadership seemed determined to show that recent Japanese actions had so inflamed popular sentiment that China had no choice but to adopt a tougher diplomatic line."[2] The website organizers soon joined student and business groups in orchestrating street protests against the Japanese. The first of these protests occurred against Japanese businesses in Shenzhen, but spread within a week to the Japanese Embassy in Beijing and consular offices and businesses in Shenzhen and Guangzhou. In previous years, the Chinese government had encouraged street protests to show its anger, for instance, over the 1999 U.S. bombing of the Chinese Embassy in Belgrade, Yugoslavia.[3] The anti-Japanese protests were encouraged by Chinese official statements that the Japanese had no one but themselves to blame. A Chinese Foreign Ministry spokesman said, "Japan must conscientiously and appropriately deal with its history of invading China [which is] a major issue of principle involving the feelings of the Chinese people."[4] These allegedly spontaneous protests by the Chinese people were called off after a couple of weeks by the government, using both persuasion and intimidation to indicate that enough was enough. Chinese citizens were warned by text messages from the police that further protests would not be tolerated.[5]

Many issues drove the problematic relations between the Chinese and Japanese in this period. These included Japanese claims to some islands and oil reserves in the South China Sea, the increased nationalism of Japanese leadership, the new textbooks already mentioned, and Japan's bid for a permanent seat in the U.N. Security Council. At the same time, China had replaced the United States as Japan's primary export market in 2004; and China's economy had "helped pull the sluggish Japanese economy out of recession."[6] We might, then, think about the anti-Japanese protests as a negotiating tool of the Chinese government in its dealings with the Japanese. Japanese commentators were more quick to blame the Chinese educational system for the protests. The protests were "testimony to the impact of the Chinese government's intensely patriotic education system that has imbued the public with anti-Japan sentiment."[7] One may wonder what will happen between the two countries when Japan's new education reform laws aimed at instilling greater patriotism get implemented and take hold.

There is a lot to discuss in this case, but let's limit ourselves to Chinese protests as a reflection of public opinion. The Internet protests and later street protests were not organized by the Chinese government. These seemed to have been genuine reflections of public opinion on Japan. Yet, the Internet and street protests would not have been tolerated for as long as they were if the Chinese government did not find them useful in constructing its policy toward Japan. One of the most basic questions in the study of public opinion and foreign policy is: Does public opinion influence and shape a government's foreign policy, or does the government influence and shape the form of public opinion on foreign policy issues? The Chinese case suggests that the answer is a little bit of both—that the relationship between the public and foreign policy decision making is complicated. The Chinese case also demonstrates that public opinion matters to governments, even in nondemocratic systems.

DIFFERENT VIEWS ON THE PUBLIC

The relationship between public opinion and foreign policy making is complicated. Scholars and policy makers offer different views on this relationship, but not views that are always compatible. Some of the early foreign policy studies on public opinion focused on whether the public held a structured, coherent view on foreign policy matters. In a 1950 study, Gabriel Almond established one strong position in the scholarship by contending that American citizens were ignorant of foreign policy issues and that their opinions lacked structure and content.[8] This left the public open to volatile mood changes. According to Ulf Bjereld and Ann-Marie Ekengren, in the 1970s other scholarship took the position that there was structure, coherence, and stability to the public's foreign policy views. Scholars taking this position set out to identify the public's belief sets on foreign policy.[9] The foundation of all of this work was in cognitive understandings of human belief sets.

For our purposes, studies that analyze the structure of the public's foreign policy beliefs are less important than studies that offer insight into how public opinion either shapes foreign policy making or is shaped by the policy makers. We are interested here in any purported impact rather than cognitive structures. There are two basic views on the relationship between public opinion and policy making. The first suggests a strong impact, and the second denies any real impact. The first view derives from the pluralist model of policy making. This view is "a 'bottom-up' approach [which] assumes that the general public has a measurable and distinct impact on the foreign policy making process. In sum, leaders follow masses."[10] The second view "representing the conventional wisdom in the literature suggests a 'top-down' process, according to which popular consensus is a function of the elite consensus and elite cleavages trickle down to mass public opinion."[11] This view is consistent with realism, as it envisions a persistent national interest pursued by elites and a passive, acquiescent, or inconsequential mass public.

Foreign policy scholars of this second approach take care to distinguish between three different publics. The first is the mass public that is not interested in foreign policy matters, holds no or only poorly informed views on foreign policy, and therefore has no impact on policy making. The second is the attentive public, which, by its name, is attentive to or interested in and informed about world affairs. But, this group only has an impact on foreign policy making if its views are articulated by interest groups whose power resources are greater than an amorphous public. Finally, there is the elite, that small section of the public that is interested, informed, and influential in the shaping of public opinion. Distinguishing the pubic by these three groups follows the realist bend of earlier studies that dismissed the public as ignorant and volatile (and, manipulable).

Ole Holsti's study of the impact of public opinion on American foreign policy cautions that the relationship between policy and public opinion is more complex than that suggested by these earlier views. Using data on public opinion, Holsti dispels the notion that the American public is unknowledgeable about or indifferent to foreign affairs; but he proposes that the public acts like a cognitive miser, making use of mental shortcuts when confronted with international issues. Recall from chapter 3 that when scholars conceptualize individuals as cognitive misers, they suggest that people do not exert great cognitive energy when confronted with new information. Instead, the new information cues preexisting shortcuts so that it matches information already "stored." Therefore, the new information is remembered in a way that is consistent with the individual's preexisting belief set. Holsti concludes that the American public makes use of cognitive shortcuts that follow a pragmatic internationalist orientation.[12]

The linkage between public opinion and policy formation is more difficult to demonstrate. Holsti says that although American policy makers tend to be more inclined to internationalism than the American public, the policy makers are restrained by their perception of what the public will tolerate. Policy makers believe the public is harder to convince about internationalist policies—especially policies that involve international cooperation and/or the possible deployment of U.S. troops abroad—and the lack of public support could jeopardize any undertaking.[13] Holsti concludes that there is no direct linkage between public opinion and policy formation, but that policy makers' perceptions of public opinion—in the immediate and future sense—set the parameters for foreign policy behavior.

Although scholars have provided evidence to the contrary, it seems intuitive that pluralistic countries—democracies—should exhibit more of the bottom-up impact of public opinion on foreign policy, while nondemocratic countries would be more likely to exhibit the top-down relationship. Public opinion should matter more in democratic states. Public opinion in nondemocracies, on the other hand, should be a nonfactor in foreign policy making, or should play at best an instrumental role for elites. The research, however, does not support these simple generalizations. Instead, public opinion is seen to have an indirect impact on policy making in democratic states, while public opinion in nondemocracies matters more than an elite-driven model would allow. This gray area is more understandable when we recall that policy makers' perceptions of public opinion are crucial.

PUBLIC OPINION IN NONDEMOCRACIES AND DEMOCRACIES

Does public opinion matter in nondemocracies as much as democracies? The short answer is yes. Democratic structures allow public opinion to manifest itself in different ways than do nondemocratic structures; but as we discussed in the last chapter, leaders of any type of regime need to pay attention to opponents and whatever resources those opponents wield. Public opinion is a political resource wielded by different actors (including the public itself) in different ways.

For an example of how public opinion matters in nondemocratic states, consider the work of Shibley Telhami on Egypt, Syria, Iraq, Jordan, Tunisia, Israel, and the West Bank in 1990 and 1991. His goal was to determine whether public opinion had any impact on the foreign policies of Arab states. In Arab countries, Telhami proposes, government legitimacy derives not from elections but from the mass public's perception of the given regime's adherence and faithfulness to powerful transnational symbols. There are two symbols that transcend borders and ideological differences among Arab states: support for the Palestinian people's right to self-determination and statehood, and anticolonialism (which translates into anti-Israeli and anti-American sentiments).[14] Arab regimes compete with one another for regional leadership, because (among other reasons such as power and prestige) obtaining regional leadership is proof of one's service to the two pan-Arab symbols.[15] Should a public perceive its government to be weak in supporting these two symbols, street protests and rioting result, and social movements opposed to the governing regime may take root. Arab governments challenge each other's leadership by attempting to manipulate public opinion in the target state through media campaigns aimed at questioning the loyalty of the target regime. "Successful" regimes are able to control the media messages to which their publics are exposed, and thereby keep people off the streets at less expense than using coercion.

Telhami gives examples of what he proposes. During the 1950s and 1960s, Egypt attained regional leadership by using military power and leverage against Israel and Western interests. But the Camp David Peace Accords with Israel in 1977–1978 removed Egypt's prestige on both transnational symbols. Egyptian president Anwar Sadat was assassinated not long afterward by fundamentalist Islamists from within Egypt. Since that time, the Egyptian government has needed to expend considerable resources to fight the internal threat posed by the organized and potent Islamic Brotherhood.

With the changes that occurred internationally at the end of the Cold War and collapse of the Soviet Union, Arab leaders worried about unimpeded U.S. dominance in the region. Telhami explains that these regimes took different views on the best way to respond to this altered order. Egyptian and Syrian leaders were convinced that the time was not right to get on the wrong side of the United States. They urged caution until a new global order emerged. The Iraqi regime proposed that the Arabs might unite to balance against U.S. domination, while the Jordanian and Palestinian leadership worried that disaster was pending because the United States and Israel would unite against Arab interests.[16] The key for each Arab regime was to portray its views—to its own and to the others' publics—in ways that demonstrated continued support for pro-Palestinian and anticolonial goals while offering a plan for dealing with impending U.S. domination.

At a regional summit in Baghdad in May 1990, the Iraqi regime attempted to claim leadership of the Arab world, broadcasting a call to the pan-Arab public to rally behind its plan for direct and specific Arab counterweight to the U.S.-Israeli threat. Telhami asserts that the Egyptian and Syrian governments were able to maintain their cautious policy by blocking the media dissemination of Saddam Hussein's message to their own publics.[17] Within a few months, Iraq had invaded Kuwait with more calls from Saddam Hussein to the pan-Arab public to rally behind Iraq's first strike at Western domination. Egyptian and Syrian leaders chose to join the U.S.-led coalition against Iraq, a move that these regimes were able to portray to their own publics as in line with the pan-Arab themes. Thus "the information campaign deprived Iraqi leaders of extensive access to the masses they sought to mobilize."[18] There were no significant public demonstrations in Egypt and Syria against the decision to join the U.S.-led fight. Conversely, Jordanian leaders did not attempt to block or counter the broadcasted Iraqi views. Most public demonstrations against the U.S.-led coalition and in favor of Iraq took place in Jordan, a country in which the leadership took no official stand in favor of either side of the war.

In the fall and winter 2000, it was again possible to see the impact of public opinion on Arab leaders. By this time, many Arab states had reached some accommodation and somewhat normalized relations with Israel and the United States. The eruption of violence between the Palestinians and Israelis (the second intifada discussed in the last chapter) put the Arab regimes in a precarious position. People throughout the Arab states were mobilized and on the streets in the tens of thousands in support of the Palestinians, calling on their governments to declare war against Israel. The Arab regimes needed to walk a dual-game tightrope—speaking in outrage about Israeli violence against Palestinians to placate their own people, while being careful not to go too far and jeopardize relations with Israel or the United States. In Yemen, the government decided to take the side of the street protestors and called for an Arab war against Israel,[19] despite the fact that U.S. military ships were using Yemen's ports for refueling at the time. Within days of this call, a terrorist attack on the USS *Cole* in a Yemeni port caused massive damage to the ship and killed sixteen U.S. service personnel.

The goal of the Arab regimes was to preempt any public protest that might take on the shape of organized political movements threatening their power at home and limiting policy options abroad. The terrorist attacks on New York City and Washington, D.C., on September 11, 2001, posed numerous public opinion management challenges to these regimes. Complicating all of this was the fact that although each Arab government still maintained state-run media that would offer the government's line to the exclusion of other views, state-run media was not alone anymore. In 1996, a satellite news channel was started in Qatar called al Jazeera. Although funded by the emir of Qatar, al Jazeera is a politically independent news channel. As al Jazeera's popularity grew in the Middle East and then in the world, and as other independent satellite channels sprung up, Arab governments had to find new ways to present their versions of events and retain the support of their publics in the face of competing media portrayals. These governments might have only looked to the democratic governments for lessons on how to manipulate free media to get the "right" message to their publics.

Let's turn to democratic systems. Recall that in the case of the Netherlands public opinion in support of a strong human rights foreign policy was channeled through human rights NGOs and the four major political parties. Democratic systems by their nature allow for more public involvement in the policy-making process. But, as already pointed out, scholars have wondered about the processes by which public opinion gets translated into influence on the foreign policy-making process in democracies. To some scholars, the articulation of public opinion by formal or informal interest groups appears to be critical to the process in which public opinion shapes policy in any type of political system.

Thomas Risse-Kappen examines the relationship between public opinion and foreign policy making in the United States, France, and other countries. He concludes that "mass public opinion mattered" in each case, in that it "set broad and unspecified limits to the foreign policy choices."[20] Public opinion has an important indirect effect as it appears that "the main role of the public in liberal democracies is to influence the coalition-building processes among elite groups."[21] Further, Risse-Kappen maintains, "For both the political elites and societal actors, mass public opinion proves to be a resource for strengthening one's position in the coalition-building process."[22] Public opinion, then, is the leverage used by elites and interest groups in establishing their claims to dominate a policy coalition.

Additionally, the degree of both societal fragmentation and centralization of political authority are critical parameters in understanding the impact of public opinion on foreign policy. In countries with great societal political fragmentation, such as France, no mass public opinion exists on foreign policy issues. French social fragmentation is "complemented" by the highly centralized nature of political authority; both conditions combine to limit severely the impact of public opinion on foreign policy making. The United States presents a different picture on these two variables. American society is politically heterogeneous, but far less so than French society. Thus it is possible to identify certain policy orientations among segments of the mass public. Whereas centralized political authorities tend to control the formation of policy networks in France, in the United States political authority is decentralized, allowing societal groups to dominate the formation of policy networks.[23] Risse-Kappen concludes that public opinion has more impact on U.S. foreign policy making than it does in the other cases for these very reasons.

How might interest groups in a heterogeneous society attain the opportunity to put their stamp on foreign policy? In his study of the impact of interest groups on the Clinton administration's China policy (a case explored in chapter 1), John Dietrich suggests that interest groups that possess broad leverage over many different policy areas are able to exert greater influence on the making of a particular policy than are single-issue groups.[24] Business and farm groups were critical to the success of the Clinton administration's policies on numerous domestic and foreign policy issues. Once these groups joined forces with the economic executive branch agencies and protrade members of Congress, this policy coalition in support of delinking China trade from human rights was unbeatable. Human rights groups, conversely, tended to be single issue, and they had less ability to link their interests to broader policy coalitions. Knowledge of their own limited leverage in the Clinton administration convinced human rights groups to back away from their prior insistence that trade be linked with human rights conditions, all toward the goal of, at minimum, staying relevant to the political game.

Similarly, Yossi Shain's study of African American and Arab American lobbies in the United States reveals that some ethnic interest groups have greater impact than others on foreign policy making when those groups are more integrated into the broader American political game. Less successful interest groups remain peripheral to the American mainstream.[25] Shain writes to counter the fear voiced by some that the rise of influential ethnic lobbies with strong ties to real or symbolic homelands will lead to a "Balkanization" of U.S. foreign policy. He suggests that the opposite is occurring: as ethnic lobbies join the American political mainstream, embracing the values and political clout associated with it, they become strong voices in support of a U.S. foreign policy that is premised on core American values.

By way of example, Shain contrasts the isolationist black power movement with the integrationist civil rights movement.

> Black Power separatists of the late 1960s advocated national liberation and rejected the civil rights movement's vision of a color-blind, integrated America. Their crusade was bolstered by the successful struggle for independence of African states and by the rise of Third World ideology. Conversion to Islam was a reaction to the perception of Christianity as "a slave religion." Yet, by the early 1970s, black separatism was already waning, as more and more black leaders . . . preached the gospel of power-sharing and pluralism and denounced Black Power as reverse racism. Moderate black leaders realized that only by playing an insider's game and embracing the American electoral system and its democratic values could they hope to become equal participants in American society.[26]

Integration into the American mainstream deepens the potential impact of ethnic lobbies on policy making because these groups' interests broaden to encompass a variety of issue areas, thereby increasing their ability to join policy coalitions. Concurrently, once ethnic interest groups demonstrate their commitment to pluralism, they no longer pose a threat to groups already in the mainstream, also increasing the likelihood of cross-group coalitions on foreign *and* domestic policy issues. To return to Shain's example:

In the African American community, the integrationists' mode of foreign affairs is best represented by TransAfrica. From its inception, TransAfrica considered African American involvement in African and Caribbean affairs to be
an additional mechanism for domestic empowerment. In the crusade to reverse America's posture toward South Africa, TransAfrica endeavored to apply Martin Luther King's domestic strategy of challenging Americans to live
up to their democratic creed.[27]

To bring together some elements discussed above, we can conclude that
public opinion matters, but scholars seem to agree that its impact on policy making is indirect. Public opinion seems to matter most when it has
been filtered through either the perceptions of elite policy makers or interest group and political party activity. But there is another actor that
needs to be considered here—the mass media.

PUBLIC OPINION AND THE "CNN EFFECT"

The above discussion of public opinion in Arab countries considered Telhami's argument that state control of media is critical to maintaining the
legitimacy of nondemocratic regimes, introducing the idea that the media
play an instrumental role for national leadership. But, as with many issues, the full story is more complicated.

There exists in the minds of some observers and policy makers a phenomenon called the "CNN effect." Political scientist and former U.S. as-
sistant secretary of defense for international security affairs Joseph Nye
explains the CNN effect in this way:

> The free flow of broadcast information in open societies has always had an
> impact on public opinion and the formation of foreign policy, but now the
> flows have increased and shortened news cycles have reduced the time for
> deliberation. By focusing on certain conflicts and human rights problems,
> broadcasts pressure politicians to respond to some foreign problems and not
> others. The so-called CNN effect makes it harder to keep some items off the
> top of the public agenda that might otherwise warrant a lower priority.[28]

Nye sees the CNN effect as real and potentially harmful to reasoned
policy making. Because the news broadcasts "24/7," the media sometimes force issues out into the open, issues policy makers would be hap-
pier to keep in the dark. This, in turn, lessens deliberation time and the
search for the most reasonable policy response.[29]

Those who believe that the CNN effect is real propose that it makes use
of public opinion. Once the media broadcast images of mass starvation,
ethnic conflict, or some other sort of mass suffering, the images arouse

strong emotions in the public. The public then turn to their elected officials and demand some strong and morally correct response. That is, the
public, aroused by images of suffering protrayed in the media, demand
that officials "do something." Elected officials, wanting to stay in the public's favor for all sorts of obvious reasons, respond with some sort of humanitarian intervention, military intervention, or whatever action is
needed in the immediate term.

This suggests that the media play a powerful role in setting the public
agenda. How powerful is this role? Jonathan Mermin poses this question
about the American media: "Journalists necessarily engage in agenda setting, in deciding out of the vast universe of events what to report and
what to ignore. *But in setting the news agenda, what rules do journalists follow?*"[30] Mermin asks an important question: How do the media decide
when to cover a story out of the many, many stories that might be covered? He suggests two possible answers. First, the media act indepen-
dently and "independent journalistic initiative" puts stories in the head-
lines.[31] Mermin cites the story of one NBC correspondent who decided on
his own to publicize forgotten stories. He single-handedly put the story of
the 1984 Ethiopian famine on the airwaves (a story covered by the BBC
but not American media), prompting an outpouring of U.S. aid to
Ethiopia. But this independent journalistic initiative is the exception
rather than the rule.

The second possible explanation for how the American media come
to cover what they cover is that "American journalists turn to politicians and government officials for guidance in deciding what constitutes news."[32] American journalists—and arguably journalists from
around the globe on issues of broad importance—take their cues from
Washington for practical reasons. Mermin offers three. First, given limited budgets and staff, reporters are assigned to newsworthy places—
Washington, D.C., would rank among the top newsworthy places on almost anyone's list. Second, on foreign policy issues, Washington
generates a plethora of information every day. Third, "considerations of
the need to establish the legitimacy of information reported and the
need for protection against the liability for inaccurate reports also encourage the use of official sources."[33]

At the same time that Washington—or any national capital—makes
practical sense as a location for budget- and personnel-strapped media
outlets, Washington also produces far too much news for the media to
cover. As Mermin puts it, "Far more stories are pitched to reporters than
end up making the news."[34] Members of the media, then, do exercise
some independent judgment about which stories to cover. Mermin suggests this about what ultimately is reported: "The news agenda in this
view is a joint production of sources and journalists."[35]

Mermin supports his conclusions with evidence of news coverage of the famine and conflict in Somalia in the eleven months leading up to the U.S. humanitarian intervention that started in November 1992. U.S. intervention in Somalia was not the result of the CNN effect, but instead "journalists worked closely with governmental sources in deciding when to cover Somalia, and how to frame the story, and how much coverage it deserved. The lesson of Somalia is not just about the influence of television on Washington; it is equally about the influence of Washington on television."[36]

When considering the "joint" agenda setting between government officials and media, can we say the balance of influence leans more toward one side or the other? We might conclude with some degree of certainty that the "power" tilts in favor of those with information—officials—although not overwhelmingly so. We can find support for the idea that the media are driven more by policy makers than policy makers are driven by the media outside the case of the United States. Tony Shaw examines the British popular press coverage of the early Cold War period in order to learn how the press contributed to the eventual consensus that developed between policy makers and the British public. At the immediate conclusion of World War II, Shaw notes, the British press were diverse in terms of political ideologies and portrayals of the Soviet Union, the United States, and the United Nations.[37] In 1947, Shaw asserts, the British press exhibited widely different views on the Truman Doctrine, the Marshall Plan for the reconstruction of Europe, and whether Soviet troops were correct to stay throughout Eastern and Central Europe.

The British government came to a different opinion regarding the Soviet Union and the United States and, Shaw explains, it decided that the press would need to be brought around to the correct view:

> All heads of Foreign Office political departments were instructed on ways to make "subtler use of our publicity machine" to ensure the publication of anti-Soviet material, including various ways of leaking information to friendly diplomatic correspondents and inspiring questions that the Foreign Office could pretend it did not want to answer.[38]

Similarly, the Foreign Office orchestrated a pro–United States, pro–Marshall Plan campaign aimed at changing press views. The aptness of the government's view regarding the Soviet Union was "demonstrated" by the Soviet-inspired communist takeover of Czechoslovakia in 1948. By 1949—just two years into a concerted government effort to manage the press message on the Cold War—the British press was unified in its portrayal of the emerging Cold War, and this portrayal was in line with the government's view.

Further, policy makers can find ways to ignore events that are covered by the media when those policy makers have already decided not to "do something." Encouraged by humanitarian NGOs on the scene, the media *did not* ignore the unfolding genocide and refugee crisis in Rwanda in the summer of 1994. Despite media attention, with the exception of France and to a lesser extent Canada, no major powers called for any type of intervention; and, in fact, the major powers worked within the U.N. Security Council to cut the presence of U.N. peacekeepers weeks before the genocide started. The French call for action, it should be noted, was in *opposition* to any U.N. operation. Media coverage made no difference because policy makers in important countries had decided that intervention would be difficult with little likelihood of success.

Similarly, international media coverage of Russian human rights violations in Chechnya during the first and second Chechen wars evoked little formal condemnation (and no action) by the United States. U.S. humanitarian aid workers attempted to cajole or shame the American government into a more forceful stand on Chechnya, but U.S. policy makers had determined already that they would not jeopardize U.S.-Russian relations on behalf of the people of Chechnya.

Ultimately, the role media play in setting the public agenda is primarily determined by "the conditions that officials themselves . . . create," according to journalist Warren Strobel.[39] Strobel examines the impact of media on the United States' decision to participate in peacekeeping and peace enforcement operations, operations in which media have freer access and thus might be able to generate more pressure among publics for the government to act. Strobel proposes that push and pull factors might be at play: the media might push governments into launching peace operations, or the media might pull governments away from certain courses of action or even cause the termination of participation in peace operations. From his study, Strobel concludes,

> Images and written accounts of the horrors of the post–Cold War world that stream into the offices of government officials do not dictate policy outcomes. Sometimes they suggest policy choices, but there is ample reason to believe that officials can reject those choices if they feel it necessary. At other times, media reports become an ally for an entire administration, or individual members of it, seeking to pursue new policies.[40]

Media, like other societal actors, can take control of a government's policy only when that government loses control:

> If officials let others dominate the policy debate, if they do not closely monitor the progress and results of their own policies, if they fail to build and maintain popular and congressional support for a course of action, if they

step beyond the bounds of their public mandate or fail to anticipate problems, they may suddenly seem driven by the news media and its agenda.[41]

This discussion is not meant to suggest that media have no power to mobilize opinion against a government's policy and cause some change to occur to that policy. Recall from our discussion of the first Chechen war in the last chapter, Russian media and other interest groups were instrumental in forcing the Russian government to end the war. Similarly, U.S. media played a crucial role in mobilizing antiwar sentiment in the United States during the Vietnam War by offering interpretations of events that did not fit the official presentation. Strobel cautioned that we should refrain from making blanket statements about the balance of power between media and government in wartime, since the United States had not yet fought a war that involved a high number of casualties in the era of real-time television coverage.[42] Strobel issued his warning before the 2003 U.S.-led invasion of Iraq. The second Chechen war may be instructive here since media access to Chechnya was controlled tightly by the Russian government. Media and public views of the second Chechen war tended to stay in line with the official view. The lesson seems to be that policy makers—once set on or against a foreign mission—usually can control or ignore the media when they stay in full control of the policy-making process. The American air campaign against the Taliban and al Qaeda in Afghanistan in late 2001 and the subsequent military operations there as well as the U.S.-led invasion of Iraq seemed informed by this lesson. The use of "embedded" journalists limited media coverage to those images that fit the government's depiction of events.

A COMPLICATED RELATIONSHIP:
GOVERNMENT, ELITE, MEDIA, AND THE PUBLIC

This last insight—that once set on a foreign policy course leaders can usually control or ignore media messages—can be expanded to include other actors. Robert Entman offers an understanding of the complicated relationship between policy makers, opposition elites, the media, and the public that combines many of the elements of state-level foreign policy analysis discussed in these last three chapters. In a nutshell, his research suggests that, "in practice, the relationship between governing elites and news organizations is less distant and more cooperative than the ideal envisions, especially in foreign affairs."[43]

The basic set up is this: When a foreign policy problem arises, someone attempts to explain the problem and its solution. That someone might be the policy makers, or what Entman calls the governing elites, or the opposition elites, or even the media. The explaining of the problem and its solution is called "framing." Sometimes the governing elite get out in front of a problem and frame it in such a way as to deny others the ability to offer a competing frame. When this happens, opposition elites and media often reinforce the frame. The single frame then "cascades" down to the public in a small and recognizable package. The public hears from multiple sources that the problem can be understood in a single way and, being cognitive misers, the public is content to buy the single frame and support it.[44]

Framing is not so easy, and it is in the framing that governing elites may get behind on an issue, opening the door to competing frames from the opposition and/or the media. Framing is the act of "selecting and highlighting some facets of events and issues and making connections among them so as to promote a particular interpretation, evaluation and/or solution."[45] Frames that work best are those that have cultural resonance, that is, frames that evoke words and images that are "noticeable, understandable, memorable, and emotionally charged" in the dominant political culture.[46] Such framing is necessary because all actors in the political context are cognitive misers and satisficers.

Successful frames depend on the stimulus: when the foreign policy event is recognizable and congruent with the political culture, then the national response is based on habit. If the governing elite have successfully matched the event with a habitual schema, it requires "almost no cognitive effort [by the public] to make the connections promoted by the administration's frame of the event."[47] In the aftermath of the September 11, 2001, attacks on the United States, the Bush administration framed the problem as a surprise terrorist attack on innocent U.S. civilians. The terrorists were evil and irrational. Those who responded to the attacks were brave heroes. The images in this frame were so easily acceptable to the American public that other elites stayed silent or echoed the administration's frame and the media also repeated the frame. Because Entman assumes that all elites and members of the media are motivated by self-interest and survival, few would dare offer competing frames for 9/11, such as those that sought to understand how American foreign policy would incite individuals to take such extreme actions. In fact, commentators who sought to understand the reasons behind the attacks were marginalized and shunned as unpatriotic.

When an event is totally incongruent with national self-image and habitual response, the public's response is to block information about the event. Elites who get out in front of the framing can capture the public's support by offering an explanation that evokes images that are more reconcilable with the national self-image. Entman proposes that the governing elite's control of the frame is the highest in situations in which the event is totally congruent or totally incongruent with the political culture. He gives two compelling examples to make his case.

In the first case, a Soviet fighter jet shot down Korean Air Lines (KAL) Flight 007, killing all 269 people on board. This occurred in September 1983. In the second case, in July 1988, a U.S. Navy ship shot down Iran Air Flight 655, killing 290 people. "In both cases, military officials misidentified a passenger plane as a hostile target; in both cases, the perpetrating nation's officials claimed that circumstances justified the attacks."[48] In the first case, Reagan administration officials got out in front of the story, depicting the events in a "murder" frame. The story of the evil Soviets (from the habitual Cold War schema) murdering innocent civilians was not hard for the American public to accept. Political survival for opposition elites and sales for the media meant that the frame was never questioned, just repeated and magnified.

In the second case, the events did not fit any habitual schema and indeed were "thoroughly at odds with Americans' national self-image." This incongruent event blocked thinking about the event, allowing the Reagan administration's explanation that the shoot-down occurred due to a technical glitch to dominate.[49] The standard expectations about opposition elite and the media hold in this case: both simply maintained the administration's frame. Indeed, the media devoted more print pages and broadcast time to discussing the "murder" frame involving the shoot-down of KAL 007 than it did to the "technical glitch" frame involving Iran Air 655.[50]

Clearly Entman is proposing what some of the scholars discussed above contend: a government can control its own response to a foreign policy event when it stays on top of the event, framing and explaining the event and the country's response to it. When policy makers let others—domestic political opponents, media—define the event, policy makers lose control of the event. Foreign policy choices in such a case are determined by actors outside the regime, if the regime cannot succeed in distracting the public in order to maintain its own foreign policy frame. Ultimately, the regime that loses control of the frame loses control of the policy.

When a foreign policy event is ambiguous, so that the dominant culture has no immediate, habitual response, opposition elites and the media may be able to offer alternative frames that win critical support among parts of the public. Entman warns that the governing elites tread dangerous waters here and may mismanage the foreign policy event (that is, let others frame the situation and the solution) "especially if it cannot find compelling schemas that support its line."[51] In the American case, the end of the Cold War shattered many dominant schemas, making the public's response to events less predictable and potentially enhancing the role of the media in framing events. In the absence of an all-encompassing schema like the Cold War, media and elites (governing and oppositional) put more time into monitoring public opinion in order to discern which events would resonate and how.[52] Ultimately, this means that understanding public sentiment becomes critical to the shaping of policy that will be supported by the public. A public that is disorganized in terms of its dominant political narrative will not respond in any uniform way to a foreign policy venture. This could be costly to the regime that attempts a foreign policy action that does not resonate as true or right with the public. The Republican Party's loss of the U.S. Congress in the 2006 elections may reflect the cost to governing elites who choose to wage a war that does not fit a dominant cultural schema.

CHAPTER REVIEW

- There is little scholarly agreement on the impact of public opinion on policy making other than that the impact is probably indirect.

- There is little scholarly and practitioner agreement on the "CNN effect," but policy makers seem to believe the effect is real.

- Scholarship on the "CNN effect" shows that it has no impact on policy once decision makers have already agreed on a course of action.

- When a government stays in control of the "framing" of a foreign policy event, it generally can control the views of the opposition, media, and the public on that event.

- When a government lets others define and explain a foreign policy event, it stands to lose control of its own response to that event.

8

Great Powers

IN THIS CHAPTER

- Position and Power
- The Elusive Concept of Power
- Who Gets to Be a Great Power?
- What Do Great Powers Do?
- The Unique Position of the United States
- American Foreign Policy under George W. Bush
- Chapter Review

Cases Featured in This Chapter

- The projection that India and China will be the great powers by 2020 and that the "map" and rules of the game of global politics will change as a result.
- How the U.S. military won the battle but not the "war" against unruly, disorganized Somalian factions in the Battle of the Black Sea, also known as the Black Hawk Down incident, in October 1993.
- The melding of neoconservative and realist foreign policy goals in the foreign policy of the George W. Bush administration.

POSITION AND POWER

The National Intelligence Council (NIC) is the U.S. intelligence community's center for medium- and long-term strategic thinking. The NIC's

purpose is to produce National Intelligence Estimates (NIEs) and unclassified "over the horizon" reports about trends in world politics. The NIC
works under and reports directly to the director of national intelligence.
During the Bush 2 administration, NIEs became notorious for what they
said, what they did not say, and what the administration read them to say.
NIEs bring together the analyses of many U.S. intelligence-gathering
agencies on particular topics. The "over the horizon" NIC reports make
use of the collective understanding of trends in the world derived from
experts from different agencies of the government and from nongovernmental experts from around the world.

In a report entitled "Mapping the Global Future," the NIC looked at
trends to get a sense of the world in 2020. The NIC concluded that four issues will shape the global landscape in 2020: contradictions in globalization, rising (and falling) powers, new challenges to the capacity of states
to govern, and pervasive insecurity. Of these, globalization is the "mega-
trend" that will "substantially shape all the other major trends."[1] Some
countries will reap great benefits from globalization while others will experience relative decline and still others will fall further and further behind. First among the winners would be China and India. These countries' economies would experience a boom that would draw global firms
and labor migrants alike to Asia.[2] The formerly rich and powerful countries—especially in Europe and Russia—will grow less rich and less powerful as their middle classes are devastated in the economic shift to Asia.

Shifting economic fortunes will cause the shifting of political fortunes
such that "how we mentally map the world in 2020 will change radically"
from current-day understanding.[3] The new global powers will do what
global powers have always done—change the rules of the game to suit
their interests. This will "usher in a new set of international alignments,
potentially marking a definitive break with some of the post-World War II
institutions and practices."[4] "Only an abrupt reversal of the process of
globalization or a major upheaval in these countries would prevent their
rise."[5] The competition for increasingly scarce oil and water between the
old centers of economic and military power and the new centers of power
will be an important feature of this landscape. Meanwhile, "over 40 countries—including many African countries, Central Asian states, and Russia—are projected to have a lower life expectancy in 2010 than they did in
1990."[6]

Ultimately, the contradictions in globalization and the changing geopolitical landscape will create destabilizing forces in much of the world.
Governments will come under increasing strain and challenge as populist
and religious identities become more attractive to the world's peoples.
The net result of these trends is pervasive insecurity.[7] Because the NIC is
part of the U.S. intelligence community, its take-away message is that the

United States would be wise to make plans now for this changing global future in order to best maintain its power and position.

"Mapping the Global Future" is a classic example of analysis poised at the system level. At the system level of analysis, we study state–state relations that occur bilaterally or multilaterally, regionally or globally. This is the level of analysis that is most commonly used in media reports of global affairs ("Today Bolivia and Venezuela announced they were forming a new kind of alliance . . ."), and thus it seems more familiar to the reader. This level of analysis might also seem more familiar because the discussion is focused more on policy outcomes—particularly behaviors—than on policy process. The primary purpose of analysts using this level is to get "outside" national borders in order to discuss the interactions of states with other states, transnational actors, and within international organizations.

It is not enough to just describe relationships between actors. We want to understand the bases of relations, the different goals being pursued by different actors, as well as the motivations behind actions. There are two fundamental questions (or two sides to a single, fundamental question) underlying much of foreign policy scholarship. Do states act the way they act in the world because of who they are (as defined within the state)? Or do states act the way they do because of where they sit in the world (as defined by their relationships with other states in the international system)? Scholars studying foreign policy at the system level stress the latter but cannot escape from the former. Foreign policy makers, too, confront this reality, as they play what scholars call the two-level, dual, or nested game.

System-level analysis that focuses on power and position derives primarily from the realist worldview, but Marxist-based accounts also are informative here. In realist system-level accounts, the focus is on how a state's position in the international system is related to its foreign policy. Sometimes the suggested relationship is causal—a country's position is said to determine its foreign policy—but, most typically, the suggested relationship is a matter of explaining which options are open to states in certain positions and what those states must and/or will do to preserve or enhance their status.

To realists, the nature of the international system conditions and encourages certain foreign policy behaviors, although it does not determine specific behaviors. A classic statement on the impact of the system level on a state's foreign policy comes from neorealist Kenneth Waltz. Waltz writes,

With many sovereign states, with no system of law enforceable among them, with each state judging its grievances and ambitions according to the dictates of its own reason or desire—conflict, sometimes leading to war, is bound to occur. To achieve a favorable outcome from such conflict a state has to rely on its own devices, the relative efficiency of which must be its constant concern.[8]

And

> In anarchy, there is no automatic harmony. . . . Because each state is the final judge of its own cause, any state may at any time use force to implement its policies. Because any state may at any time use force, all states must constantly be ready either to counter force with force or to pay the cost of weakness. The requirements of state action are, in this view, imposed by the circumstances in which all states exist.[9]

In a realist world, anarchy requires a foreign policy stance that is always watchful for encroachments on one's security and power and for opportunities to advance one's security and power. This applies to all states no matter their type or position in the system, although more-powerful states can have more impact on anarchy than less-powerful states can.

The last statement is important because realists place their primary, if not exclusive, emphasis on the study of powerful states. The system level of analysis is the level of choice for realism, and the subject of choice is that group of states that have some shaping impact on the system. This is true for classical realists as well as for those neorealists who study international relations through the lens of international political economy. These scholars focus on the states at and near the top of the power hierarchy. For instance, Charles Kindleberger contends that a state's size determines its ability to stabilize or disrupt the international economic system. "Large" countries have the capability to stabilize the system, "middle" countries can damage or disrupt the system, and "small" countries have no impact at all on the system.[10] Because the focus is on expected systemic impact, the study of small countries yields no interesting lessons and so lacks analytical value to scholars such as Kindleberger. Not all foreign policy scholars take this position, but those who study foreign policy at this level admit that position in the system opens opportunities for some states—the more powerful—and closes opportunities for others.

The terms used here—large, middle, and small countries, or great, middle, and small powers—can be misleading. For example, when foreign policy scholars speak of "small states," they are not necessarily suggesting anything about the geographical size of the state, its population, or the level of the institutional development of its governance structures. Instead, something is implied about how the country's size, population, economy, and so forth position the state in respect to other states. Similarly, foreign policy discussions of "weak states" may not necessarily suggest anything about the internal features of countries and their governments (as is suggested by the terms failed state and failing state, for example). Instead, the state is weak in relation to other state actors. System-level analysis focuses on the power-based relationships between international actors.

Another knotty aspect of the use of categories such as great, middle, and small is that there is rarely agreement among scholars or policy makers about which states fit which categories because the categories themselves are often a little "fuzzy." For instance, recall the "pre-theory" of foreign policy proposed by James Rosenau and discussed in earlier chapters. In Rosenau's pre-theory, he offered eight ideal nation-types that he developed from a simple "large country" versus "small country" starting point. Rosenau's purpose, remember, was to get the ball rolling on systematic, comparative foreign policy research, and so he did not offer—nor did he need to offer—any definition of large and small. He had in mind that the United States, Soviet Union, India, and China were large countries, while Holland (Netherlands), Czechoslovakia, Kenya, and Ghana were small countries. Unfortunately, other analysts have been content to offer similarly impressionistic designations of state type without any greater definitional precision.

THE ELUSIVE CONCEPT OF POWER

Much of the imprecision in categories of states derives from a problem that resists resolution: there is no agreement among analysts about the definition of the elemental, fundamental concept of "power." Power is one of the defining features of international politics, according to realists, liberals, and Marxists. But none of these three dominant perspectives has ever reached consensus within their ranks about this critical concept. This failure is not limited to international politics; one of the more prominent international relations scholars, Robert Gilpin, noted that this is endemic to the broader study of politics. Gilpin declared that the "number and variety of definitions (of power) should be an embarrassment to political scientists."[11]

When Rosenau divided states into large and small, developed and underdeveloped, and open and closed, he had in mind the idea that we can array states based on measurements of certain attributes or resources. More powerful states, for instance, are those with larger, more industrialized national economies and larger, better-equipped, better-trained national militaries. We might also add that more powerful states have healthier, better-fed, better-educated citizenries. Indeed, we could keep adding different measurable attributes to this list, depending on what we as analysts believe to be important. From this, we can say that power derives from or is the summation of these tangible resources of the state. Tangible aspects of power create a certain level of state capability.

But capability does not translate directly into influence. A highly capable state may not be able to influence the foreign or domestic policies or behaviors of other states. How states translate capability into the ability to make other states modify their behavior is a long-standing puzzle.[12] Contributing to this puzzle is the fact that history provides many examples of very powerful states that lost wars to far less powerful actors. The U.S. failure in Vietnam during the 1960s and early 1970s and the Soviet failure in Afghanistan in the 1980s are two prominent, noteworthy examples. To be sure, powerful states sometimes can have their behavior changed by actors whose power capabilities seem miniscule in comparison. For example, consider the "Battle of the Black Sea," which took place in October 1993 between U.S. "peacekeepers" and "civilians" of various loyalties in Mogadishu, Somalia.

Somalia's government had collapsed in 1991, leaving the country without any widely accepted central political authority. From 1991 until this book went to press in 2008, Somalia has been a textbook example of a failed state. Upon the collapse of the government, various armed factions competed violently for control, with none having sufficient power to conquer the others. In the midst of political disarray and civil war, a famine of enormous proportions hit Somalia. International food-relief efforts were stymied and then hijacked by the armed factions, causing humanitarian assistance groups and international media to call for international intervention.

In April 1992 the United Nations dispatched a peacekeeping operation—the United Nations Operation in Somalia (UNOSOM I)—to help NGOs conduct humanitarian relief activities. Traditional peacekeepers carry small weapons for self-defense, but they have no authority to enforce order or compel anyone to stop undesirable behavior. Local compliance with rules established by U.N. peacekeepers is totally voluntary. Having no authority to use power, UNOSOM I was unable to create and maintain a cease-fire, ensure the delivery of food relief, or even protect itself from hostile fire. By the end of 1992, it was clear that the mission was a failure.

The humanitarian disaster in Somalia had only deepened, so the U.N. peacekeeping operation was replaced by a U.N.-approved, muscular multinational force called the United Task Force (UNITAF) in December 1992. This force was under U.S. command and control and was composed of twenty-eight thousand U.S. troops and seventeen thousand troops from other countries. UNITAF, acting under liberal rules of engagement that permitted the use of force to compel acceptable behavior, was able to impose temporary calm and order, helping NGOs get food relief into about 40 percent of the country. After several successful months, UNITAF was disbanded and a second U.N. peacekeeping operation (UNOSOM II) followed in May 1993. This peacekeeping mission operated under similar, mostly limited rules of engagement, much as the first U.N. mission, but it was mandated to perform disarmament and reconciliation tasks. Violence reemerged, and once again relief efforts and peacekeepers were threatened.[13]

The violence escalated in Somalia. In one episode in early June in Mogadishu, twenty-four Pakistani peacekeepers were killed by the Habr Gidr armed faction (the Somali National Alliance army) led by General Mohamed Farah Aidid. In another episode, a U.S. Black Hawk helicopter had been shot at and disabled. The head of the U.N. mission, retired U.S. admiral Jonathan Howe, ordered a drastic change in some of the peacekeepers' orders in response to this violence. Because peacekeeping troops are volunteered by their national governments, U.N. military and civilian commanders hold precarious and shifting power/authority over these troops. Howe could not issue orders to all of the U.N. peacekeepers in Somalia, but he could "order" the U.S. contingent to modify its mission and behaviors. The Clinton administration, U.S. commanders in the field, and Howe determined that the violence against peacekeepers could not be tolerated and so U.S. troops were ordered to capture General Aidid and his top advisers. This order was to be accomplished through the use of military force. The U.S. forces, ostensibly part of the U.N. peacekeeping operation, were under U.S. command and control for this new mission.

In the late summer 1993 and into the fall, U.S. Rangers and Delta Force members, using armored vehicles and Black Hawk attack helicopters, conducted many "snatch-and-grab" operations against the leaders of Habr Gidr. These snatch-and-grab raids were conducted with massive force and resulted in the deaths of many Somalis and considerable destruction in Mogadishu. General Aidid, however, eluded capture—while his local popularity soared. On October 3, 1993, an afternoon snatch-and-grab operation went badly awry when the people of Mogadishu decided to fight back against the Americans. (A gripping account of the Battle of the Black Sea can be found in Mark Bowden's excellent book *Black Hawk Down*.[14]) Using rocket-propelled grenades, combatants loyal to Aidid shot down two of the Black Hawk helicopters. The 120 elite soldiers and surviving Black Hawk crew members were pinned down in a firefight in the Black Sea area of Mogadishu until early the next morning. Eighteen American soldiers were killed and seventy-three were wounded. Approximately five hundred Somalis were killed and over a thousand were wounded. Somalis celebrated their victory by dragging the dead and mutilated bodies of several American GIs through the city streets. Images of this were broadcast around the world.

In terms of the number of deaths and casualties sustained by each side in the Battle of the Black Sea, the Americans did not lose. In fact, the snatch and grab operation was a success, as two senior Aidid advisers and others from Habr Gidr were arrested and detained, and the pinned-down American troops were rescued successfully by dawn on October 4. We might conclude, then, that American power was flexed successfully over the far less powerful Habr Gidr clan. In terms of tangible, measurable power capabilities, the accounting sheet would clearly present a favorable balance for the Americans. Yet we must look beyond this battle—but not very far beyond it—in order to ascertain whether this flexing of overwhelming U.S. military capability translated into observable changes in the target's behavior or circumstances. The Battle of the Black Sea did not contribute in any way to the ultimate capture of Aidid and the pacification of Somalia. Instead, the Battle of the Black Sea caused the immediate reversal of U.S. policy so that Aidid was no longer pursued as a criminal, his senior advisers were released, and within months the U.S. military was tasked with providing protective transport for Aidid as he traveled to a U.N.-sponsored peace conference. This change in U.S. policy took effect the day after the Battle of the Black Sea, at which time the United States also announced that it would withdraw completely from Somalia by March 1994.

Ultimately, American interests in Somalia were limited and could not be balanced against American casualties. With limited interests and limited tolerance for casualties, we can conclude that American resolve was also limited. The Somalis, on the other hand, were completely resolved against the American military presence. In terms of this accounting sheet, the United States was far less powerful than the Somalis. Analysts are in agreement about this: power is both tangible and intangible. Tangible power can be listed and tallied—the number of well-armed and well-trained elite troops, the number of Black Hawk helicopters and related supporting air cover, the number of armored personnel carriers, and so on—but intangible power cannot be listed and tallied nor even understood or estimated until the firefight occurs. This points to another critical characteristic of power: power is contextual and situational. Analysts can make educated guesses about how powerful one actor might be over another, but the elusive nature of intangible power and the importance of context means there can be no final word on which actors are more and which are less powerful until after an event has occurred.

WHO GETS TO BE A GREAT POWER?

Despite the elusiveness of power, we continue to define great, middle, and small powers in terms of measurable power capabilities. So, which countries get to be great powers? We might be inclined to use membership in certain "elite" international organizations as proof of a country's ranking and position. For example, we might decide that the permanent members of the U.N. Security Council—the United States, Russia, Great Britain, France, and China—are the states that should properly be designated "great powers." These states were the victors of World War II (with the French resistance earning France its title as victor), and created for themselves a privileged position in the new United Nations with the special power of the veto. Some modifications within this group have been allowed by the group. The China seat was held by the Republic of China or Taiwan until 1971 when the People's Republic of China assumed that seat. Similarly, the Soviet Union was an original member of the "Big Five," but upon its dissolution its seat went to Russia and not to any of the other fourteen independent countries created out of the former Soviet Union.

These self-made modifications notwithstanding, the possibility of adding permanent members to the Security Council has been and remains a controversial topic. Other countries have become powerful actors on the world stage—and certainly are great powers using some definitions—yet remain outside permanent membership. As discussed in the last chapter, Japan is the second-largest financial contributor to the United Nations, yet it is only periodically a member of the Security Council sometimes occupying one of the ten two-year, rotating, nonpermanent seats. India is the world's largest democracy by population, a major participant in U.N. peacekeeping activities, and, just like the Big Five, it possesses nuclear weapons. Indonesia is the world's fourth-largest country by population and the largest Muslim country. We could continue to name strong candidates for permanent membership to the Security Council and great power designation—none of which are ever likely to achieve the same status as the Big Five. Why? Because adding permanent members to the Security Council requires a change to the U.N. Charter, and all changes to the U.N. Charter require the approval of three-quarters of the General Assembly membership and the agreement of the Big Five. Each of the Big Five maintains opposition to the possibility of admitting certain other states to the permanent membership, and all maintain opposition to sharing the veto with any other state. This is what great powers do—they block rising great powers using whatever means available.

What if we decided to use other criteria besides Security Council permanent membership for great power designation? For example, what if possession of nuclear weapons earned a state great power status? Then the great powers would include the Security Council permanent five—the United States, Russia, Great Britain, France, and China—as well as India,

Israel, Pakistan, and North Korea. There would be very little beyond nuclear weapons characterizing this group. Consider the data presented in Table 8.1. The Human Development Index (HDI) is produced by the U.N. Development Programme using data on life expectancy, gross domestic product per capita (GDP/cap, measured in purchasing power parity, or what money would buy given the local costs of goods and services), literacy rates, and a package of many other indicators measuring the quality of life for human beings in 177 countries. Two of the HDI individual indicators are included in this table.

Table 8.1.   Comparative Indicators for Selected States

Country	Human Development Index Rank (n = 177)	Life Expectancy in Years	GDP/capita (PPP in US$)	Nuclear Weapons State
Afghanistan	NR (.312 score)	42.9	632	No
Australia	3	80.9	31,794	No
Brazil	70	71.7	8,402	No
China	81	72.5	6,757	**Yes**
France	10	80.2	30,386	**Yes**
Iceland	1	81.5	36,510	No
India	128	63.7	3,452	**Yes**
Indonesia	107	69.7	3,843	No
Israel	23	80.3	25,864	**Yes**
Japan	8	82.3	31,267	No
Nigeria	158	46.5	1,128	No
North Korea	NR	66.8	1,527	**Yes**
Norway	2	79.8	41,420	No
Pakistan	136	64.6	2,370	**Yes**
Russia	67	65.0	10,845	**Yes**
Sierra Leone	177 (.336 score)	41.8	806	No
South Africa	121	50.8	11,110	No (but did)
UK	16	79.0	33,238	**Yes**
US	12	77.9	41,890	**Yes**
Venezuela	74	73.2	6,632	No
Zimbabwe	151	40.9	2,038	No

Source: United Nations Development Programme, *Human Development Report 2007–2008,*
   http://hdrstats.undp.org/countries (accessed December 5, 2007).
Notes: Italicized countries are permanent members of the U.N. Security Council. Boldfaced countries have
   nuclear capacity. PPP = purchasing power parity.

In Table 8.1, we see that the overall HDI rankings for the nuclear weapons states vary greatly. France, the United States, the United Kingdom, and Israel are in the top twenty-five. But consider the placement of Big Five members Russia, ranking sixty-seventh (forty-four spots after Israel), and China, ranking eighty-first (fifty-eight spots after Israel). India and Pakistan do much worse, ranking in the third quartile, and the U.N. Development Programme's data on North Korea are too incomplete to earn it a ranking at all. The countries with the highest rankings—Iceland, Norway, and Australia (1, 2, and 3 respectively)—are neither nuclear weapons states nor permanent Security Council members.

The disparity among the nuclear weapons states gets more distinct when we look at life expectancy in years and GDP/capita. Israel has a slightly higher life expectancy than any of the Big Five nations; there is a fifteen-year difference between the life expectancy of the average Israeli and the average Russian. Russia's life expectancy is less than North Korea and just above Pakistan and India. In terms of GDP/capita, the United States, United Kingdom, France, and Israel are wealthy states. Russia's GDP/capita is well below these four, and China's is well below Russia's. India, Pakistan, and North Korea are low-income countries by this indicator.

Ranking countries in terms of who possesses nuclear weapons or in terms of national wealth can create more questions than may be resolved. Should Russia and China be ranked among the great powers? The standard answer is yes, although these countries are not so "great" by the indicators used in the HDI. Should India, Pakistan, Israel, and North Korea be ranked among the great powers? The standard answer is no, although these countries belong to the exclusive club of nuclear weapons states. Yet it does not make much sense intuitively to group these four countries together. Thus we are left again with the imprecise nature of power. This imprecision is unavoidable but not too problematic, given that our focus at this level of analysis is more on power relations than on absolute power.

WHAT DO GREAT POWERS DO?

Realists, liberals, and Marxists—with some disagreement over the specifics—agree that the international system is defined by the number and actions of great powers, especially their actions vis-à-vis other great powers. What is a "great power?" The *Penguin Dictionary of International Relations* offers this round-about description:

> In addition to military and economic strength, great powers normally have global if not universal interests and are usually characterized as possessing

the political will to pursue them. The United States, for example, although long regarded by others as a great power, has not always displayed the political will to behave like one, especially during the period until 1917 and between 1921 and 1941. It was only after the Second World War that the United States consistently and self-consciously adopted this posture.[15]

We are also told this about the origins of the concept:

> The term itself can be traced back to fifteenth-century Italian politics but the first time it was adopted as an orthodox diplomatic concept was with the signing of the Treaty of Chaumont in 1817. As a result of the Congress of Vienna (1815) five states, Austria, Britain, France, Prussia and Russia, had informally conferred on themselves great power status. The intention was that these states acting in concert would adopt a managerial role in relation to the maintenance of order in the European state system.[16]

Great powers, then, are states with extraordinarily large military and economic capabilities, global political interests, *and* the will to protect and maintain those interests. The Congress of Vienna great powers named themselves to this designation in mutual recognition of the power they held, and they linked this designation to the job description of maintaining the European state system. These great powers did not act out of altruism but out of their own self-interests. Yet these interests were defined more broadly than those of other states. The desired order served their interests and required their maintenance.

Great powers use force to promote goals beyond their immediate national self-defense, and this sets them apart from the small powers. Consider Edward Luttwak's distinction between small and great powers:

> To struggle for mere survival was the unhappy predicament of threatened small powers, which had to fight purely to defend themselves and could not hope to achieve anything more with their modest strength. Great powers were different; they could only remain great if they were seen as willing and able to use force to acquire and protect even non-vital interests, including distant possessions or minor additions to their spheres of influence. To lose a few hundred soldiers in some minor probing operation or a few thousand in a small war or expeditionary venture were routine events for the great powers of history.[17]

Moreover, Luttwak adds, "Great powers are in the business of threatening, rather than being threatened. A great power cannot be that unless it asserts all sorts of claims that far exceed the needs of its own immediate security, including the protection of allies and clients as well as other less-than-vital interests."[18]

Luttwak defines "great powers" as those states with overwhelming power resources who display "a readiness to use force whenever it [is] advantageous to do so and an acceptance of the resulting combat casualties with equanimity, as long as the number [is] not disproportionate."[19] Finally, and importantly, Luttwak explains that "great powers [are] strong enough to successfully wage war without calling on allies."[20]

Not only are great powers defined by their willingness to use force, but great powers *arise* through the use of force. The great powers of the twentieth century, explains Ian Lustick, engaged in large-scale state-building wars in their formative years. Lustick expands on Charles Tilly's description of state building in the West, a description summarized in the idea that "war made the state, and the state made war."[21] In the European state-building experience, political units were engaged in an ongoing fight to survive. The need to raise money to field armies, necessary for basic protection and the defeat of opponents and ultimately for the acquisition of increasing amounts of territory, led the early European states to institutionalize. Taxation and conscription could only be successfully accomplished through the consolidation of internal control, and both were necessary for the consolidation of external power. Lustick asserts that European and North American states were free of international constraints such as U.N. Charter prohibitions against the use of force, and thus they were able to amass the necessary power capabilities to be strong internally and externally. The unrestricted use of force was necessary for building great power capabilities and achieving great power status. By the twentieth century, international prohibitions against such use of unrestricted force—prohibitions designed by the existing great powers—kept other great powers from rising in places such as the Middle East.[22]

Traditionally, a great power policy of denying other potential great powers entailed the use of military force. Unique to great power behavior in the twentieth century, however, was the use of force in tandem with the construction of global international organizations such as the United Nations. These institutions and their attendant principles locked other states into "antibelligerency norms" that, in turn, limited the ability of these states to amass sufficient power capabilities to challenge the established great powers.[23] Thus, while the European and North American great powers, as well as China and Japan to some extent, used war to increase their land and resource holdings and make them great powers, the norms and institutions established by the (Western) great powers in the twentieth century denied other countries this same route to greatness.

Indeed, twentieth-century institutions and norms, particularly those embodied in the mid-century creation, the United Nations, have been used *to justify* the use of force by great powers against potential challengers. For example, Iraq's invasion of Kuwait in 1990 resulted from the inability of the two countries to reach agreement on key points of contention. Central to their dispute were terms of the repayment of debts incurred by Iraq to Kuwait during the decade-long Iraq-Iran war. When the Iraqi leader Saddam Hussein could not persuade Kuwait to accept more agreeable repayment terms, he decided to settle differences with Kuwait through invasion and occupation. Perhaps the Iraqi leader had in mind the U.S. invasion of Panama in December 1989 after the U.S. government could not get the Panamanian leader Manuel Noriega to comply with American wishes. The Iraqi invasion of Kuwait, however, was condemned by the members of the United Nations as a violation of key principles of the U.N. system. When Iraq refused to comply with U.N. demands to vacate Kuwait, the U.N. Security Council gave its blessing to the United States and a multinational coalition to use force against Iraq to compel it to act by the established rules.

This description of great powers thus far is essentially derived from realist accounts, but we need only modify it slightly to make it read as a Marxist account or an account positing that economic interests are primary to understanding foreign policy choices. Marxists would argue that states described as great powers are the product of global elite economic interests. Global economic elites—acting through their agents the states—form a global core or centre that protects established wealth and assists in the acquisition of even greater wealth. International institutions are built by this rich club to impose restrictions on others to keep them out and dependent. Should states on the periphery attempt to challenge this system—or gain entrance into the rich club—international organizations are used to punish the challengers. The use of U.N. principles to justify the war against Iraq is an example of this.

Similarly, great powers impose relationships on lesser powers that serve to undermine the consolidation of power and legitimacy within those states, thereby establishing the need for the continued presence of powerful external actors in the domestic affairs of those weak regimes. To protect British access to Kuwaiti oil, Britain formed a patron–client relationship with the Kuwaiti monarchy in 1899 that lasted off and on until the early 1960s. In this, Britain secured its oil interests and British troops guaranteed the security of the Kuwaiti regime from both external and internal threats.[24] The cliency relationships between Britain and Kuwait and the United States and Saudi Arabia are discussed in the next chapter.

Thus, great powers are states with enormous power capabilities and the demonstrated willingness to use those capabilities whenever necessary. Great powers are especially attuned to potential threats to their status and constantly guard against rising powers. Allies might restrain great powers from doing what they must do, and so a watch must be kept on allies as well as challengers. Allies and challengers alike are constrained by the web of institutions used by great powers that lock countries into a status quo that feeds the military and economic power of these great powers.

THE UNIQUE POSITION OF THE UNITED STATES

From 1945 to approximately 1989, the international system was described as a bipolar system. Prior to 1945, the international system was described as a multipolar system. A bipolar system has two great centers of power led by two major powers. A multipolar system has three or more major powers—classical realists would say such a system must have five powers to be a properly functioning balance-of-power system. The relationships between great powers at the top of the international system set the parameters for what all others states could do.

At the conclusion of the Cold War that characterized the 1945–1989 bipolar system, foreign policy makers and foreign policy scholars began deliberating what the shape of the "new world order" would be. There was agreement that, after the collapse of the Soviet Union, there was only one superpower remaining in the world and that the international system was unipolar. For scholars and policy makers alike, a central point of debate was whether unipolarity was a short-term phenomenon or could be maintained for the longer term. Some analysts argued that the system would naturally tend to multipolarity because other powerful states in the system would attempt to stop any single state from becoming or remaining predominant. The goal for the United States in this situation would be to manage the rise of other powers while conserving its own power resources. Others suggested that unipolarity might be maintainable and a worthy goal. Again, the goal for the United States would be to manage the system in order to stay on top.

This debate was and still is over which "grand strategy" the United States should employ. Robert Art explains that "a grand strategy tells a nation's leaders what goals they should aim for and how best they can use their country's military power to attain these goals."[25] Christopher Layne explains that "grand strategies must be judged by the amount of security they provide; whether, given international systemic constraints, they are sustainable; their cost; the degree of risk they entail; and their tangible and intangible domestic effects."[26] For the United States, selecting the appropriate grand strategy means making decisions about whether it is worth it to try to maintain unipolarity or whether a multipolar system might be better for the long-term preservation of American national interests.

To understand the strategic options available to the United States as the single superpower, it is helpful to understand the American grand strategy pursued in the previous international system. An important part of American grand strategy post-1945 was defined by the Cold War competition with the Soviet Union. This should be familiar to the reader. The other critical part of post-1945 grand strategy is perhaps less familiar but

just as important to understanding the current situation. American foreign policy elites concluded that World War II, like World War I, arose because of the restrictive trading policies of the major states. Restrictive
trade policies impeded the collective ability to "grow" economies and
amass wealth. American policy makers sought to eliminate the causes of
major power war by creating a global liberal economic regime to support
a global free-trade system.

The part of American grand strategy that focused on the Soviet Union
and the communist threat was embedded in a realist framework, but the
part of the strategy devoted to the construction of a global free-trade system was embedded in a liberal worldview. These are not necessarily contradictory impulses. The liberal view is that states can and will pursue
their own national interests, but these interests are best pursued in cooperation with other states. At the same time, those who threaten this vision
of global free trade—which during the Cold War meant the Soviet Union
and its communist allies—need to be treated as enemies.

Benjamin Schwarz argues that building and maintaining a global free-
trade system required the United States to convince the major powers (on
the Western side of the Cold War) that their interests could be blended
profitably together. Germany and Japan were special targets for U.S. policy, as these countries had waged wars on other countries because they
had been excluded from the fruits of previous international systems.[27]
Creating a liberal world order meant guarding against the possibility that
one or more major powers might turn away from the cooperative union
in pursuit of narrow national interests. Schwarz contends that the United
States decided that if it were to pay the costs of security for the major
powers—especially Germany and Japan, but all the others as well—it
would be able to keep these powers happy with the system and keep
them in the system. The United States would "relieve" these countries of
the burden of high defense costs, thereby relieving them of the military
capacity to return to individualistic great power behavior. In Schwarz's
words, the United States would "protect the interests of virtually all potential great powers so that they need not acquire the capability to protect
themselves—that is, so those powers need not act like great powers."[28]

This grand strategy would entail clear costs for the United States, but
America would gain in the long run as the global economy flourished. In
Europe, the foreign policy behavior associated with this strategy was the
establishment of a strong U.S. military presence in Europe through the
North Atlantic Treaty Organization. NATO would constrain the European
states from pursuing unilateral foreign policies, while pulling Germany
firmly into the fold. In Asia, the United States established a significant
military presence in Japan, while the Japanese government developed a
national security policy that was founded primarily on a U.S.-Japanese

defense arrangement. Christopher Layne—a critic of this strategy—sums it up this way: "The logic of the strategy is that interdependence is the paramount interest the strategy promotes; instability is the threat to interdependence; and extended deterrence is the means by which the strategy deals with this threat."[29]

Both Schwarz and Layne contend that this grand strategy is too costly to maintain for very long. For Schwarz, the strategy dangerously allows and encourages other states to grow economically at the expense of the superpower. Layne worries about both expense and the problem of "strategic overextension." That is, this grand strategy requires the United States to actively address threats to the international order whether these occur in the core or periphery. The danger of this is twofold: the United States could become engaged militarily in far too many peripheral areas, stretching itself too thin and draining its resources; and the United States might promise to protect the interests of others but fall short, thereby undermining its international credibility and eroding its intangible power.

After the terrorist attacks of September 11, Schwarz and Layne—writing together—suggest that a third danger in this grand strategy had revealed itself: "Those who undertook [the terrorist attacks] acted with cool calculation to force the United States to alter specific policies—policies that largely flow from the global role America has chosen." Schwarz and Layne intone,

> We need to come to grips with an ironic possibility: that the very preponderance of American power may now make us not more secure but less secure. By the same token, it may actually be possible to achieve more of our foreign policy goals by means of a diminished global presence.[30]

The lesson they take from the attacks of September 11 is that the United States does not need to remain predominant and engaged in the world. Instead, the United States should disengage and "pass the buck" for maintaining the international system to others.

Schwarz and Layne propose that the United States employ a grand strategy called "offshore balancing." Stephen Walt advocates the same policy. All these scholars belong to the "multipolarity is inevitable" camp. As Walt explains, U.S. unipolarity, or "primacy" "fosters fear and resistance when its power is misused."[31] During the George W. Bush administration, power often was misused. The Bush strategy was to pursue global hegemony

> in which the United States tries to run the world more or less on its own. In this strategy, the United States sets the agenda for world politics and uses its power to make sure its preferences are followed. Specifically, the United States decides what military forces and weapons other states are allowed to

possess and makes it clear that liberal democracy is the only form of government that the United States deems acceptable and is prepared to support. Accordingly, American power will be used to hasten the spread of democratic
rule, to deny WMDs to potential enemies, and to ensure that no countries are
able to mount an effective challenge to America's position.[32]

Arguably, the spread of democracy has taken a back seat to the other
goals.

Walt proposes that the United States adopt a grand strategy that "pre-
serves its current position for as long as possible."[33] Offshore balancing is
a strategy in which American power is deployed only when its vital interests (at home and in Europe, "industrialized Asia," and the Persian
Gulf) are threatened. To protect these interests, the United States does not
need to keep its troops positioned in critical regions; it only needs to ensure that those regions do not fall under the control of peer competitors.
U.S. military intervention would occur only when regional actors could
not maintain their regional power balances or in the case of genocide or
mass murder (if the costs of such humanitarian intervention are acceptable).[34] The benefits of offshore balancing are many:

> Offshore balancing is the ideal grand strategy for an era of American pri-
> macy. It husbands the power upon which this primacy rests and minimizes
> the fear that this power provokes. By setting clear priorities and emphasiz-
> ing reliance on regional allies, it reduces the danger of being drawn into un-
> necessary conflicts and encourages other states to do more for us. Equally
> important, it takes advantage of America's favorable geopolitical position
> and exploits the tendency for regional powers to worry more about each
> other than about the United States. But it is not a passive strategy and does
> not preclude using the full range of America's power to advance its core in-
> terests.[35]

Robert Art disagrees with offshore balancing, advocating instead a
grand strategy of selective engagement. This grand strategy is based on
the assumption that America's unparalleled power will not last and that
"America's ability to shape the world is now at its peak."[36] The United
States should not miss this opportunity to use its unprecedented power to
shape the world. The United States should remain militarily engaged in a
peacetime footing in the Persian Gulf, Europe, and Asia to protect its vital interests. American vital interests include realist and liberal internationalist goals (the realist goals come first, but Art insists the liberal goals
are also important).[37] These goals, in order of importance, are: (1) The
United States needs to prevent an attack on the homeland. (2) The United
States needs to prevent great power Eurasian wars. (3) The United States
needs to ensure its secure access to "reasonably priced" oil. (4) The United

States should work to preserve an open international economy. (5) The United States should foster democracy and respect for human rights, and take action to stop genocide and mass murder. (6) The United States should work to protect the global environment.[38]

> In sum, all six of its interests can best be pursued if the United States remains militarily strong, militarily engaged, forward-based, and allied with key nations. None of these interests would be well served if the United States were to sheathe its sword, cut loose from its alliances, and bring its military forces home.[39]

Although they advocate different grand strategies, both Walt and Art contend that what they want is a return to a traditional American grand strategy. In some ways, they both are correct; great powers, including the United States, have always picked their fights to advance their own interests. But they would have the United States take different military postures in the world in order to pursue this great power tradition.

AMERICAN FOREIGN POLICY UNDER GEORGE W. BUSH

The post–Cold War administrations of George H. W. Bush and Bill Clinton used essentially the same grand strategy of selective engagement. The George W. Bush administration, by its own admission, experienced a sea change on some aspects of its grand strategy from pre- to post–September 11. The pre–September 11 Bush 2 administration appeared to be following a stay-at-home and go-it-alone strategy. After 9/11, Bush adopted a "you're with us or you're with the terrorists" or a "my way or the highway" global hegemony strategy that contained elements of neoconservatism and stark realism (more on this later). Both periods, however, were marked by the Bush administration's preference for unilateralism.

The new administration promptly announced that it would review a number of "flawed" international treaties and agreements, unilaterally withdrawing from those that did not fit an America-first worldview. The Kyoto Treaty on global warming was one of the first to go. Protocols on biological and chemical weapons were also to be reviewed with the goal of "untying" the hands of the United States—and this idea become critical to policy after 9/11. The 1972 Antiballistic Missile (ABM) Treaty between the United States and Soviet Union/Russia was abrogated. And, the administration proceeded to build (or try to build) a missile defense that many critics proclaimed was both a practical impossibility and a move that would destabilize mature nuclear deterrence. The administration also made a public point of "unsigning" the Rome Statute that created the International Criminal Court (ICC), although it could have just left the treaty unratified and ignored it. And the administration left the United Nations waiting for more than half a year to learn who the new U.S. ambassador would be.

Dismaying allies, the Bush 2 administration announced early on that it would withdraw troops from Europe, especially from NATO peacekeeping operations there. After 9/11, the administration pursued this same policy, even threatening to veto U.N. reauthorization of peacekeeping in Bosnia. The United States agreed not to veto Bosnian peacekeeping if the Security Council would put a one-year ban on ICC investigations and prosecutions involving any "current or former officials or personnel from a contributing State not a Party to the Rome Statute over acts or omissions relating to a United Nations established or authorized operation." The Security Council approved such a limitation on the ICC for a year starting in July 2002, and renewed it again the following July for twelve more months. By mid-summer 2004 no suspensions were requested because only a handful of U.S. military personnel were deployed in U.N.-led or U.N.-authorized peace operations. The Ottawa Treaty, or the land mine ban treaty, also came under the scrutiny of the Bush 2 administration. The Clinton administration had not signed the ban but had pledged to stop all use of land mines by 2006. In March 2004, the Bush administration revoked this pledge, reserving the right to use land mines where it deemed necessary.

Similarly, the Bush administration put a damper on Korean unification talks—a blow to ally South Korea—when it repudiated and denigrated North Korean peace efforts in the spring and summer of 2001. It would not be until after the Bush administration named North Korea to the "axis of evil" and after the North Koreans kicked out IAEA inspectors and built operational nuclear weapons that the Bush administration would return to multilateral talks with North Korea. On the Israeli–Palestinian conflict, Bush officials announced early in the administration that they wanted peace in the Middle East but would not remain engaged in diplomatic efforts as long as the parties themselves made no progress; meanwhile, the violence between the sides grew worse. The Bush administration made a weak effort to reengage in the Middle East peace process in late fall–early winter 2001 when the conflict threatened to disrupt Bush plans for a larger war on terrorism, but its reengagement manifested symptoms of attention deficit disorder. Finally, not until the fall of 2007, when the president was in his full "lame duck" glory, did he and the secretary of state arrange a one-day peace conference in Annapolis, Maryland. The conference lasted for a few speeches, and then Bush sent the parties off to go talk about talking about future talks.

The September 11, 2001, terrorist attacks on the United States caused the Bush 2 administration to take another look at the world. Stay-at-home unilateralism was jettisoned for global hegemony and "my way or the highway" bullying. The new policy was influenced by two camps within the administration. The first was the neoconservative camp, which thought 9/11 was an opening for the United States to use might to create right in the world. Neoconservatives claimed to be disaffected liberals. They believed that democracy and human rights could be coercively imposed and saw the post–9/11 world as a blank canvas for the United States to paint upon (if painting can be done with cruise missiles). Ridding the world of the Taliban and even al Qaeda was less important to them than ridding the Middle East of nondemocratic regimes, starting with Saddam Hussein's in Iraq. Neoconservatives lived by the notion of "perpetual war for perpetual peace" without noting the irony in this idea.[40]

The second camp that influenced the new Bush policy was the realist camp led by Vice President Dick Cheney. Francis Fukuyama, a neoconservative who quit the group, suggests that some of Cheney's cadre were better categorized as "Jacksonian nationalists." Fukuyama defines Jacksonian nationalists as those who seek narrow national interests, distrust multilateralism, and tend toward nativism and isolationism.[41] Certainly the short-tenured U.S. ambassador to the United Nations, John Bolton, fits this characterization. Cheney, however, was less isolationist and nativist than he was power-seeking and calculating, so we'll consider him to be in the realist camp. These realists saw great possibility in co-opting the neoconservative democracy-promotion goals (as distorted as they were) in order to pursue raw power aimed at enhancing U.S. primacy far into the next century. September 11 was their opening, too, for reshaping the map of the Middle East to secure access to the world's greatest oil reserves. First, Iraq's oil could be controlled through regime change there, then the options included regime change in Saudi Arabia (also on the neoconservative wish list) to control its oil *or* regime change in Iran to control its oil and its claims to Caspian Sea oil reserves. During the Clinton administration, Cheney served as head of Halliburton Oil. In this capacity, he actively lobbied the U.S. government to lift sanctions on Iran so Halliburton could help Iran build a pipeline from the Caspian Sea to the Persian Gulf. As vice president, Cheney's was the loudest voice calling for forced regime change in Iraq, and later in Iran. The power of the vice presidency, the loftier goals of the neoconservatives, and the opening of 9/11 created endless possibilities for the realist camp.

In between these camps sat the president. George W. Bush achieved a wide reputation as strikingly lacking in curiosity, a cognitive miser of the first magnitude. He eschewed the "fact-based reality" that others lived in. Reality to Bush was about faith, taking strong stances based on that faith, and never looking back or reflecting. He also was an oilman with family and friends deeply involved in the oil industry. The narratives the neo-conservatives had to tell and the narratives the realists had to tell merged and were accepted by Bush without question.

The merger created the so-called "Bush Doctrine" announced in the September 2002 National Security Strategy (NSS) of the United States of America and elaborated in his second inaugural address. The 2002 NSS declared that the United States had the unilateral right to engage in preventive war to eliminate potential future threats. The 2002 NSS also retained the great power right to use force to ward off future military competition with all other states. The Bush Doctrine was expanded in the second inaugural address of January 2005. With this expansion, "ending tyranny" in the world became a vital security interest of the United States. "We are led, by events and common sense, to one conclusion: The survival of liberty in our land increasingly depends on the success of liberty in other lands. The best hope for peace in our world is the expansion of freedom in all the world."[42]

The real-world results of this policy involved protracted wars in Afghanistan and Iraq, and constant threats of a "World War III" with Iran over its nuclear weapons program. In late November 2007, a new National Intelligence Estimate (NIE) was released that indicated that Iran had stopped pursuing nuclear weapons in 2003 as a result of international pressures.[43] Despite this, in the same week that the NIE was released, the U.S. president said twice publicly that Iran posed a growing danger to the world and must be dealt with.

A less obvious result of the global hegemony strategy has been the achievement of U.S. nuclear primacy.[44] Nuclear primacy is the condition in which one state has the nuclear weapons capability to strike an enemy with a disarming attack. That is, the forces of country A are so powerful and accurate and the forces of B so much smaller and less technologically advanced (perhaps even degraded) that A can attack B and disarm B. If country A has nuclear primacy, it can "win" a nuclear war ("winning" in this context ignores the environmental consequences of a nuclear war). Short of war, A can threaten and bully other competitor states until they either capitulate or rush to counter the imbalance. Nuclear primacy ends the situation of stable nuclear deterrence and ends the restraining assumptions found in MAD. Keir Lieber and Daryl Press have produced some stunning research findings in which they conclude that the American nuclear arsenal had become so enhanced by an accuracy revolution and the next-nearest competitor's arsenal (Russia) had become so degraded that the era of mutual assured destruction likely was over by 2006.[45] Lieber and Press ran a computer model "of a hypothetical US attack on Russia's nuclear arsenal using the standard unclassified formulas that defense analysts have used for decades." Their model showed that "a simplified surprise attack would have a good chance of destroying every Russian bomber base, submarine, and ICBM."[46] America's nuclear primacy will, of course, threaten others, causing them to attempt to bandage their hemorrhaging national security positions. This, in turn, increases the likelihood of preemptive attacks by potential rivals, a likelihood the United States must be prepared to *pre*-preempt.[47] And so it goes.

Lieber and Press think it is unlikely that nuclear primacy was achieved in order to deal with the threat of nonstate actors such as terrorist groups. The kinds of "almost continuous improvements" that have been made to the U.S. arsenal would only be useful against peer competitors—or challenging great powers. This is, of course, part of the Bush Doctrine, to meet peer competitors with military force if need be. This is what a great power should do, according to this adopted grand strategy of global hegemony.

In time Bush's neoconservative supporters started to abandon him for misunderstanding and poorly executing their ideas, especially in the botched occupation of Iraq. They were also disappointed by the lack of carry-through on the democracy-promotion mission in places like Saudi Arabia. The neoconservatives left the administration one-by-one (either literally, for those who had administration posts, or figuratively, for those who wrote in neoconservative periodicals) and the vacuum was filled by Cheney's winner-take-all realism and Bush's faith-based rigidity. Internationally, countries in the Iraq war coalition started peeling away almost from the start, but with growing urgency after things turned bad as the insurgency took hold in 2004. Tony Blair had ordered that British troops stand down and then begin withdrawing long before he left office. In the fall of 2007, one of Bush's strongest and most hawkish supporters, Australian prime minister John Howard, was soundly beaten in a reelection bid despite Australia's strong economy. Foreign policy issues—Iraq and the Kyoto Treaty—led voters to switch parties.

By the time this book is published, readers may be able to begin to assess how much damage the Bush global hegemony grand strategy did to U.S. reputation and influence in the world. Power is not just measured in numbers of troops, weapons, and bombers, but in intangibles as well. Reputation and influence are critical dimensions of any state's ability to thrive in world affairs. The global hegemony grand strategy has made the United States many enemies, made old friends of the United States wistful for a different era (and threatened by some of the same forces unleashed by American bullying), and has left far too many of the world's people wondering when bad karma would catch up with the United States. And then there are the disaffected and the angry, such as Osama bin Laden and people who follow his example. We've come a long, hard way from the 1990s when Josef Joffe wrote that

America is differen.t . . . It irks and domineers, but it does not conquer. It tries to call the shots and bend the rules, but it does not go to war for land and glory. . . . Those who coerce or subjugate others are far more likely to inspire hostile alliances than nations that contain themselves, as it were.[48]

The next U.S. administration would be wise to put some time into re-thinking American grand strategy and repairing what damage global hegemony has done to American reputation and military readiness. It may be worthwhile to begin at different starting points rather than the old realist questions about whether the world is inevitably multipolar and how the United States should try to hang on to its power. The questions that might underscore a more sustainable, more cooperative world order might begin by acknowledging the connections between peoples and the common problems and dreams that bind us together. For, as Richard Falk has said, "If you fail to ask the right questions, it is impossible to find the right answers."[49]

CHAPTER REVIEW

- Realists focus on the great powers in the international system be-cause these states have the ability to shape the system and write the rules for all other states.

- Great powers are states who use force to promote interests beyond their own vital national interests.

- Power is an elusive concept; it has tangible and intangible elements and is defined by the situation at hand.

- A grand strategy is a policy employed by a great power in which mil-itary power is used to promote national interests and global goals.

- Realists disagree over whether multipolarity is inevitable, and there-fore the United States should adjust its grand strategy to save its re-sources, or whether unipolarity is maintainable, and therefore the United States should capitalize on its present predominance to stay on top indefinitely.

9

The Other Powers

IN THIS CHAPTER

- Penetrated Systems
- Rising Great Powers
- Secondary Powers
  What Kind of Power Is the European Union?
- Middle Powers and Good International Citizens
- Small Powers and Client States
- Chapter Review

Cases Featured in This Chapter

- India's benevolent great power strategy as it extends its power into Central Asia.
- How France and Germany seek to deny each other singular great power status while seeking to attain such status together.
- The patron–client relationship of Great Britain and Kuwait and how Kuwait traded a strategic patron for the economic patron of oil.
- Libya's strategy of using its military-political dependence on the United States as a cover for taking full national control of its natural resources.
- The patron–client relationship between the United States and Saudi Arabia and how that relationship causes mutual problems for each side.

PENETRATED SYSTEMS

A primary issue facing analysts of non–great powers is understanding
how much control states have over their foreign policy choices. We might
imagine a continuum: On one end, states are totally constrained in their
choices by lack of power. Perhaps these states are technical or virtual dependencies or colonies. On the other end of the continuum, states are totally free in their choices, answering to no one but their own constituents.
There are still some states that are dependencies, so states with little to no
control over their foreign policies are not hard to imagine. But, no state is
totally free from foreign linkages—not the most autarkic (like North Korea) or the most powerful (the United States). Thus is it hard to imagine a
state that is totally free to do what it chooses to do in its foreign policy.
Most states sit somewhere along the continuum rather than at the opposing ends; thus states have varying degrees of control over their foreign
policy choices.

What contributes to a state's level of control? States are limited in their
range of foreign policy choices by geography, wealth, and military power.
States also are limited by the fact that, in an era of globalization, "foreigners" and foreign interests are everywhere. James Rosenau put this a
bit more eloquently over forty years ago when he wrote that all states are,
to some degree, "penetrated political systems":

> A penetrated political system is one in which *nonmembers of a national society
> participate directly and authoritatively, through actions taken jointly with the soci-
> ety's members, in either the allocation of its values or the mobilization of support on
> behalf of its goals.* The political processes of a penetrated system are conceived
> to be structurally different from both those of an international political sys-
> tem and those of a national political system.[1]

Denoting a system as "penetrated" does not suggest anything about its legitimacy or type of government. Indeed, Rosenau assumes that "penetrated processes are conceived to be legitimate and authoritative for the
society in which they unfold."[2] That is, beyond nativists, no one is much
surprised by the presence of foreign interests in a society's domestic political processes. Rosenau proposes that all "national societies can be organized as penetrated political systems with respect to some types of issues—or issue-areas—and as national political systems with respect to
others."[3] That is, on some issues, all countries must accommodate the participation of nonnationals in policy making.

To some states, accommodating nonnationals in policy making poses no
particular threat. In countries with a history of being on the downside of a
colonial or imperial relationship, however, accommodating non-nationals

may be particularly noxious. Countries whose autonomy has been sharply limited in the past will not open their arms in welcome to the continued presence of others whose interests may not be close to their own. Globalization makes the "problem" of penetration, to those states that see political penetration as a problem, more acute. Globalizing forces and actors (such as international banks) increase the number of foreigners who get a voice in policy making and lessen the ability of governments to protect their national economies and cultures.

In this chapter, we review some more conceptually fuzzy categories of states and their expected foreign policy behaviors. We will attempt to arrive at a broad understanding of how international position and foreign penetration impose constraints as well as create opportunities for states' foreign policy choices.

RISING GREAT POWERS

In the previous chapter, we discussed the realist view that great powers will use whatever means they have to stop other great powers from rising. In the past, this has often meant preventive war in which great powers attempt to hold down challengers with force. But great powers do not need to wage war against rising or would-be great powers to hold them in check. In the example of the U.N. Security Council permanent membership, the Big Five are able to block the entry of any other country to their powerful ranks. International organizations and international rules may be more efficient than war for protecting the great powers against would-be great powers. This lesson was fully absorbed and put into practice by the great powers who constructed the twentieth-century international institutions that still dominate the landscape today—the United Nations, the World Bank, the International Monetary Fund, the World Trade Organization, and so on.

Preventive war, then, may be an inefficient or short-term fix compared to constructing a web of long-term interlocking international institutions and regulations. It is also the case that great power war may have become what John Mueller has called "obsolescent" or "sub-rationally unthinkable."[4] The great powers and their relevant friends, this liberal internationalist argument goes, have come to realize that war between them serves no good and most certainly would interrupt critical economic interdependencies between them. Nuclear weapons, too, especially during the alliance-loaded Cold War, make great power war an irrational foreign policy choice.[5]

What, then, might great powers do when confronted with rising challengers? War might be unthinkable (although the Bush Doctrine asserted that preventive war is America's right), but there are other instruments of statecraft that might help great powers deal with power transitions. For example, a great power may attempt to accommodate a rising great power by forging a new, mutually rewarding relationship with the rising power. Accommodation acknowledges both the newcomer's enhanced status and the established status of the recognized great power, something that both might desire. The U.S.–Indian nuclear treaty discussed in chapter 6 can be seen in this light. India stood to gain much more from the treaty than the United States, but the United States could gain the good wishes and partnership of a grateful India as the global landscape shifts. And, recall from the last chapter that India is seen as one of the two significant world powers in the era to come, according to the CIA's National Intelligence Council. Accommodation might dissuade the rising power from being a peer competitor and may even dissuade the rising power from becoming friendly with an existing peer competitor. The expectation, though, is that other great powers will move to accommodate the rising power as well, thereby accelerating its rise. Accommodation as a policy does not stop the rise of new great powers. It only gives existing great powers a little more control over the process.

If, for the sake of the argument, warfare is no longer acceptable as a way to prevent the rise of challengers, then it seems logical to conclude that warfare is no longer acceptable as a way to rise into the ranks of the great powers. But, just as established great powers have other ways to block or manage the rise of challengers, so too do challengers have other tools of statecraft to assist in their ascendancy.

Consider India again, but this time in relation to Central Asia. Stephen Blank explains that "Central Asia's large gas and oil reserves and India's rising demand for energy sources . . . [suggest] a naturally complementary relationship."[6] Yet Pakistan and China are also keen to increase their influence in Central Asia. To become the predominant power in Central Asia, "India has utilized all the classical and modern tools of influence building, security assistance, trade, diplomatic support, and even the forging of close relationships, if not alliances with major regional actors."[7] India's general policy toward states in its "extended security horizon," including Central Asia, has been that of a benevolent great power. The policy is that India "should unilaterally grant its neighbors concessions in trade and economics without expecting strict reciprocity."[8] This benevolence, according to Blank, would amend for "India's earlier more overtly hegemonic approach to issues of regional economics and cooperation." How best to win friends in a dangerous neighborhood? India's choice has been to engage in a two-part process that takes full advantage of globalization. First, India opened its own market to foreign arms manufacturers from Russia, France, Israel, and the United States in order to develop an indigenous, sophisticated arms industry. Then, India sought to win friends and control of long-term relationships through arms sales and technology transfers to states in Central Asia.[9]

But Central Asia is not the stopping point for India on its path to great power status. Much of the momentum for its expansion comes from India's domestic economic growth and demand. "India's energy deficit, rising domestic demand, and need to sustain high growth rates, make securing reliable long-term sources of energy a vital strategic priority. The pursuit of energy sufficiency and markets in Asia impels Indian leaders to look seriously at Central Asia, East Asia, and the Middle East and attempt to influence trends there."[10] India's rising fortunes make it an attractive partner, not a threatening power, to most countries in these regions. And India's policy of unilateral concessions to smaller powers demonstrates that it knows how to make use of soft power.

Giving India's "omnidirectional" extension of power, the Bush administration's pursuit of the nuclear treaty with India makes strategic sense. India's reach into critical energy zones is proceeding apace. Rather than compete with China and Russia and India in these zones, the United States offered India a deal it should not be able to refuse in order to tag along on India's rise and gain access to energy supplies that will help the United States maintain its own power and status.

SECONDARY POWERS

There isn't much scholarly agreement on the concept of "secondary powers," certainly not to the degree that there is on great or middle powers. Secondary powers is a term that is used to designate countries who have sufficient resources and power to sit near the top of the international hierarchy of states but, for different reasons, do not sit precisely at the top. During the Cold War, when the United States and the former Soviet Union were "superpowers," this secondary category included some very powerful states—such as the United Kingdom and France, two nuclear weapons states with permanent membership in the U.N. Security Council—and some relatively powerful states—such as Canada and Australia. Since the collapse of the Soviet Union and the start of the unipolar era, this category is still a catch-all, taking in different great powers. The basic difference between a secondary power and a rising great power is that secondary powers do not aspire to lead or control their regions or the international system. But even this distinction is not hard and fast.

Some secondary powers are countries that have decided to forgo the pursuit of great power status for a variety of reasons. For example, Japan is currently a country of considerable economic strength but limited military capacity. Politically, Japan has been content to play key follower to the United States in global affairs. Militarily, Japan relies on its special defense arrangement with the United States and on the U.N. collective security system for protection. Although political and military avenues to great power status are closed off to Japan (or closed off *by* Japan, depending on one's perspective), it does pursue economic great power status. This is particularly manifested in Japanese trade policy vis-à-vis the United States. Eric Heginbotham and Richard Samuels suggest that, in its pursuit of economic goals, Japan poses a significant challenge to the United States. Politically and militarily Japan agrees to occupy a secondary status, but economically it pursues great power status.[11] Scholars have some difficulty categorizing a state such as Japan because of its split personality on standard power indicators.[12] Indeed, without military power, Japan is said not to be a "normal" power. This reflects the traditional orientation of most international relations scholars and the general resistance to new categories of international actors.

France and Germany provide more examples of states that have accepted secondary status, primarily as a way to check the great power aspiration of one another and perhaps to achieve some extraordinary status together. Michael Loriaux proposes that both countries pursued a policy of geopolitical internationalism in the aftermath of World War II and on the path to European Union. Essentially, Loriaux's idea is that both countries pursued realist policies based on geostrategic interests, but both decided that the best way to pursue power politics was through cooperation, or internationalism. This geopolitical internationalism bound Germany and France into a supranational Europe, thereby denying either or both singular great power status, while ensuring their mutually supported pursuit of key national interests and collective status enhancement. As Loriaux explains:

> The Germans showed generally strong support for [European] multilateralism, but only because those arrangements provided the most expeditious way to regain the equality of status with the victorious powers and curry Western support for territorial reunification. France, however, continued to work to institutionalize its cartel relationship with Germany and to construct a viable European rival to the Atlantic alliance, because this was the most expeditious way to maximize control over the way Germany used its resources.[13]

For France, especially, the pursuit of European integration was seen as the most effective way to keep a watch on its enduring rival, Germany. For both countries, European integration or union was a means by which great power status could be achieved collectively when individual great power status was unachievable. From this, we might say that secondary powers are countries that cannot singly achieve great power status and so are willing to (permanently?) trade away that goal in exchange for collective empowerment.

British post–World War II foreign policy was and still is about trading individual great power status for a special position of its own devising. The first conceptualization of this was Winston Churchill's "three circles" that might compensate for Britain's lost empire: Britain would be a link or a bridge between the British Commonwealth, the transatlantic relationship with the United States, and continental Europe.[14] Much later, Tony Blair proposed that Britain's special relationship with the United States made it ideally suited to be the pivotal power between America and Europe.[15] The unpopularity of the Iraq war in Europe and Blair's decision to remain steadfast with Bush put a wedge between Britain and Europe, preventing the pivot from playing any kind of role. According to William Wallace, Britain should give up on the special relationship and focus on European integration as "the necessary foundation for British influence over global political developments."[16] Blair's replacement in 10 Downing Street, Gordon Brown, has seemed to agree, putting less emphasis on the special relationship with America and more emphasis on repairing the divide with Europe.

What Kind of Power Is the European Union?

If France, Germany, and Britain see their individual powers greatly enhanced by being members of the European Union, what kind of power is the European Union? In the summer of 2005, when proposals were afloat to add permanent members to the U.N. Security Council, one idea was to add an EU seat. The EU seat would be occupied at different times by different EU members (although not the French or British, who had their own seats), reflecting the collective importance of the European Union in world affairs. This idea was not supported by all the EU members, such as Germany, who sought its own seat, but it was supported by the smaller powers in the European Union. Like all proposals to expand the permanent membership, this one also failed.

Unlike proposals from individual countries, the nature of the European Union no doubt clouded the picture for Security Council membership. The European Union, in some ways, is like the United Nations: it is an international organization. But the European Union is also quite *un*like the United Nations: it is a supranational organization in which member states recognize the overarching authority of some EU structures and laws. The European Union does not take sovereignty away from its member states, but is said instead to take power from the pooled sovereignty of its member states. And, by pooling their sovereignty, members gain enhanced power.

The European Union began under a different name with a much more limited membership and a unique purpose. The European Coal and Steel Community proposed to eliminate the causes of war between France and Germany (and their immediate neighbors) by pooling resources for the collective good rather than having states fight for exclusive control of them. That is, the community was begun and continues to exist as a way to "civilize conflict" among its member states. Europe, as a community, was also to be a civilizing place between Europeans. And, Europe was to be an exemplar of civilization to the world.[17]

In time, some European scholars have called the European Union a "civilian power." The European Union is distinguished from other actors because it is "not only a *civilian* power (in the sense that it doesn't have military instruments at its disposal) but (also) a *normative, civilizing* or *ethical* power within the international system."[18] As a "civilian" or "normative" power, the European Union promotes norms and values such as cooperative conflict resolution, the rule of law, and a human security ethic through nonmilitary foreign policy instruments.[19] Indeed, Helene Sjursen notes that EU members and scholars see the European Union as an exemplar for a post-Westphalian world order in which state boundaries slip away.[20]

It is not hard to miss the hegemonic aspirations embedded in this civilizing mission. Ian Manners proposes that Europeans should drop the neocolonialism of the phrase "civilian" or "civilizing" power in favor of the category of "normative power." In "Normative Power Europe," Manners argues that what distinguishes European norm diffusion is the "relative absence of physical force in the imposition of norms."[21] Of course, if one is imposing norms, then there is still a coercive quality to one's actions, no matter how well intentioned. For Sjursen, this is a fatal flaw with scholarly efforts to categorize the European Union as a special kind of normative power:

> If power is, as it is usually defined, the ability to make others do what they would not otherwise do, the concept of normative power appears a contradiction in terms. "Power" alludes to "coercion"; "normative" alludes to "legitimacy." How do we know that the EU's use of—normative—power is legitimate as is implied in this concept?[22]

Whether one uses the term civilian power or normative power to describe the European Union, crucial to such a designation is the intentional absence of a military face in EU foreign policy. But the European Union has acquired and is acquiring greater military capacity to pursue its policy of "preventive engagement." Preventive engagement is claimed to be different from American "preemptive engagement," but Manners doubts whether this claim can hold water.[23] Manners sees international events—the 9/11 attacks on the United States, the March 11, 2004, terrorist attacks in Madrid, crises over the Iraq war, and a greater and more authoritative European imprimatur in Bosnia Herzegovina—combining to accelerate the militarization of EU foreign policy along the lines advocated by a hawkish Brussels-based network of "military-industrial" experts.[24] Sjursen agrees that increased militarization of EU foreign policy will remove any doubt about whether the European Union is a special kind of "normative" power. Instead, the deepening of military capabilities will give the European Union the ability to pursue policies akin to those of traditional great powers.[25]

The movement from normative or civilian power to aspiring great power is not one that should surprise too much. As discussed above, French, German, and British aspirations to global influence are bound up in the hope that EU membership will provide such influence, long after each state's singular great power status has eroded. The problem for Britain, France, and Germany is that their international positions have yet to take form. There is too much flux at the top of the system two decades after the collapse of the last international system (as reflected in the debate over whether U.S. grand strategy should accept multipolarity or attempt to maintain unipolarity). This uncertainty plays out in the individual foreign policies of the more powerful EU member states as well as in their on-again, off-again efforts to forge a single EU foreign policy.

MIDDLE POWERS AND GOOD INTERNATIONAL CITIZENS

Of all the categories we will consider, "middle power" is at once the best defined and most belittled. This belittling comes largely from scholars in states that are self-declared middle powers. "Middle power diplomacy" involves international mediation, peacekeeping, consensus building within international organizations, and other similarly cooperative behaviors. According to some analysts, middle power diplomacy (i.e., the foreign policy behaviors of the middle powers) derives from a moral imperative found in the political cultures of the middle powers (Canada, Australia, Sweden, Norway, Denmark, and so forth). This moral imperative is to serve as international "helpful fixers," extending their own social policies on the redistribution of wealth, peaceful conflict resolution, and so on, outward. To other observers, middle powers play their roles because of their position in the international distribution of power, especially vis-à-vis the great powers. Middle powers are not capable of directing the system—as are the great powers—but neither are they the weakest members of the international system. Thus their foreign policy derives from their in-between status.

"Middle power" is a self-identification taken up sometimes by Canadians, Australians, Swedes, Norwegians, Dutch, and Danes, and, as of the 1990s, (South) Koreans, to explain their own countries' roles and positions in the world. The self-identification goes back to the interwar period; "middle power" was a designated category within the League of Nations system (1920–1946), but not a particularly popular one. Brazilian delegates threatened to end their participation in League activities if Brazil were designated as being in the middle of anything. Indeed, Brazil quit the League in 1926, only a few years into its existence.

At the half-century mark, Canadian diplomats set their sights on carving out a role for Canada in the architecture of the post–World War II era. "Middle power" would designate both what certain states had contributed to the Allied war effort—important, albeit secondary, resources and energies—and what these states would contribute to maintaining the postwar international system. As the United Nations took shape, Canadians and Australians began promoting the codification of middle power status into the U.N. Charter based on this functional criteria. The great powers—the soon to be Big Five or "Perm Five"—had no particular interest in delineating categories for non–great powers. And countries relegated by the self-described middle powers to small power status had no interest in seeing another layer constructed atop them.[26] This functionally based, status-seeking claim by the Canadians, Australians, and others, was rejected, but the notion of the middle power was not.

The self-identified middle powers did not go back to stand among the ranks of the non–great powers—not entirely. Instead, they internalized the idea of the middle power and began conforming their external behaviors to role expectations. In time, middle power diplomacy became defined as the "tendency to pursue multilateral solutions to international problems, [the] tendency to embrace compromise positions in international disputes, and [the] tendency to embrace notions of 'good international citizenship' to guide . . . diplomacy."[27] In line with this, middle powers were self-defined as states that committed their relative affluence, managerial skills, and international prestige to the preservation of international peace and order. Middle powers were the coalition builders, the mediators and go-betweens, and the peacekeepers of the world. Middle powers, according to the diplomats and scholars of these states, performed internationalist activities because of a moral imperative associated with being a middle power—middle powers were the only states that were able and willing to be collectively responsible for protecting the international order, especially when smaller states could not and greater powers would not.[28]

How did this moral imperative get imported into what, in the first instance, was a status-seeking project? One quick answer is that the "imperative" was already present. The self-declared middle powers already possessed a sense of moral superiority and certitude that required a unique foreign policy stance. Going hand in hand with this do-gooder impulse was the equally strong impulse to demonstrate to the world that middle powers were like great powers, but were not great powers. As J. L. Granatstein explains, in regard to Canada:

> Canadian policy in the postwar world would try to maintain a careful balance between cooperation with the United States and independent action. This was especially true at the United Nations. And peacekeeping, while it often served U.S. interests, to be sure, nonetheless had about it a powerful aura of independence and the implicit sense that it served higher interests than simply those of the United States, or even the West.[29]

The packaging of middle power diplomacy in a moral wrapping was not intended to obfuscate the essentially interest-based, status-seeking nature of the middle power project. Middle power scholars, particularly, never shied from this element of middle power diplomacy. Middle powers were devoted to the preservation of international norms and principles because they clearly benefited from a routinized international system. Further, middle power internationalism earned these states much deserved prestige. Even as middle powers proclaimed that their internationalism made them different from the great powers, middle powers also acknowledged that they generally were *active followers* of the great powers. Middle power scholars Andrew Cooper, Richard Higgott, and Kim Richard Nossal have coined a term to describe this behavior: "followership." This phrase is chosen to both be similar and dissimilar to the term "leadership."[30]

"Middle power," then, is a self-declared role that contains both status-seeking, self-interested behavior (securing a coveted international position) and moralistic/idealistic elements (being a good international citizen). Thus both realist and liberal elements characterize this role. Post–World War II efforts to attain international recognition for the middle power label failed, yet the middle powers maintained the identity and elaborated on the role expectations attendant to it. It is not difficult to find statements from the prime ministers or foreign ministries of middle powers saying: Middle powers act in certain ways, and therefore we must act in certain ways. Yet the middle power imperative did not blind these states to real-world constraints and dangers, and so it also is not difficult to find statements that take the following form: Middle powers act like this, we are a middle power so we naturally want to act like this, but unfortunately, this is not a prudent time for such actions. Imperative—a sense of duty coming from within the country's national culture to do some good in the world—and position—where one is positioned or where one desires to be positioned in the international hierarchy of states—have long been two sides of the middle power coin, equally at play in explaining middle power diplomacy.

It is important to stress here that the self-identified middle powers were never "revisionist" states for all the efforts they made to distance themselves from the relevant great power (i.e., the United States). From the start of the post–World War II order, these states were content with the status quo and were more concerned that this order would be upset by the great powers through nuclear war than they ever were concerned about their secondary status in it.

Another key point is that middle power studies all have emphasized middle power vulnerability to changes in the central great power relationship. Problems arise for middle powers when changes occur in the relations between the central great powers, or when the central great powers themselves change. The end of the Cold War, the collapse of the Soviet Union, and the uncertainty over whether unipolarity will be maintained has caused anxiety among the middle powers that has yet to be resolved. This anxiety produces ambivalence about the role middle powers should play in the world. This ambivalence is demonstrated most remarkably in the retreat of middle powers from U.N. peacekeeping.[31]

SMALL POWERS AND CLIENT STATES

Here we will think of small powers as countries in situations of near total penetration, penetration that spans the range of political issue areas, both domestic and foreign. How policy makers might find some room for independent policy making in this penetrated position is a topic for analysts of small powers. Small power foreign policy is examined in terms of whether and how small powers may find openings to pursue independent foreign policies. Most of the scholarship on small power foreign policy comes from the liberal and Marxist schools, as realists are largely dismissive of small states. Realists only focus on states that can make an impact on the international system; small states, according to realists, cannot individually or collectively have such an impact and thus can be disregarded.

The starting point for any observer of small power foreign policy is the acknowledgment that the range of opportunities for independent, self-interested behavior is more limited than that of any of the more powerful states. Small powers are boxed in by virtue of their relative weakness, but they are not powerless. Maria Papadakis and Harvey Starr contend that small states have some power over their foreign policy choices and ultimate fates, but this power is contingent on the opportunities present in the international system and the willingness of the leaders of small states to take advantage of those opportunities.[32] In this way, small states are like secondary states and great powers; international conditions must be ripe for action and leaders must be inclined to act.

Davis Bobrow and Steve Chan assert that some small powers have greater ability than other small powers to create opportunities for themselves. Distinguishing among small powers is necessary for analysts since this category—like the related categories "Third World" or "developing countries"—contains the majority of the world's countries. Except in the most abstract sense, it would be impossible to generalize about the foreign policy behavior of this classification of states, since so many different states "belong" here. Bobrow and Chan contend that some small states are more powerful than others because they "have been able to carve out for themselves a special niche in the strategic conceptions, political doctrines, and domestic opinions of their chief ally."[33] These states derive power from manipulating the very relationship in which they are the dependent partner. Israel and South Korea are small powers that have been especially successful in defining their importance to the United States and taking great advantage from this.

Let's examine how a small power might manipulate its relationship with a great power by examining the scholarship of Mary Ann Tétreault on Kuwait and of Martin Sampson III on Libya. Tétreault defines a small state as one whose small territory, population, and resource base make it virtually impossible for it to defend itself against external attack.[34] Defense is the first, most basic duty of any government. A government that cannot defend its country against external threats is a government that lacks fundamental legitimacy. It is also a government that will not be in charge of a country for very long. Other national goals are important, but without basic defense, all other goals fall by the wayside.

In order to guarantee Kuwait's external security against the Ottoman Empire, and to prop it up internally as well, the Kuwaiti Mubarak regime (1896–1915) entered into a cliency relationship with Great Britain in 1899.[35] Tétreault defines cliency as a "strategic relationship between a strong state and a weak one."[36] Although the power relationship is asymmetrical, cliency is reciprocal. Great Britain, the patron, gained a secure base in the Persian Gulf region from which to check the expanding German presence in the Middle East and, in 1913, all rights to the "rumored" Kuwaiti oil reserves. Kuwait, the client, gained external security from the Turks and internal order through the presence of British troops. Cliency "placed a severe limitation on Kuwait's sovereignty, but it preserved the existence of Kuwait."[37] Cliency did not preserve all of Kuwait, though, as its size would ultimately be pared down through various treaties designed and mediated by, ironically, the British.[38] That the Kuwaiti regime was able to engage such a relationship indicates that Kuwait was not a completely powerless small state.

The cliency relationship remained relatively stable until the early 1940s, about the time that Kuwait's oil production took off. Tensions between client and patron over the division of oil revenues and British control of the Kuwaiti economy and entanglement in Kuwaiti political affairs led the Kuwaiti regime to begin seeking another patron around 1950.[39] The "patron" eventually found was oil and economic interdependence.

Tétreault posits that the Kuwaiti leadership placed its faith in oil and economic interdependence, rather than strategic interdependence with another country. She explains:

> Substituting oil for cliency seemed to be a reasonable strategy from the perspective of Kuwaiti rulers. If the primary domestic goal of cliency was to acquire instruments enabling the government to meet domestic demands with a minimal loss of autonomy, oil was even more useful than cliency for obtaining such instruments. Oil revenues not only enabled the ruler to buy off domestic elites quite openly and to retain his independence from domestic society as the source of state income, but they also expanded his resources so astronomically that he could create a huge constituency supporting the regime by making the whole population of Kuwait dependent on the state. In the external realm, the shift from cliency to oil was trickier, but the same strategy applied. Oil revenues were used to buy off the most dangerous of the state's external enemies, also quite openly. In addition, they were used to mobilize an international constituency of supporters of Kuwait by creating foreign aid dependencies.[40]

Kuwait's new "patron" was soon to be tested. The British–Kuwaiti cliency relationship ended in 1961 with the full and formal independence of Kuwait. Almost immediately, Iraq declared Kuwait part of Iraq and moved troops into place to back this claim. This prompted the quick return of British troops. Then British troops were replaced with Arab League troops as a condition to Kuwait's membership in this organization. Thus Kuwait's Arab neighbors became its protectors, and Kuwait became the financial benefactor of the Arab states.[41] Kuwait made the shift from a military client to an economic patron at a time when international institutions such as the Arab League and the United Nations were being formed, binding states into a series of agreements on acceptable and unacceptable foreign policy behavior. At the same time, the booming, oil-hungry world economy ensured Kuwait adequate resources to maintain loyal friends in the Arab world. Beyond the Arab world, growing Western oil dependence sealed Kuwait's importance.

The international political and economic environments were also important variables in two different Libyan regimes' efforts to set an independent foreign policy course. Libya became an independent state in 1951, just as global politics entered the Cold War era and the postwar industrial appetite for oil exploded. As described by Martin Sampson, Libya faced three constraints on independence. First, Cold War politics imposed a nonchoice on the Libyan monarchy, as Middle Eastern monarchies generally aligned with the United States. Second, Western multinational corporations—Exxon, Mobil, Texaco, Standard Oil, Gulf, Shell, British Petroleum, and French Campagnie—held near total control of the oil wealth of the region. These multinational corporations (MNCs) operated together to limit new oil production in order to maintain the petroleum price structure and their own profits. Third, the monarchy had little internal support or legitimacy and a poor resource base to draw on for governing. Sampson concludes:

> In 1951 Libya would seem to have been as dependent and powerless a country as one could imagine—a country that had few foreign policy choices and virtually no possibility of affecting the systems and structures of the outside world. This was not a country from which one would expect foreign policy innovation, or even a foreign policy that would have much impact.[42]

Yet, the Libyan monarch, King Idris, did engage in foreign policy innovation, or, to put it differently, he read the opportunities in the system and was willing to try to exploit them. Libya was not an oil producer at independence, but it was thought to possibly possess significant oil reserves. King Idris wanted to tap into the potential oil riches, but without giving oil MNCs too much control of the Libyan fields. Politically, Idris was constrained by Cold War politics, but he turned these constraints into opportunities that in turn were put toward the service of transforming Libya into a wealthy oil producer and exporter.

Idris's policy contained two elements: he would pursue a conventional political/military strategy that would enable him to pursue an unconventional economic strategy. First, Idris signed agreements with the United States and Britain allowing both countries to build military bases in Libya. The American base was built within a short distance of Idris's palace, ensuring internal protection for Idris if needed. This base, Sampson reports, was the largest U.S. base outside U.S. territory with the exception of the base in Danang, South Vietnam.[43] This conventional political–military strategy gave Idris international "cover" to pursue his second, more important strategy.

Because Libya's oil industry was still in its nascency, Idris was able to exert strong control over its development. In 1955, the Petroleum Law divided Libya into many small oil exploration zones, which were opened to the oil MNCs for bidding. Winners of bids had to begin exploration within a specified time frame and, if oil was found, the MNCs' control over the field would be reduced over a period of ten years until ownership was returned to the Libyan state.[44] This caused oil MNCs to rush into the exploration and exploitation of the oil reserves, which in turn caused Libya to jump from a nonplayer in oil production in the 1950s to the third-largest Middle Eastern oil producer by the mid-1960s.[45] Additionally, Idris opened the Libyan economy to all who wanted a part of the action, including Eastern bloc countries and China. The Libyan economy thus was developed rapidly by a diversity of foreign investors, with little cost and much gain for Libya's economic independence.

King Idris saw clear opportunities in the situation confronting Libya in the 1950s and clear constraints. He used the political constraints of the Cold War as opportunities to buy protection and insulation for his economic goals. U.S.–Libyan relations were so secure and comfortable for the United States that the American government felt no threat in Libyan economic policies. Ultimately, though, Idris was not immunized against internal opponents who disagreed with the trade-offs he made. In September 1969, a group of young nationalist military officers deposed Idris in a bloodless coup. Their chosen leader was Colonel Muammar Qaddafi.

Sampson's reading of the Qaddafi era is that it was made possible by the innovations of Idris. Libya's economic independence and new wealth ultimately empowered those opposed to political dependence on the West. The Qaddafi regime negotiated an end to the American and British military presence in Libya in 1971 and set Libya on a socialist-Islamic path by 1973. In time, Qaddafi moved Libya to the Soviet side of the Cold War while supporting a strongly anti-Western, pro-Arab, pro-Islamic foreign policy stand. Qaddafi set Libya's political-military foreign policy on its head, yet he maintained Idris's economic policies.[46] In particular, Qaddafi used the 1955 Petroleum Law to pressure individual oil MNCs into paying Libya higher and higher revenues from oil production. This had a multiplier effect throughout the region, as Sampson explains:

> [Qaddafi] soon had the oil companies paying Libya more revenue per barrel of oil than other countries were receiving. Libya's success encouraged leaders of other Middle Eastern oil states to demand an increase in the royalties the [oil] monopoly consortia paid to them—to which the companies eventually agreed. Libya would then pressure the companies for even higher prices, would receive them, and then the other oil states of the Middle East would renew their quest for higher royalties. In a very real sense the 1970 to 1972

maneuvering in the Middle East among oil companies and oil exporting states over higher royalty payments was made possible by the independent oil policy that the Libyan monarchy had left to [Qaddafi]. What appeared to be an aggressive and innovative foreign policy change by the [Qaddafi] regime was in fact grounded in the policy of [Qaddafi's] predecessor; he had only extended the exploitation of the structural seams that was initiated by King Idris.[47]

In a brief span of twenty years or so, Libyan leaders saw opportunities and took full advantage of them, revising Libya's position in the region and world. Sampson concludes, "Under two different regimes Libya's foreign policy change has made it important out of all proportion to what would have been expected from structural predictions of Libya's foreign policy."[48]

The examples of Kuwait and Libya demonstrate how small powers can manipulate their circumstances in order to gain greater—even disproportionate—power. Yet not all small powers are presented with the same opportunities and endowed with the same resources. Libya and Kuwait possess critical natural resources, and insightful leaders in each country found ways to leverage this resource and external relations in ways that served their own independent foreign policies. Small powers without such an economic resource need to look elsewhere for ways to exploit the system and gain greater independence. Some small states can draw on their geostrategic location for such leverage—as in the cases of Israel and South Korea mentioned in brief earlier. But many small states possess neither an economic resource nor geostrategic importance that can be manipulated to their advantage. These small states better fit the notion of "powerless" states.

Even the "success" stories have within them cautionary tales. Idris was secure from international threats because of the deal he struck with the United States. Yet this deal was the source of Idris's fall from power. The terms and extent of American penetration of Libyan politics gave rise to the 1969 nationalist-socialist-Islamist coup. Around the time that Britain and Kuwait embarked on a cliency relationship, Britain forged a similar relationship with Iran. Subsequently, the United States assumed the role of Iran's patron. This relationship ultimately generated a popular uprising in Iran, resulting in the 1979 revolution and the founding of the first Islamic republic in modern history. Certainly for the old ruling monarchies in Libya and Iran, cliency had enormous short-term gains and enormous long-term drawbacks.

The patron–client relationship between the United States and Saudi Arabia serves as another example, one with serious implications for September 11, 2001, and beyond. The cliency relationship between these two states goes back to World War II when the Franklin Delano Roosevelt administration sought to secure access to Saudi oil supplies. Michael Klare suggests that this relationship constitutes the "roots" of the terrorist attacks of September 11. This relationship was also seen as crucial to American post–World War II power:

> American strategists considered access to oil to be especially important because it was an essential factor in the Allied victory over the Axis powers. Although the nuclear strikes on Hiroshima and Nagasaki ended the war, it was oil that fueled the armies that brought Germany and Japan to their knees. Oil powered the vast number of ships, tanks and aircraft that endowed Allied forces with a decisive edge over their adversaries. . . . It was widely assumed, therefore, that access to large supplies of oil would be critical to U.S. success in any future conflicts.[49]

Roosevelt administration planners scanned the globe for sufficient oil reserves to guarantee U.S. and European needs and future prosperity. They decided that Middle East oil reserves fit the bill. As Klare describes,

> In one of the most extraordinary occurrences in modern American history, President Roosevelt met with King Abd al-Aziz Ibn Saud, the founder of the modern Saudi regime, on a U.S. warship in the Suez Canal following the February 1945 conference in Yalta. Although details of the meeting have never been made public, it is widely believed that Roosevelt gave the King a promise of U.S. protection in return for privileged American access to oil—an arrangement that remains in full effect today and constitutes the essential core of the U.S.-Saudi relationship.[50]

In return for such access, the United States extended a security guarantee to the House of Saud, promising protection from external and internal challengers. The 1990 Iraqi invasion of neighboring Kuwait posed a serious external military threat, which the United States answered with a massive military response known as the Persian Gulf War. Internal threats to the Saudi government are managed by the Saudi Arabian National Guard. The National Guard "protects the kingdom from its internal enemies and guards important strategic facilities, such as oil installations."[51] Training the National Guard, as of 2001, was the job of a Virginia-based U.S. military consulting firm, whose paid advisers included former president George H. W. Bush and his secretary of state, James Baker.[52] Through the use of private U.S.-based military and security firms, the United States promotes continued Saudi dependency.

This dependency is further demonstrated in Saudi arms imports from the United States. According to the journalist Aram Roston, as of 2001, Saudi Arabia was the world's largest arms importer; weapons constituted some 40 percent of Saudi import dollars. Roston asserts, "The U.S. philosophy is to guarantee the kingdom's safety while also making sure the Saudis buy the best of everything, at top dollar."[53] The deepening military entanglements with the United States and the growing external debt of the Saudi regime is said to have caused deep resentment among the Saudi people, including former Saudi citizen Osama bin Laden. Following a pattern used by Britain in its relationship with Kuwait, Iraq, and Iran until the mid-twentieth century, the United States and Saudi Arabia find themselves in a mutually advantageous and mutually troublesome relationship. The "power" that the ruling regime of a small state derives from a cliency relationship, we might conclude, is finite, and potentially fatal on one or both sides of the nested game.

CHAPTER REVIEW

- Because of globalization all countries have penetrated political systems to some degree.

- Some scholars propose that great power war is obsolete. Established great powers have institutional and diplomatic methods by which they can block or manage the rise of new great powers.

- Secondary powers are states that have great power attributes, but not great power aspirations.

- The European Union is an entity that defies easy categorization. Some scholars call it a "civilian" or "normative" power because its foreign policy has not made use of military force.

- Middle power is a well-defined, self-described role in which states act as mediators, go-betweens, and peacekeepers. When the international system is ill-defined, middle powers have a difficult time maintaining their "good international citizenship."

- Small powers may "punch above their weight class" by attracting an interested great power to a strategic relationship. This might take the form of a patron–client relationship in which both parties stand to gain (or lose) from the arrangement.

10

Conclusion: A Nested Game with Many Players

IN THIS CHAPTER

- A Tangled Tale of Pinochet
- Between Domestic and International Politics in an Era of Globalization
- Nonstate Actors on the Rise
- Concluding Thoughts and a Message to Those in Power

Cases Featured in This Chapter

- A tangled tale in which a Spanish judge, the London Metropolitan Police, human rights groups, victims of torture, and a host of others bring Augusto Pinochet before the world to answer for his regime's human rights abuses.
- Al Qaeda's use of linkage actor strategies in its attacks on the United States.
- How Al Gore, the U.N. Intergovernmental Panel on Climate Change, the Nobel Peace Prize Committee, and the ten thousand–strong Bali Conference put the global hegemon on notice about global warming.

A TANGLED TALE OF PINOCHET

In the summer of 1996, a Spanish group called the Association of Progressive Prosecutors filed a criminal complaint in a Spanish court against

Chilean citizen Augusto Pinochet. The complaint alleged that Pinochet was responsible for the murder or disappearance of seven Spanish citizens while he was the military dictator of Chile from 1973 to 1990. The prosecutor of the case expanded the indictment to include charges of genocide, murder, and torture of Chileans and non-Chileans. Spanish judge Baltazar Garzón issued an arrest warrant for Pinochet.[1]

Twenty-five years earlier, Socialist Party leader Salvador Allende was elected president of Chile. Allende had won a plurality of votes in a three-way election, and then won a run-off election in the Chilean congress to become president. He took power in a country suffering from economic depression; it was also deeply divided politically. Allende's economic agenda was, thus, welcomed by many, and opposed by many others. Some non-Chileans were unhappy with the election as well. U.S. multinational corporations (MNCs) doing business in Chile felt their economic interests threatened by indications that Allende would move to nationalize some of the industries controlled by MNCs. And, U.S. national security adviser Henry Kissinger is reported to have made this remark in response to Allende's election: "I don't see why we need to stand by and watch a country go Communist due to the irresponsibility of its own people."[2]

By 1972 Chile was in an economic crisis and the streets were beset with protests and strikes. Meanwhile, the U.S. Nixon administration undertook a destabilization plan that involved, among other things, CIA support for the Chilean military's orchestration of unrest and lawlessness. A generalized strike in Santiago was met with Allende declaring a state of emergency. Allende turned to General Augusto Pinochet to restore order to the capital. When Pinochet did so, Allende named him chief of the army in August 1973.[3] The next month, Pinochet led a military attack against the presidential palace. Salvador Allende and his closest advisers were killed or committed suicide during the attack. With the Allende government so dispatched, Chile was plunged into seventeen years of military dictatorship led by Pinochet. According to official Chilean records, more than three thousand people were tortured and murdered or "disappeared" during these years.[4] In the early years of this brutal regime, then secretary of state Henry Kissinger visited Pinochet in Chile and assured him that he could ignore U.S. congressional protests about human rights abuses in Chile. Kissinger's message to Pinochet was encouraging: then U.S. president Gerald Ford stood firmly behind him.[5]

The domestic politics of Chile were important to several successive U.S. administrations. Many international and "domestic" actors—Chilean and non-Chilean, state representatives and nonstate actors—get entangled in this tale, as the introductory paragraph to this chapter suggests. The tangled tale of Pinochet will help us return to the primary themes of *The New*

Foreign Policy, reinforcing the importance of multilevel foreign policy analysis, while bringing into focus the nonstate actors who play an increasingly critical role in shaping states' foreign policies. Now, back to our tale.

When he overthrew the elected government of Chile in 1973, Pinochet vowed that it would be a generation before Chile returned to democracy.[6] In 1989 Pinochet allowed national elections, which he lost, and so he stepped out of the presidency in 1990. Throughout Latin America in the preceding decade or so, there had been a "return to the barracks" as military governments relinquished control and democracy swept over the region. The Chilean military leaders, like military leaders elsewhere, negotiated "golden parachutes" to ease their way out of politics. Pinochet's golden parachute came in the form of "senator for life" status, with limited immunity from prosecution and a permanent presence in Chilean politics (albeit a decidedly low-key one). Although many Chileans and non-Chileans believed that Pinochet's deal meant that justice would be forever denied, Chilean political leaders believed the deal was the best way to move Chile into a democratic future.

In the fall of 1998, Augusto Pinochet underwent back surgery in London. While he was recuperating, the London Metropolitan Police arrested him on the warrant issued by Spanish judge Garzón. The British police, a domestic institution whose purpose is to uphold British law inside Britain, arrested a former Chilean head of state for crimes allegedly committed in Chile on a warrant issued by a Spanish judge in Spain. Why would the British police carry out an arrest warrant issued by a Spanish judge? Great Britain, Spain, and Chile were/are all signatories to the U.N. Convention against Torture and Other Cruel, Inhuman, and Degrading Treatment or Punishment. The convention became binding on all three countries in 1988. Once ratified at home, international treaties take on the force of domestic law and are upheld within national territory by the same state agents—the police and the courts—that uphold domestic law. Legal proceedings commenced in Britain to extradite Pinochet to Spain.

Spain's extradition request to the British government was joined by Switzerland, Belgium, and France, while Germany and Sweden opened their own investigations into allegations against Pinochet. Chile, on the other hand, protested Pinochet's arrest and requested that he be allowed to return to Chile. Chile's protest was based on the principle that heads of state and former heads of state enjoy immunity from prosecution. This was the same claim made by Pinochet's lawyers as they attempted to stop his extradition to Spain and win his release from British custody.

The issue of immunity for heads of state and former heads of state (or their representatives) is an extremely contentious one. New millennium efforts to establish the International Criminal Court (ICC) for prosecuting crimes against humanity and war crimes were met with strong opposition by some states who feared the ICC could be turned against them as a political tool. The United States, in particular, opposed the ICC for this reason. (Bill Clinton signed the ICC treaty, but George W. Bush "unsigned" it in spring 2002.) Countries opposed to the ICC argue that their own domestic legal systems are adequate for ensuring justice in cases of true war crimes and that an international legal authority is unnecessary. These states are reluctant to cede traditional state authority to a supranational or international organization.

Six of the European states involved in this tangled tale—Great Britain, Spain, Belgium, France, Germany, and Sweden—are members of the European Union. As EU members, these states already assented to supranational authority on particular issues. For instance, individual rights are privileged in the EU system to the extent that community citizens have legal recourse to challenge *domestic* laws that are claimed to be in conflict with EU legislation.[7] Community citizens may bring their challenges in domestic courts or within the European Court of Justice (ECJ) framework.[8] Thus Great Britain, Spain, Belgium, France, Germany, and Sweden erased one important line dividing domestic from international. Their membership in the EU and ECJ *and* their obligations under the U.N. Convention against Torture and Other Cruel, Inhuman, and Degrading Treatment or Punishment *required* them to investigate allegations against Pinochet.

By international accord, including the Rome Statute that gave life to the ICC, diplomatic immunity cannot be claimed in cases of human rights violations because even heads of state—*particularly* heads of state—must recognize and protect human rights. In the words of the British Law Lords who ruled on the Pinochet case:

> International law has made plain that certain types of conduct, including torture and hostage-taking, are not acceptable conduct on the part of anyone. This applies as much to heads of state, or even more so, as it does to everyone else; the contrary conclusion would make a mockery of international law.[9]

Chile's argument against the extradition was premised on the idea of state immunity, although the government's real goal was to maintain democracy in Chile against some strong domestic political forces. Chilean leaders were in an uncomfortable dual or nested game. On one side were the European states with whom Chile wanted favorable economic and political relations. Also, Chilean leaders sought to maintain a good international reputation, especially in regard to its international commitments; the Chilean government was a signatory of the 1998 Rome Statute and, under the Pinochet regime, Chile had signed the U.N. Convention against Torture.

On the other side of this nested game was a divided domestic political arena: many Chilean citizens and citizens' groups demanded that justice be done in the Pinochet case while the military and its supporters wanted the past to remain in the past. As a democracy, the government of Chile was bound to listen to the many voices of its people and to the rule of law—and in both regards, the government was highly conflicted. The possibility of a return to military rule was an unfortunate reality that figured into the calculations of Chile's civilian leaders, as were the legal commitments made to Pinochet and his cadre as the price of returning to democracy.

Chile's leaders appealed to the Spanish government to intercede and save Chile from this difficult situation. Since the early 1980s, Spain had cultivated a special relationship with its former colonies in Latin America, and it was on the basis of that special relationship that the Chilean leaders made their appeal. But the Spanish government did not intercede on Chile's behalf, out of respect for both its own relatively young democratic system and its commitments to the European Union and the U.N. Convention.

Chilean leaders also appealed to another international actor with whom it had a special relationship: the Roman Catholic Church. Since Pinochet's arrest in October 1998, Chilean leaders had appealed to the Vatican—even directly to the pope—to ask the British authorities to allow Pinochet to return to Chile. In Latin American international relations, there is a long history of mediation and arbitration by the Vatican. The Vatican holds religious and historical importance in Latin America, giving it considerable diplomatic power and influence. In February 1999, it was revealed that the pope and his representatives had appealed to the British government for "leniency for humanitarian reasons and in the interests of national reconciliation in Chile."[10] The Vatican also endorsed Chile's claim that diplomatic immunity barred the prosecution of Pinochet on any charges stemming from his rule.

If you have not been keeping a scorecard, one will be provided shortly! This tale became more tangled as the case moved to British court in October 1998.[11] What is important to note in the following discussion is the variety of actors—state, nonstate, and individual—involved, rather than trying to keep track of the particulars. Pinochet's lawyers brought an action of habeas corpus before the London High Court to win Pinochet's release. The London High Court agreed that Pinochet had diplomatic immunity from the charges, but it ruled that he would remain under arrest while an appeal was heard. The Crown Prosecution Service (an agent of the British government) brought an appeal on behalf of the Spanish government. The appeal was heard by a five-member panel convened by the House of Lords. In this hearing, several human rights organizations—Amnesty International, Redress Trust, the Medical Foundation for the Care of Victims of Torture, and Human Rights Watch (in a more restricted fashion)—were permitted to intervene in the case, as was a British doctor who had been tortured in Chile and the family of a British citizen who disappeared in Chile during the Pinochet era. Meanwhile, the Spanish government filed a formal extradition request with British home secretary Jack Straw.

The House of Lords rejected the previous court's ruling and declared that Pinochet was not protected by diplomatic immunity. The Law Lords, however, restricted the charges to those that occurred after 1988—the year that the Convention against Torture was incorporated into British law. The home secretary, in response, announced that the extradition would go forward. In December 1998, Pinochet appealed the Law Lords' ruling after it was revealed that one of the ruling judges had a formal affiliation with Amnesty International, one of the interveners. The first ruling was set aside and the implicated judge was disqualified from the case. But, in an unprecedented move, Amnesty International was allowed to participate in the oral arguments in a second hearing. The government of Chile was also allowed to make arguments before the court. In March 1999, a seven-judge panel of Law Lords ruled again that Pinochet was not entitled to diplomatic immunity.

Over the course of the next year, the extradition process played out with Pinochet's lawyers and the Chilean government making repeated requests for Pinochet's release, citing his medical condition as the reason. In early January 2000, the home secretary declared that a medical review panel had found Pinochet mentally unfit to stand trial, and so he would be released to return to Chile.[12] Belgium and a group of human rights organizations filed an appeal against the ruling, but this only extended Pinochet's stay in London by another month or so. In March 2000, Pinochet was released from detention and returned home aboard a Chilean air force plane. Within a week of Pinochet's return to Chile, in an odd twist of fate, Ricardo Lagos was elected Chile's second socialist president, the first having been Salvador Allende.[13]

Eventually Augusto Pinochet was stripped of his immunity from prosecution and made to stand trial in Chile for crimes committed while in office. A 2002 Chilean Supreme Court ruling found that Pinochet was too ill to be prosecuted, but in 2006 the Court reversed this ruling. Pinochet died in December 2006, facing pending human rights and financial corruption prosecutions. He lived out his life in freedom once released from British arrest. A former political prisoner under Pinochet was elected to the presidency that same year—that former political prisoner was also the third socialist and first woman president of Chile, Michelle Bachelet.

Despite the fact that Pinochet was never found guilty by a legal authority for his government's human rights abuses, international human rights groups hailed the Pinochet case as an important step forward for the protection of human rights everywhere. The case became the model for similar NGO efforts to bring dictators to justice, as in the case made by Human Rights Watch against Hissene Habre, the former ruler of Chad.[14] The case brought to the forefront one of the U.S. government's worst fears when former secretary of state Henry Kissinger was asked to give evidence to a French judge investigating the murder of French citizens in Chile during the Pinochet dictatorship.[15] What Kissinger knew about Pinochet's Chile and what Kissinger (and his bosses, Presidents Nixon and Ford) approved or aided in remain of great interest to state and nonstate actors who support the International Criminal Court.

BETWEEN DOMESTIC AND INTERNATIONAL POLITICS IN AN ERA OF GLOBALIZATION

Many questions of domestic and international politics are linked in the tangled tale of Pinochet, including:

- How do the citizens of a country seek protection against human rights abuses by their own government? How do noncitizens seek protection? How might individuals seek redress when their rights have been violated? From whom would individuals seek redress?
- Who is to judge the validity of the claim made by national leaders that acts that appear to be human rights violations are efforts to protect national security against internal threats to the state?
- Should democratic leaders make deals with former dictators in order to protect a fledgling democracy? If such deals are made, does this mean that some citizens have special rights over others? Is this a democracy? Can democratic leaders make deals with former dictators regarding the rights of noncitizens?
- Should the leaders of a country in democratic transition be allowed to "silence" opponents whose activities pose a threat to the development of the democracy?
- What principles or interests should inform the relationship between democratic and nondemocratic governments?
- What rules should inform the relationship between states and nonstate actors?
- Should countries help other countries undergoing democratization? Would such help constitute interference in the state's domestic affairs?

- Should states be held responsible for their obligations under international conventions and treaties such as those within the U.N. system? How? What authority would enforce such obligations?
- Is there a need for an international criminal court if international treaties entered into have the effect of domestic law? How can an international criminal court be structured so as not to become a political instrument used by states against their opponents or used by nonstate actors against states?

Some of these issues are more clearly in the realm of foreign policy and some are more clearly domestic, but all have implications in both. It is the nature of global politics in the new millennium that makes this true. Indeed, consider this description of the Pinochet case written in 1999 by President Ricardo Lagos and Heraldo Muñoz:

> In recent years, it has become commonplace to think of globalization solely in terms of transnational finance. The economic well-being of countries such as Brazil, Mexico, and South Korea ebbs and rises on the decisions made by international speculators and foreign investors. Recognizing the growing interdependence of national economies, we use terms such as the Tequila Effect and Asian flu to describe the global contagion that allows financial crises to spread unimpeded across borders. But Pinochet's detention in London has shown that globalization has now expanded from economic affairs to the institutions of politics and justice.[16]

Lagos and Muñoz continue, "Chile enjoys the unique status of having been buffeted by both forms of global contagion—with diametrically opposite results."[17] In the 1980s, the Latin American debt crisis and the resulting disruption to economies throughout the region put Chileans on the street protesting their economic distress. In response—and giving way to internal and external critics—Pinochet began to relax political restrictions on opposition. A prodemocracy movement took off at the same time that Chile's economy began to slowly recover, but Pinochet could not recover his iron grasp. Forces at the international and domestic levels combined to compel Pinochet to call a referendum on his rule, which he lost.

The second "buffeting" of Chile involved the arrest of Pinochet. Lagos and Muñoz, writing before Pinochet returned to Chile, note that "in Chile the [arrest] has created strong political tensions and threatens to fracture further a society that remains deeply embittered and divided over Pinochet's legacy."[18] Chile's new democracy was put under a severe test by the same forces of globalization that helped loosen Pinochet's control.

Globalization is much larger, penetrating, and pervasive a project than any previous international systems have offered. Even states that have been the most hostile to a global free trade system and to the Westernization of world culture have indicated that there are few alternatives to globalization. Globalization has caused and will continue to cause major foreign and domestic policy restructuring for the world's states. Globalization, with all its faults and promises, is now a conditioning feature of all states' policies. But states are not the only actors affected by globalization. Nonstate actors have been empowered by globalization even as many of them rise up to protest globalization's darker side. Some nonstate actors are rising up to speak out on behalf of people left behind in globalization. Not all of these nonstate actors have the same goals or use the same resources; the more extreme of these—symbolized by Osama bin Laden's al Qaeda terrorist network—seek to eliminate globalization and its perceived companion, Westernization.

NONSTATE ACTORS ON THE RISE

Let's consider the many different actors present in the tangled tale of Pinochet. Like the earlier tangled tale of Tibet, the Pinochet case involves more actors than just states. The international actors involved in the tale of Pinochet include:

- Chile, Great Britain, Spain, France, Belgium, Switzerland, Sweden, and the United States
- the United Nations, European Union, and European Court of Justice (all by implication)
- the Roman Catholic Church/Vatican
- international human rights groups: Amnesty International, Human Rights Watch, Redress Trust, Medical Foundation for the Care of Victims of Torture
- Chile-based human rights groups
- Spain-based human rights groups
- UK-based human rights groups
- the Spanish Association of Progressive Prosecutors
- the Spanish legal system
- the British legal system/House of Lords
- General Augusto Pinochet
- Spanish Judge Baltazar Garzón
- British Home Secretary Jack Straw
- U.S. Secretary of State Henry Kissinger
- the British doctor tortured in Pinochet's Chile
- the family of the British citizen "disappeared" in Pinochet's Chile
- the other victims of torture and murder in Pinochet's Chile

This list, like the list of issues already mentioned, is far from complete; but it demonstrates a key point: the "stuff" of foreign policy involves many different actors. It would be impossible to try to understand the issues involved in the Pinochet case just from the perspective of the involved states. The issues go beyond state interests and state actors.

NGOs played critical roles in the arrest of and the case made against Pinochet. The important roles played by NGOs increased the net power of citizen groups and forwarded the notion of a global citizenry, while diminishing the strong grip of states on their own domestic affairs. Similarly, large and sometimes confrontational interest group protests at the World Trade Organization meetings in Seattle (1999) and Prague (2000) and at the Summit of the Americas in Montreal (2001) and the International Monetary Fund meeting in Genoa (2001) signaled that citizens will attempt to exert control over the process of globalization in order to minimize its human toll.

Amnesty International, a key player in the Pinochet case, declared in its fortieth anniversary annual report that "globalization is no excuse for states to shirk their human rights responsibilities."[19] The report states that the work of Amnesty International and the targets of its work have changed to meet the new era:

> The human rights challenges which arise from globalization have stimulated Amnesty International to expand its work by promoting the human rights agenda within the business community, confronting multinational corporations and insisting that companies engage in protecting human rights—particularly those active in countries where there are massive human rights violations.

Further,

> The potential conflict between the pursuit of profit and the protection of human rights has led Amnesty International to communicate its concerns with the international financial institutions, like the World Bank, which is in a position to exert great influence over national economic and political agendas.[20]

Beyond increasing the power of NGOs vis-à-vis states, globalization also opens the door to greater empowerment of international organizations (IOs). Lagos and Muñoz argue that the empowerment of IOs is critical to ensuring that the globalization of human rights norms not lead to the destabilization of fledgling democracies or to more great power politics. They write,

> With the indictment and detention of Pinochet, it is now clear that the erosion of national borders is fast becoming a fait accompli. But just as economic globalization relies on international institutions such as the World Trade Organization to regulate the system and level the playing field, so too does the globalization of justice require mechanisms to minimize potential chaos.[21]

For Lagos and Muñoz, the ICC is the mechanism that "meets the dual objective of curtailing impunity on serious human rights violations and, at the same time, of ensuring just and fair processes subjected to clear rules that are accepted voluntarily by all countries."[22]

Globalization—a force that no state can fully resist—undermines the grip of states on both their foreign and domestic policies while opening the door for NGO and IO empowerment. Beyond the empowerment of NGOs and IOs, globalization can be a force for citizen empowerment through the efforts of "transnational advocacy networks" such as that illustrated in the Pinochet case. "Transnational advocacy networks" is the term coined by Margaret Keck and Kathryn Sikkink to refer to groups "working internationally on an issue who are bound together by shared values, a common discourse, and dense exchanges of information and services."[23] The tangled tale of Pinochet prompts us to think about the impact of these rising networks of nonstate actors on states' foreign and domestic policy making and the strategies these groups employ.

Karen Mingst provides such a framework in her work on "linkage actors." Mingst uses Rosenau's definition of "linkage" to mean "any recurrent sequence of behavior that originates in one system and is reacted to in another."[24] She offers seven categories of linkage actors:

1. Government negotiators engaged in the nested game between domestic and international politics.
2. International organizations, whether acting as agents in their own right or as agents of states.
3. International courts, especially the European Court of Justice, which enjoys supranational jurisdiction.
4. Transgovernmental coalitions between agencies of different states acting cooperatively toward a common goal.
5. Individuals involved in "track two" or informal diplomacy, such as the representative of the Vatican or a former head of state.
6. Nongovernmental organizations.
7. Epistemic communities, which are, as Mingst quotes Peter Haas, "network[s] of professionals with recognized expertise and competence in a particular domain and an authoritative claim to policy-relevant knowledge within that domain or issue area."[25]

Linkage actors utilize four strategies to influence state policy. The first strategy is the power approach. This entails making diplomatic contacts at the ultimate decision-making levels in a high-stakes game of influence. Because failed efforts can come at a great loss of the linkage actor's credibility, Mingst warns, this strategy should not be overplayed. In our example of the Pinochet case, the Vatican effort to convince the British government to release Pinochet on humanitarian grounds illustrates a nonstate actor utilizing a power approach.

The second strategy employed by linkage actors is the technocratic approach. This entails, among other things, the use of the linkage actor's knowledge and expertise of the procedural mechanisms of domestic and international courts to force state compliance with international agreements. In the Pinochet case, a coalition of human rights groups in Chile and Spain led by a group of Spanish prosecutors used those prosecutors' expert knowledge of Spanish law to establish the grounds for the original arrest warrant. Similarly, the human rights NGOs that intervened in the hearings in the British House of Lords used expert knowledge of British and international law to argue against Pinochet's claim of diplomatic immunity.

The third linkage actor strategy is coalition building. Building a coalition that contains many different linkage actors and their resources ensures a stronger, more effective tool to change state policies. The coalitions of European governments and human rights organizations and of British human rights organizations and private British citizens who had suffered under the Pinochet regime are illustrations of effective coalition building.

Finally, the fourth strategy is grassroots mobilization. This entails building widespread public involvement in the cause, especially when the "public" spans multiple national borders. Generally such a strategy involves the use of large-scale public education efforts designed to mobilize the public to demand a response from officeholders. Although Pinochet was not made to stand trial in Spain, the case was seen as a victory for the larger cause: publicity generated by the case educated people worldwide on their rights and on the costs of violating those rights. Moreover, the case served to educate global citizens on the notion that heads of state and former heads of state did not enjoy unlimited diplomatic immunity on human rights issues, thereby standing this old notion on its head.

As nonstate actors rise in importance and power, foreign policy analysts will need to incorporate them into foreign policy studies. The realist notion that nonstate actors are simply instruments of state interests and the Marxist notion that nonstate actors are simply instruments of economic elite interests do not cover the range of nonstate motivations, behaviors, and power we see displayed in the tangled tale of Pinochet. Nonstate actors use features of globalization—such as global communications—to protect individuals against states even while recognizing that globalization itself poses dangers to individuals. Globalization offers such paradoxes—it offers avenues for strengthening the hands of citizens and NGOs against the traditional state structure and against states while also offering more reasons for citizens and NGOs to be alarmed. States, too, may reap the benefits of globalization while also experiencing erosion of sovereignty. States may also engage a darker side of globalization by claiming they cannot act to protect their poor or their environment because the globalization tide is inevitable and overwhelming.

September 11, 2001, presented us with another paradox of globalization that cannot and should not be ignored. For many people in the world, globalization seals the indictment against the United States and the West while it also potentially presents the means by which the Western world system can be destroyed. Osama bin Laden and his terrorist network, al Qaeda, stand in opposition to the U.S.-dominated world economic and political systems and to the Americanization of world culture. At the same time, al Qaeda is the full beneficiary of globalization with associated groups, cells, and operatives in some sixty countries who share resources, finances, and expertise globally. As *Washington Post* reporters Karen DeYoung and Michael Dobbs explain,

> A defining characteristic of the movement's development has been its success in combining two seemingly incompatible sources of strength: a conservative interpretation of Islam and a comfort with aspects of the modern world that have given birth to a highly mobile, popular, wealthy, technologically savvy transnational enterprise.[26]

The groups that together form al Qaeda have become "models of globalization."

The al Qaeda network operates in much the same way as any linkage actor, yet its stakes and methods are extreme, as are its goals. Certainly the 1993 bombing of the World Trade Center, the attacks on the U.S. Marines barracks in Saudi Arabia in 1996, the 1998 bombings of the U.S. embassies in Kenya and Tanzania, and the attack on the USS *Cole* in 2000 can all be characterized as extreme versions—even ultimate versions—of the power approach described above. September 11 demonstrated that this particular linkage actor will go where even the strongest state opponent of the United States will not. Further, the terrorist attacks of September 11 took considerable technocratic expertise—the second linkage actor approach discussed above. How else could the hijackers fly jumbo commercial aircraft into the World Trade Center and Pentagon? Everything about the September 11 attacks required precise, long-term planning and execution, considerable knowledge of building structures and airport security, not to mention absolute commitment to the cause. Coalition building, the third approach, is the way in which al Qaeda arose and continues to attract adherents and spin-off organizations. As governments attempt to undermine this terrorist network, they are finding it to be a diverse and knotty web that combines humanitarian assistance groups, governments, terrorist training bases, and various legitimate and illegitimate financial concerns. Finally, the network that took on the United States finds its strength and its next round of front-line troops in grassroots mobilization, or in the "rage, poverty, and hope-lessness in neighborhoods throughout the Middle East and sub-Saharan Africa."[27]

Like all other linkage actors, global terrorists must work within the con-fines of the international state system. This is yet another paradox of glob-alization: it erodes the importance of states while it accentuates the power of states. In 1991, Saudi Arabia expelled Osama bin Laden because he had issued a *fatwa* against the government, denouncing the regime as illegiti-mate. From then until 1996, Osama bin Laden and his entourage of *mu-jahideen* (holy warriors left over from the successful 1980s Afghani war against the Soviets) resided in Sudan. Around 1996 bin Laden chartered a jet and took his entourage and financial assets to Afghanistan.

Osama bin Laden was forced or encouraged by states to relocate several times. States—fully functional states—retain control over who resides within their borders. Afghanistan was, perhaps, a much better refuge for bin Laden, since the ruling Taliban regime was extraordinarily sympa-thetic to him, his cause, and his money. Plus, the Taliban did not have full control over the country, so its own position was precarious, giving it less relative power over bin Laden than the Saudi or Sudanese governments had and making it far more dependent on bin Laden's fighters and assets.

Bin Laden and al Qaeda were not the only actors in this "war" bound by the state system. The American war against international terrorism was constrained by the power retained by other states. For example, the first arrests in the September 11 attacks came in Spain. In mid-November 2001, eight men were arrested and charged with complicity in the attacks in an indictment released by a Spanish investigative judge, Baltazar Garzón—the same judge who issued the indictment that led to Augusto Pinochet's arrest in London. Spanish authorities had been investigating an al Qaeda cell that had formed in 1994 in Madrid. Phone intercepts in-dicated that the individuals in the cell had helped plan the September 11 attacks with some of the hijackers.[28]

Although the arrest of the al Qaeda cell for complicity in the attacks should have been very good news, it actually posed some diplomatic dif-ficulties for the Bush administration. As part of the administration's evolving plans for the war on international terrorism, Bush announced that he would use military tribunals to try any foreign nationals on charges stemming from September 11. This announcement was met with criticism from all sides of the political spectrum within the United States and as well as from the closest American allies. Within days of the an-nouncement of the arrests of the cell, the Spanish Foreign Ministry an-nounced that "Spain could extradite detainees only to countries that offer defendants the legal guarantees provided by Spanish courts."[29] Military tribunals would not offer the same legal guarantees, making extradition to the United States highly unlikely. Moreover, none of the other EU countries could be expected to extradite suspects to the United States for the same reason. Because the death penalty would be an option in these U.S. tribunals, extradition of suspects from Europe would violate EU policy against the death penalty. Although Spain and the broader European Union were supportive of U.S. efforts in the war against international terrorism, they were not prepared to sacrifice their own national and EU laws and principles in the process.

In the years after the September 11 terrorist attacks on the United States there have been multiple other spectacular terrorist attacks by al Qaeda–affiliated or al Qaeda–inspired groups. One particularly bad attack was launched at commuter trains in Madrid, Spain, on March 11, 2004. This attack killed nearly two hundred and wounded another two thousand. As the United States and others seem no closer to arresting Osama bin Laden and the leaders of al Qaeda, groups inspired by the September 11 attacks continue to proliferate. These groups, including some of the insurgents fighting against U.S. forces in Iraq and Afghanistan today, continue to make use of the linkage actor strategies as they wage asymmetrical war against states. Indeed, the use of strategic communications—especially the use of the Internet and other media—is said to be one of the most important assets of insurgents and terrorist groups. The use of strategic communications—a technocratic approach—demonstrates these groups' persistence and their strength in the face of more powerful state actors and contributes to the recruitment of more individuals and affiliated groups—the grassroots mobilization approach.[30]

CONCLUDING THOUGHTS AND A MESSAGE TO THOSE IN POWER

A final case example illustrates the complicated nature of foreign policy making—how it involves both domestic and international actors and interests and how, more and more, it involves nonstate actors playing critical roles in the shaping of states' foreign policies.

In 2006, former U.S. vice president Al Gore released an Academy Award–winning and box-office hit documentary called *An Inconvenient Truth*. In some ways, this documentary was like a PowerPoint presentation by an ardent environmentalist. Yet, this PowerPoint presentation was also produced by and starred the former vice president of the United States, the man who won the popular vote for the presidency in 2000. That is, this presentation featured someone who was larger than life as its star.

In this documentary, Gore described how—if the present rate of carbon emissions is not just reduced, but reversed—the world will undergo irreversible climate change with cataclysmic effects across much of the world. The environmental groups that had long warned against global warming finally were aided in their efforts by Al Gore. Gore, a track-two diplomat *not* representing the views of the current U.S. administration, upped the power of the grassroots and coalition-building efforts of environmentalists by his power approach. Gore was not alone in his efforts. *An Inconvenient Truth* and related international activities were backed by the growing body of evidence being assembled by the U.N. Intergovernmental Panel on Climate Change (IPCC).[31] That is, Al Gore attached his international presence and access to the highest power circles to the technocratic work of the climate change epistemic community, a community of some six hundred scientists working in one hundred countries whose work was coordinated by the head of the IPCC, Rajendra Pachauri.[32] This powerful transnational advocacy network was joined in late 2007 by the Nobel Peace Prize Committee, when it awarded the Nobel Peace Prize to Gore and the IPCC. You might call it a "bandwagoning" of nonstate groups and international organizations (the United Nations particularly) that could not be easily ignored by the state actors.

And it *was not* ignored by state actors. In December 2007, delegates from 187 countries—some ten thousand state officials, environmentalists, and industry lobbyists—participated in a two-week convention in Bali, Indonesia, on how to cut greenhouse emissions. The goal of the Bali convention was to produce an international agreement that would take the international community beyond the expiration of the Kyoto Protocol in 2012. Early in the conference, the U.S. delegation ran into difficulties with the developing countries, who demanded that the eventual pact "measure not only poorer countries' steps, but also the effectiveness of financial and technological assistance from wealthier ones."[33] During the acrimonious meeting, the U.S. delegation was booed as it tried to block proposals. The European states and environmental groups threatened to boycott a future Bush administration international meeting on the climate if the United States did not agree to the Bali plan. Prior to the Bali meeting, the chair of the White House Council on Environmental Quality had told a reporter about Bali that "The US will lead, and we will continue to lead, but leadership also requires others to fall in line and follow." As U.S. obstinacy at the Bali meeting grew, not a friend rose to defend the U.S. point of view. Indeed, beyond being booed, the U.S. delegation was rebuked by Kevin Conrad, the negotiator from Papua New Guinea, who said, "If for some reason you are not willing to lead, leave it to the rest of us. Please, get out of the way."[34]

In the end, a compromise position was struck; but it was a compromise that gave the Bush administration nothing but a "see you later." The Bali Action Plan provides a two-year timetable of talks to shape the follow-on to Kyoto with much stronger requirements for states to follow. The path may look like another compromise to just continue talking, but the two-year period was chosen because at its midpoint a new U.S. president would be elected. Al Gore had encouraged the Bali negotiators to look beyond the Bush administration. The head of the U.S. NGO the National Defense Council, who served in the Clinton administration, said that "the US will field a new team in the second half [of the Bali process]. And there are good odds that the next president will get serious on global warming."[35] The U.S. delegation agreed to the two-year process (what choice did it have?) and the rest of the world would wait and plan various strategies to convince the U.S. electorate and the soon-to-be-elected U.S. president to stop standing alone and come to the table to address the urgent issue of global warming.

The resolution of the Bali process—an international process involving states, industry, and environmental groups, among many others—will wait for the resolution of U.S. domestic politics. And then the new U.S. president will be expected to send a delegation to the table that reflects U.S. interests in rejoining the community and getting a handle on climate change. This move by the new U.S. president will signal the grand strategy the United States will follow, setting the stage for the next round of international politics. This example is a perfect blending of the kinds of questions and forces at play in the making of foreign policy.

And so we'll stop, where we started, with some simple statements about foreign policy:

- Foreign policy is made and conducted in complex domestic and international environments.
- Foreign policy results from the work of coalitions of interested domestic and international actors and groups.
- Foreign policy issues are often linked and delinked, reflecting the strength of various parties and their particular concerns.
- The stuff of foreign policy derives from issues of domestic politics as well as foreign relations.
- Foreign policy analysis needs to be multilevel and multifaceted in order to confront the complicated sources and nature of foreign policy.

Notes

PREFACE

1. Jessica T. Mathews, President, Carnegie Endowment for International Peace, "The Situation in Iraq," Testimony before the U.S. House Armed Services Committee, July 18, 2007, 3, available at http://armedservices.house.gov/pdfs/FC071807/Mathews_Testimony071807.pdf.

2. "The Terrorism Index," *Foreign Policy*, September–October 2007, available at http://www.foreignpolicy.com/story/cms.php?story_id=3924 (accessed December 1, 2007).

3. Daniel Maliniak, Amy Oakes, Susan Peterson, and Michael J. Tierney, "Inside the Ivory Tower," *Foreign Policy*, March–April 2007, 63, 64.

CHAPTER 1

1. Jonathan Mirsky, "The Dalai Lama on Succession and on the CIA," *New York Review of Books*, June 10, 1999, 48.

2. Jim Mann, "China Issue: Early Test for Clinton," *Los Angeles Times*, January 25, 1993, D1.

3. John W. Dietrich, "Interest Groups and Foreign Policy: Clinton and the China MFN Debates," *Presidential Studies Quarterly* 29, no. 2 (1999): 285.

4. Dietrich, "Interest Groups," 286.

5. Nicholas D. Kristof, "Chinese Apparently Halt Rights Talks with U.S.," *New York Times*, November 25, 1992, A12.

6. Mann, "China Issue."

7. Dietrich, "Interest Groups," 288.

8. "Approval Likely on China Trade Status—with Restrictions," *USA Today*, May 26, 1993, 4B.

9. Steven A. Holmes, "World Moratorium on Nuclear Tests Is Broken by China," *New York Times*, October 6, 1993, A1.

10. Dietrich, "Interest Groups," 289.

11. Dietrich, "Interest Groups," 292.

12. In this same year, the Clinton administration changed its policy on humanitarian intervention, backing away from campaign pledges and early administration policy. This change went hand in hand with a redefining of when the United States would assist the United Nations in such interventions, repudiating the earlier policy of being a better, more helpful member of the U.N. community (i.e., having a policy committed to multilateralism).

13. Leon Hadar, "Clinton Firm on Delinking China Trade, Human Rights," *Business Times* (Singapore), December 19, 1995, Lexis-Nexis.

14. Robert D. Putnam, "Diplomacy and Domestic Politics: The Logic of Two-Level Games," *International Organization* 42, no. 3 (1988): 427–69.

15. Karen Mingst, *Essentials of International Relations* (New York: Norton, 1999), 139.

16. Charles F. Hermann, "Foreign Policy Behavior: That Which Is to Be Explained," in *Why Nations Act*, ed. Maurice A. East, Stephen A. Salmore, and Charles F. Hermann (Beverly Hills: Sage, 1978), 25.

17. Hermann, "Foreign Policy Behavior," 26.

18. Hermann, "Foreign Policy Behavior," 34.

19. Bruce Russett, Harvey Starr, and David Kinsella, *World Politics: The Menu for Choice*, 6th ed. (New York: St. Martin's, 2000), 117.

20. Russett, Starr, and Kinsella, *World Politics*, 117.

21. Deborah J. Gerner, "The Evolution of the Study of Foreign Policy," in *Foreign Policy Analysis: Continuity and Change in Its Second Generation*, ed. Laura Neack, Jeanne A. K. Hey, and Patrick J. Haney (Englewood Cliffs, N.J.: Prentice-Hall, 1995), 18.

22. James N. Rosenau, "Pre-theories and Theories of Foreign Policy," in *Approaches to Comparative and International Politics*, ed. R. Barry Farrell (Evanston, Ill.: Northwestern University Press, 1966).

23. J. David Singer, "The Level-of-Analysis Problem in International Relations," in *The International System: Theoretical Essays*, ed. Klaus Knorr and Sidney Verba (Princeton: Princeton University Press, 1961).

24. The realist worldview has many variants, including neorealism or structural realism, as well as balance-of-power versus balance-of-threat arguments. For an interesting presentation of the variations in realism, see Ethan B. Kapstein and Michael Mastanduno, eds., *Unipolar Politics: Realism and State Strategies after the Cold War* (New York: Columbia University Press, 1999).

25. Liberalism is one of the many labels applied to this worldview. It has been known as idealism, pluralism, and neoliberal institutionalism. For an example of this worldview compared with realism, see Daniel Deudney and G. John Ikenberry, "Realism, Structural Liberalism, and the Western Order," in Kapstein and Mastanduno, *Unipolar Politics*.

26. Marxism has variants of its own: neo-Marxism, structuralism, dependency theory, world-systems theory. For a comprehensive overview of Marxism as compared with realism and liberalism, see Paul R. Viotti and Mark V. Kauppi, *International Relations Theory: Realism, Pluralism, Globalism, and Beyond* (Boston: Allyn & Bacon, 1999).

27. Deborah J. Gerner, "Foreign Policy Analysis: Renaissance, Routine, or Rubbish?" in *Political Science: Looking to the Future*, vol. 2, *Comparative Politics, Policy, and International Relations*, ed. William Croty (Evanston, Ill.: Northwestern University Press, 1992), 126.

28. Gerner, "Foreign Policy Analysis," 126.

29. Gerner, "Foreign Policy Analysis," 128.

30. Howard Wiarda, "Comparative Politics Past and Present," in *New Directions in Comparative Politics*, ed. Howard J. Wiarda (Boulder, Colo.: Westview, 1984).

31. Laura Neack, Jeanne A. K. Hey, and Patrick Haney, "Generational Change in Foreign Policy Analysis," in Neack, Hey, and Haney, *Foreign Policy Analysis*, 5.

32. Wiarda, "Comparative Politics," 12.

33. Neack, Hey, and Haney, "Generational Change," 5.

34. Neack, Hey, and Haney, "Generational Change," 6.

35. Gerner, "Foreign Policy Analysis," 130.

36. Richard Snyder, H. W. Bruck, and Burton Sapin, *Decision-Making as an Approach to the Study of International Politics*, Foreign Policy Analysis Series, no. 3 (Princeton: Princeton University Press, 1954); and Snyder, Bruck, and Sapin, eds., *Foreign Policy Decision Making* (New York: Free Press, 1963).

37. Charles F. Hermann and Gregory Peacock, "The Evolution and Future of Theoretical Research in the Comparative Study of Foreign Policy," in *New Directions in the Study of Foreign Policy*, ed. Charles F. Hermann, Charles W. Kegley, and James N. Rosenau (Winchester, Mass.: Unwin Hyman, 1987), 22–23.

38. Snyder, Bruck, and Sapin, *Foreign Policy Decision Making*, 65, as quoted in James E. Dougherty and Robert L. Pfaltzgraff Jr., *Contending Theories of International Relations: A Comprehensive Survey*, 5th ed. (New York: Longman, 2001), 554.

39. Hermann and Peacock, "Evolution and Future of Theoretical Research," 23.

40. Rosenau, "Pre-theories."

41. Rosenau, "Pre-theories," 115–16.

42. Rosenau, "Pre-theories," 124.

43. Hermann and Peacock, "Evolution and Future of Theoretical Research," 23.

44. Neack, Hey, and Haney, "Generational Change."

45. Robert O. Keohane and Joseph S. Nye, *Power and Interdependence: World Politics in Transition* (Boston: Little, Brown, 1977).

46. Neack, Hey, and Haney, "Generational Change," 7.

CHAPTER 2

1. Joe D. Hagan, "Domestic Political Regime Changes and Third World Voting Realignments in the United Nations, 1946–84," *International Organization* 43, no. 3 (1989): 508.

2. Hans J. Morgenthau, *Politics among Nations*, brief ed., rev. Kenneth W. Thompson (New York: McGraw-Hill, 1993), 5.

3. Michael D. McGinnis, "Rational Choice and Foreign Policy Change: The Arms and Alignments of Regional Powers," in *Foreign Policy Restructuring: How Governments Respond to Global Change*, ed. Jerel A. Rosati, Joe D. Hagan, and Martin W. Sampson III (Columbia: University of South Carolina Press, 1994), 69.

4. McGinnis, "Rational Choice and Foreign Policy Change," 70.

5. George Kennan, quoted in Graham Allison and Philip Zelikow, *Essence of Decision: Explaining the Cuban Missile Crisis*, 2nd ed. (New York: Longman, 1999), 28.

6. James E. Dougherty and Robert L. Pfaltzgraff Jr., *Contending Theories of International Relations: A Comprehensive Survey*, 5th ed. (New York: Longman, 2001), 553.

7. Richard Snyder, H. W. Bruck, and Burton Sapin, "Decision-making as an Approach to the Study of International Politics," in *Foreign Policy Decision Making: An Approach to the Study of International Politics* (New York: Macmillan, 1962).

8. Allison and Zelikow, *Essence of Decision*, 17.

9. Allison and Zelikow, *Essence of Decision*, 18.

10. Allison and Zelikow, *Essence of Decision*, 19.

11. Allison and Zelikow, *Essence of Decision*, 30.

12. Glenn H. Snyder, "The Security Dilemma in Alliance Politics," *World Politics* 36, no. 4 (July 1984): 461.

13. Ben D. Mor, "Nasser's Decision-making in the 1967 Middle East Crisis: A Rational-choice Explanation," *Journal of Peace Research* 28, no. 4 (1991): 359–75.

14. For details on the Suez Crisis, see Michael G. Fry, "The Suez Crisis, 1956," *Pew Case Studies in International Affairs*, no. 126 (Washington, D.C.: Georgetown University School of Public Service, 1989).

15. U.N. peacekeeping troops can only be placed within a country with the permission of that country's government, if there is one. This consent requirement is necessary because the United Nations recognizes the key principle that all states are sovereign. Sovereignty means that there is no higher authority than a state in its territory. Placing foreign troops in a country without the consent of the government would constitute an invasion and would only be permissible under certain narrow and relatively untested provisions of the U.N. Charter.

16. Mor, "Nasser's Decision-making," 371–72.

17. Charles F. Hermann, Janice Gross Stein, Bengt Sundelius, and Stephen G. Walker, "Resolve, Accept, or Avoid: Effects of Group Conflict on Foreign Policy Decisions," *International Studies Review* 3, no. 2 (Summer 2001): 156.

18. Deborah Sontag, "No Optimism about Mideast Talks," *New York Times*, September 6, 2000, A13.

19. Robin Wright, "Attack on Iraq May Be Outcome Hussein Wants," *Los Angeles Times*, January 31, 1998, A1.

20. See Kenneth Waltz's side of the debate presented in Scott D. Sagan and Kenneth N. Waltz, *The Spread of Nuclear Weapons: A Debate Renewed*, 2nd ed. (New York: W.W. Norton, 2002).

21. Dougherty and Pfaltzgraff, *Contending Theories*, 562.

22. Karen Mingst, *Essentials of International Relations* (New York: Norton, 1999), 68.

23. Robert L. Jervis, "Hypotheses on Misperception," *World Politics* (April 1968); reprinted in *American Foreign Policy: Theoretical Essays*, ed. G. J. Ikenberry (Glenview, Ill.: Scott, Foresman, 1989), 477.

24. Jervis, "Hypotheses on Misperception," 477.

25. Jerel Rosati, "The Power of Human Cognition in the Study of World Politics," *International Studies Review* 2, no. 3 (Autumn 2001): 49.

26. Alex Mintz, "Applied Decision Making: Utilizing Poliheuristic Theory to Explain and Predict Foreign Policy and National Security Decisions," *International Studies Perspectives* 6, no. 1 (February 2005): 94–95.

27. David Brulé, "Explaining and Forecasting Leaders' Decisions: A Poliheuristic Analysis of the Iran Hostage Rescue Decision," *International Studies Perspectives* 6, no. 1 (February 2005): 99–113.

28. Mintz, "Applied Decision Making," 94.

29. Brulé, "Explaining and Forecasting Leaders' Decisions," 100.

CHAPTER 3

1. Stephen Benedict Dyson, "Personality and Foreign Policy: Tony Blair's Iraq Decisions," *Foreign Policy Analysis* 2, no. 3 (July 2006): 289.

2. Dyson, "Personality and Foreign Policy."

3. Louise Grace Shaw, "Attitudes of the British Political Elite towards the Soviet Union," *Diplomacy & Statecraft* 13, no. 1 (March 2002): 63–64.

4. Shaw, "Attitudes of the British Political Elite towards the Soviet Union," 70.

5. Michiko Kakutani, "All the President's Books," *New York Times*, May 11, 2006, E1.

6. Margaret G. Hermann and Joe D. Hagan, "International Decision Making: Leadership Matters," *Foreign Policy*, Spring 1988, 126.

7. Hermann and Hagan, "International Decision Making," 135.

8. Patrick J. Haney, "The Submarines of September: The Nixon Administration and a Soviet Submarine Base in Cuba," *Pew Case Studies in International Affairs*, no. 372 (Washington, D.C.: Georgetown University School of Public Service, 1996).

9. Haney, "Submarines of September," 3.

10. Kenneth Waltz, *Man, the State, and War* (New York: Columbia University Press, 1959), chaps. 2 and 3; Jerel Rosati, "A Cognitive Approach to the Study of Foreign Policy," in *Foreign Policy Analysis: Continuity and Change in Its Second Generation*, ed. Laura Neack, Jeanne A. K. Hey, and Patrick J. Haney (Englewood Cliffs, N.J.: Prentice-Hall, 1995), 51.

11. Robert L. Jervis, "Hypotheses on Misperception," *World Politics* (April 1968); reprinted in *American Foreign Policy: Theoretical Essays*, ed. G. J. Ikenberry (Glenview, Ill.: Scott, Foresman, 1989), 461.

12. Jervis, "Hypotheses on Misperception," 462.

13. Irving L. Janis, *Crucial Decisions* (New York: Free Press, 1989); *Groupthink: Psychological Studies of Policy Decisions and Fiascoes* (Boston: Houghton Mifflin, 1982).

14. Kakutani, "All the President's Books."

15. Rosati, "A Cognitive Approach," 50.

16. Jerel Rosati, "The Power of Human Cognition in the Study of World Politics," *International Studies Review* 2, no. 3 (Autumn 2001): 50.

17. For an elaboration on five stereotypical images of outside actors, see Richard K. Herrmann and Michael P. Fischerkeller, "Beyond the Enemy Image and Spiral Model: Cognitive-Strategic Research after the Cold War," *International Organization* 49, no. 2 (1995): 415–50.

18. Ole R. Holsti, "Cognitive Dynamics and Images of the Enemy: Dulles and Russia," in *Image and Reality in World Politics*, ed. John C. Farrell and Asa P. Smith (New York: Columbia University Press, 1967), 17, as discussed in Rosati, "A Cognitive Approach," 55.

19. Kakutani, "All the President's Books." See also Richard A. Clarke, *Against All Enemies: Inside America's War on Terror* (New York: Free Press, 2004).

20. Kakutani, "All the President's Books."

21. Jack S. Levy, "Learning and Foreign Policy: Sweeping a Conceptual Minefield," *International Organization* 48, no. 2 (1994): 283.

22. Janice Gross Stein, "Political Learning by Doing: Gorbachev as Uncommitted Thinker and Motivated Learner," *International Organization* 48, no. 2 (1994): 172.

23. Stein, "Political Learning," 172.

24. Matthew S. Hirshberg, "The Self-Perpetuating National Self-Image: Cognitive Biases in Perceptions of International Interventions," *Political Psychology* 14, no. 1 (1993): 80.

25. Hirshberg, "Self-Perpetuating National Self-Image," 85.

26. Hirshberg, "Self-Perpetuating National Self-Image," 91.

27. Office of the Press Secretary, "President Outlines Steps to Help Iraq Achieve Democracy and Freedom," Remarks by the President on Iraq and the War on Terror, United States Army War College, Carlisle, Pennsylvania, May 24, 2004.

28. Office of the Press Secretary, "President Commemorates Veterans Day, Discusses War on Terror," Tobyhanna Army Depot, Tobyhanna, Pennsylvania, November 11, 2005.

29. Office of the Press Secretary, "President Participates in Discussion on War on Terror," Kentucky International Convention Center, Louisville, Kentucky, January 11, 2006.

30. Keith Shimko, "Foreign Policy Metaphors: Falling 'Dominoes' and 'Drug Wars,'" in Neack, Hey, and Haney, *Foreign Policy Analysis*, 73.

31. Phil Reeves, "Sharon Appeals to America Not to 'Appease' Arabs," *Independent* (London), October 5, 2001, 15; Alan Sipress and Lee Hockstader, "Sharon Speech Riles US," *Washington Post*, October 6, 2001, A1.

32. Reeves, "Sharon Appeals to America," A1.

33. Allison Astorino-Courtois, "The Cognitive Structure of Decision-making and the Course of Arab-Israeli Relations, 1970–1978," *Journal of Conflict Resolution* 39, no. 3 (1995): 420.

34. Peter Suedfeld, Michael D. Wallace, and Kimberly L. Thachuk, "Changes in Integrative Complexity among Middle East Leaders during the Persian Gulf Crisis," *Journal of Social Issues* 49, no. 4 (1993): 183–84. See also Philip E. Tetlock, "Integrative Complexity of American and Soviet Foreign Policy Rhetoric: A Time-Series Analysis," *Journal of Personality and Social Psychology* 49 (1985): 165–85.

35. Astorino-Courtois, "Cognitive Structure of Decision-making," 420; Stephen G. Walker and George L. Watson, "Integrative Complexity and British Decisions during the Munich and Polish Crises," *Journal of Conflict Resolution* 38, no. 1 (1994): 3–23.

36. Astorino-Courtois, "Cognitive Structure of Decision-making," 421.

37. Scott Crichlow, "Idealism or Pragmatism? An Operational Code Analysis of Yitzak Rabin and Shimon Peres," *Political Psychology* 19, no. 4 (1998): 684.

38. Alexander George, "The 'Operational Code': A Neglected Approach to the Study of Political Leaders and Decision-making," in *American Foreign Policy: Theoretical Essays*, ed. G. John Ikenberry (Glenview, Ill.: Scott, Foresman, 1989), 486. Reprinted from the original article, which appeared in *International Studies* 13, no. 2 (1969).

39. Stephen G. Walker, Mark Schafer, and Michael D. Young, "Presidential Operational Codes and Foreign Policy Conflicts in the Post-Cold War World," *Journal of Conflict Resolution* 43, no. 5 (1999): 613.

40. Crichlow, "Idealism or Pragmatism?" 689.

41. Ibrahim A. Karawan, "Sadat and the Egyptian-Israeli Peace Revisited," *International Journal of Middle East Studies* 26, no. 2 (1994): 249–66.

42. Karawan, "Sadat and the Egyptian-Israeli Peace," 252.

43. Interview, Newport, Kentucky, October 29, 2007.

44. Margaret G. Hermann, "Explaining Foreign Policy Behavior Using the Personal Characteristics of Political Leaders," *International Studies Quarterly* 43, no. 1 (March 1980), 8.

45. Dyson, "Personality and Foreign Policy"; Vaughn P. Shannon and Jonathan W. Keller, "Leadership Style and International Norm Violation: The Case of the Iraq War," *Foreign Policy Analysis* 3, no. 1 (2007): 79–104.

46. Hermann, "Explaining Foreign Policy Behavior," 11–12.

47. Hermann, "Explaining Foreign Policy Behavior," 12.

48. Shannon and Keller, "Leadership Style and International Norm Violation," 80.

49. Shannon and Keller, "Leadership Style and International Norm Violation," 97–98.

50. Dyson, "Personality and Foreign Policy," 294.

51. Dyson, "Personality and Foreign Policy."

CHAPTER 4

1. Margaret G. Hermann and Charles F. Hermann, "Who Makes Foreign Policy Decisions and How: An Empirical Inquiry," *International Studies Quarterly* 33, no. 4 (December 1989): 362. See also Ryan K. Beasley, Juliet Kaarbo, Charles F. Hermann, and Margaret G. Hermann, "Leaders, Groups, and Coalitions: Understanding People and Processes in Foreign Policymaking," *International Studies Review* 3, no. 2 (Summer 2001): 217–50.

2. Hermann and Hermann, "Who Makes Foreign Policy Decisions and How," 363.

3. Hermann and Hermann, "Who Makes Foreign Policy Decisions and How," 366.

4. Hermann and Hermann, "Who Makes Foreign Policy Decisions and How," 365.

5. Hermann and Hermann, "Who Makes Foreign Policy Decisions and How," 363.

6. Charles F. Hermann, Janice Gross Stein, Bengt Sundelius, and Stephen G. Walker, "Resolve, Accept, or Avoid: Effects of Group Conflict on Foreign Policy Decisions," *International Studies Review* 3, no. 2 (Summer 2001): 134.

7. Hermann, Stein, Sundelius, and Walker, "Resolve, Accept, or Avoid," 134.

8. Esra Çuhadar-Gürkaynak and Binnur Özkeçeci-Taner, "Decisionmaking Process Matters: Lessons Learned from Two Turkish Foreign Policy Cases," *Turkish Studies* 5, no. 2 (Summer 2004): 46.

9. Irving L. Janis, *Victims of Groupthink* (Boston: Houghton Mifflin, 1972); *Groupthink: Psychological Studies of Foreign Policy Decisions and Fiascoes*, rev. ed. (Boston: Houghton Mifflin, 1982).

10. Janis, *Groupthink*, 176.

11. Hermann, Stein, Sundelius, and Walker, "Resolve, Accept, or Avoid," 140.

12. Hermann, Stein, Sundelius, and Walker, "Resolve, Accept, or Avoid," 140.

13. Mark Schafer and Scott Crichlow, "Antecedents of Groupthink: A Quantitative Study," *Journal of Conflict Resolution* 40, no. 3 (September 1996): 429.

14. Hermann, Stein, Sundelius, and Walker, "Resolve, Accept, or Avoid," 146, fig. 2.

15. Hermann, Stein, Sundelius, and Walker, "Resolve, Accept, or Avoid," 146, fig. 2.

16. International Crisis Group, "Conflict History: Iran," March 2006, http://www.crisisgroup.org (accessed Nov. 8, 2007).

17. "Country Profile: Iran," BBC News, October 9, 2007, http://newsvote.bbc.co.uk (accessed Nov. 8, 2007); "Iran: Who Holds the Power?" BBC News, no date, http://newsvote.bbc.co.uk (accessed Nov. 8, 2007).

18. Gareth Smyth, "Fundamentalists, Pragmatists, and the Rights of the Nation: Iranian Politics and Nuclear Confrontation," *A Century Foundation Report* (New York and Washington, D.C.: The Century Foundation, 2006).

19. International Crisis Group, "Conflict History: Iran."

20. Ray Takeyh, "Time for Détente with Iran," *Foreign Affairs*, March–April 2007, online version, http://www.foreignaffairs.org (accessed Nov. 9, 2007).

21. International Crisis Group, "Conflict History: Iran."

22. Smyth, "Fundamentalists, Pragmatists, and the Rights of the Nation," 17.

23. Ali Akbar Dareini, "Resignation of Iranian Nuclear Envoy Could Signal Hardening Stance in Atomic Dispute," Associated Press, October 20, 2007.

24. Takeyh, "Time for Détente with Iran."

25. Takeyh, "Time for Détente with Iran"; see also Smyth, "Fundamentalists, Pragmatists, and the Rights of the Nation."

26. Ali Akbar Dareini, "Departure of Nuclear Negotiator Leads Some Conservatives to Criticize Iran's President," Associated Press, October 23, 2007.

27. Takeyh, "Time for Détente with Iran."

28. Smyth, "Fundamentalists, Pragmatists, and the Rights of the Nation," 17.

29. Takeyh, "Time for Détente with Iran."

30. Hermann and Hermann, "Who Makes Foreign Policy Decisions and How," 364.

31. Hermann and Hermann, "Who Makes Foreign Policy Decisions and How," 368.

32. Graham Allison and Philip Zelikow, *Essence of Decision: Explaining the Cuban Missile Crisis*, 2nd ed. (New York: Longman, 1999), 256.

33. Allison and Zelikow, *Essence of Decision*, 256.

34. James E. Dougherty and Robert L. Pfaltzgraff Jr., *Contending Theories of International Relations: A Comprehensive Survey*, 5th ed. (New York: Longman, 2001), 557.

35. Çuhadar-Gürkaynak and Özkeçeci-Taner, "Decisionmaking Process Matters."

36. Çuhadar-Gürkaynak and Özkeçeci-Taner, "Decisionmaking Process Matters," 50.

37. Çuhadar-Gürkaynak and Özkeçeci-Taner, "Decisionmaking Process Matters," 51.

38. Çuhadar-Gürkaynak and Özkeçeci-Taner, "Decisionmaking Process Matters," 52.

39. Çuhadar-Gürkaynak and Özkeçeci-Taner, "Decisionmaking Process Matters," 53.

40. Christopher Torchia, "Turkey Lawmakers OK Possible Attack," Associated Press Online, October 18, 2007; and Yesim Borg and Asso Ahmed, "Turkey Threatens Incursion After Kurds Kill 12 Troops," *Los Angeles Times*, October 22, 2007.

41. Joshua Partlow and Amit R. Paley, "Turkey Sends Soldiers into N. Iraq," *Washington Post*, February 23, 2008, A11; and Joshua Partlow, "A Kurdish Society of Soldiers," *Washington Post*, March 8, 2008, A1.

CHAPTER 5

1. Ulf Hedetoft, "National Identity and Mentalities of War in Three EC Countries," *Journal of Peace Research* 30, no. 3 (1993): 295.

2. Hedetoft, "National Identity," 292.

3. Hedetoft, "National Identity," 295.

4. Peter R. Baehr, "Trials and Errors: The Netherlands and Human Rights," in *Human Rights and Comparative Foreign Policy*, ed. David P. Forsythe (New York: United Nations University Press, 2000), 52.

5. James N. Rosenau, "Pre-theories and Theories of Foreign Policy," in *Approaches to Comparative and International Politics*, ed. R. Barry Farrell (Evanston, Ill.: Northwestern University Press, 1966), 133.

6. Maurice A. East and Charles F. Hermann, "Do Nation-Types Account for Foreign Policy Behavior?" in *Comparing Foreign Policies: Theories, Findings, and Methods*, ed. James N. Rosenau (New York: John Wiley and Sons for Sage, 1974), 272.

7. East and Hermann, "Do Nation-Types Account for Foreign Policy Behavior?" 299.

8. "The Globalization Index," *Foreign Policy,* November–December 2007, 68–76.

9. The Fund for Peace and *Foreign Policy* magazine, "The Failed States Index," *Foreign Policy*, July–August 2007, 54–63.

10. Vision of Humanity, "The Global Peace Index," www.visionofhumanity .com (accessed Nov. 26, 2007).

11. Vision of Humanity, "The Global Peace Index."

12. "First Global Peace Index Ranks 121 Countries," PRNewswire, May 30, 2007, www.prnewswire.com (accessed Nov. 26, 2007).

13. "Norway Rated Most Peaceful Nation," BBC News, May 30, 2007, http:// news.bbc.co.uk.

14. Matthew S. Hirshberg, "The Self-Perpetuating National Self-Image: Cognitive Biases in Perceptions of International Interventions," *Political Psychology* 14, no. 1 (1993): 78.

15. Hirshberg, "Self-Perpetuating National Self-Image," 78.

16. J. L. Granatstein, "Peacekeeping: Did Canada Make a Difference? And What Difference Did Canada Make?" in *Making a Difference: Canada's Foreign Policy in a Changing World Order*, ed. John English and Norman Hillmer (Toronto: Lester, 1992), 223.

17. Granatstein, "Peacekeeping," 223–24.

18. The Canadian government Web site provides a detailed, comprehensive discussion of all that goes into Canada's Human Security foreign policy. See http://geo.international.gc.ca/cip-pic/cip-pic/humansecurity-en.aspx (accessed Nov. 26, 2007).

19. Hirshberg, "Self-Perpetuating National Self-Image," 87.

20. Hirshberg, "Self-Perpetuating National Self-Image," 96.

21. Alastair Ian Johnston, "Realism(s) and Chinese Security Policy in the Post-Cold War Period," in *Unipolar Politics: Realism and State Strategies after the Cold War*, ed. Ethan B. Kapstein and Michael Mastanduno (New York: Columbia University Press, 1999), 288.

22. Johnston, "Realism(s) and Chinese Security Policy," 289.

23. Daniel Bar-Tal and Dikla Antebi, "Beliefs about Negative Intentions of the World: A Study of Israeli Siege Mentality," *Political Psychology* 13, no. 4 (1992): 634.

24. Peter J. Katzenstein and Nobuo Okawara, "Japan's National Security: Structures, Norms, and Policies," *International Security* 17, no. 4 (1993): 87.

25. Yozo Yokota and Chiyuki Aoi, "Japan's Foreign Policy toward Human Rights: Uncertain Changes," in Forsythe, *Human Rights and Comparative Foreign Policy*, 127.

26. Katzenstein and Okawara, "Japan's National Security," 92.

27. Katzenstein and Okawara, "Japan's National Security," 97.

28. Paul Wiseman, "Nationalism Gains Strength in Japan; Candidates Push to Rearm Country and Rewrite History," *USA Today*, July 27, 2007, A6.

29. Anthony Faiola, "Japan Upgrades Its Defense Agency; New Laws Widen Mission, Require Schools to Foster Patriotism," *Washington Post*, December 16, 2006, A15; Norimitsu Onishi, "Japanese Lawmakers Pass Two Laws that Shift Nation Away from Its Postwar Pacifism," *New York Times*, December 16, 2006, A10.

30. Joseph Coleman, "Japan Brings Back Patriotic Education, Upgrades Defense Agency to Full Ministry," Associated Press, December 15, 2006.

31. Norimitsu Onishi, "Governing Party in Japan Suffers Election Defeat," *New York Times,* July 30, 2007, A1.

32. Kozo Mizoguchi, "Japan Halts Indian Ocean Mission," Associated Press, washingtonpost.com, November 1, 2007; Blaine Harden, "Japan's New Premier Stymied by Old Issue," *Washington Post,* November 1, 2007, A12.

33. Blaine Harden, "Japan's Leader Cites Limits in Global Security Abilities; Fukuda, on Eve of Visit, Stresses US Relations," *Washington Post,* November 13, 2007, A12; Mari Yamaguchi, "Japanese Lower House OKs Bill to Resume Curtailed Indian Ocean Naval Mission," Associated Press, November 13, 2007; Michael Zielenziger, "Our Reluctant Ally: The US-Japan Alliance, Once so Solid, has Frayed under the Bush Administration," *Los Angeles Times,* November 16, 2007, A35.

34. Michael Doyle, "Kant, Liberal Legacies, and Foreign Affairs," *Philosophy and Public Affairs* 12, no. 3 (1983): 205–35.

35. T. Clifton Morgan, "Democracy and War: Reflections on the Literature," *International Interactions* 18, no. 3 (1992): 198.

36. Brett Ashley Leeds and David R. Davis, "Beneath the Surface: Regime Type and International Interaction, 1953–78," *Journal of Peace Research* 36, no. 1 (1999): 7.

37. Leeds and Davis, "Beneath the Surface," 8; Morgan, "Democracy and War," 199.

38. David P. Forsythe, "Democracy, War, and Covert Action," *Journal of Peace Research* 29 (1992): 385–95; Laura Neack, "Linking State Type with Foreign Policy Behavior," in *Foreign Policy Analysis,* ed. Laura Neack, Jeanne A.K. Hey, and Patrick J. Haney (Englewood Cliffs, N.J.: Prentice Hall, 1995), 220–21.

39. Bruce Russett, *Grasping the Democratic Peace: Principles for a Post-Cold War World* (Princeton, N.J.: Princeton University Press, 1993).

40. Bruce Russett, "Bushwacking the Democratic Peace," *International Studies Perspectives* 6, no. 4 (November 2005): 396.

CHAPTER 6

1. "Democratic Baggage," *Economist,* August 23, 2007, 40.

2. "On the Blink," *Economist,* October 25, 2007, 50.

3. Laura Neack, *Elusive Security: States First, People Last* (Lanham, Md.: Rowman & Littlefield, 2007), 98.

4. Sam Dolnick, "Communist Parties Relent in Opposition to Landmark US-India Nuclear Deal," Associated Press, November 17, 2007.

5. "Democratic Baggage," *Economist,* 40–41; Madhur Singh, "India's Nuclear Discord," *Time,* September 3, 2007, 17.

6. Dolnick, "Communist Parties Relent"; see also Penny MacRae, "Indo-US Nuclear Pact Not Out of Woods: Analysts," Agence France Presse, November 18, 2007; and "The Real Deal? Indian Politics," *Economist,* November 24, 2007.

7. Peter F. Trumbore and Mark A. Boyer, "International Crisis Decisionmaking as a Two-Level Process," *Journal of Peace Research* 37, no. 6 (November 2000): 680.

8. Trumbore and Boyer, "International Crisis Decisionmaking as a Two-Level Process," 680.

9. Joe D. Hagan, "Domestic Political Explanations in the Analysis of Foreign Policy," in *Foreign Policy Analysis*, ed. Laura Neack, Jeanne A.K. Hey, and Patrick J. Haney (Englewood Cliffs, N.J.: Prentice Hall, 1995), 122.

10. Hagan, "Domestic Political Explanations," 137, figure 8.1.

11. Hagan, "Domestic Political Explanations," 128.

12. Hagan, "Domestic Political Explanations," 131.

13. Hagan, "Domestic Political Explanations," 129.

14. Keith B. Richburg, "Clashes Resurge at Sacred Sites, 9 Palestinians Killed in 'Day of Rage,'" *Washington Post*, October 7, 2000, A1.

15. Edward D. Mansfield and Jack Snyder, "Democratization and the Danger of War," *International Security* 20, no. 1 (1995): 13–15.

16. Edward D. Mansfield and Jack Snyder, "Incomplete Democratization and the Outbreak of Military Disputes," *International Studies Quarterly* 46, no. 4 (December 2002): 532.

17. Mansfield and Snyder, "Democratization and the Danger of War," 26.

18. Mansfield and Snyder, "Democratization and the Danger of War," 33.

19. Mansfield and Snyder, "Incomplete Democratization," 530.

20. Mansfield and Snyder, "Incomplete Democratization," 531.

21. Mansfield and Snyder, "Incomplete Democratization," 532.

22. Mansfield and Snyder, "Incomplete Democratization," 532.

23. Mansfield and Snyder, "Democratization and the Danger of War," 90.

24. Neil MacFarlane, "Realism and Russian Strategy after the Collapse of the USSR," in *Unipolar Politics: Realism and State Strategies after the Cold War*, ed. Ethan B. Kapstein and Michael Mastanduno (New York: Columbia University Press, 1999), 236.

25. Rajan Menon, "In the Shadow of the Bear: Security in Post-Soviet Central Asia," *International Security* 20, no. 1 (1995): 149–81.

26. Menon, "In the Shadow of the Bear," 157.

27. Menon, "In the Shadow of the Bear," 158–59.

28. Menon, "In the Shadow of the Bear," 160.

29. Maria Persson Lofren, "Russia: Mothers for Peace Oppose Sons in War," Inter Press Service, October 2, 1996.

30. "Putin Flies into Grozny in Fighter Bomber," Deutsche Presse-Agentur, March 20, 2000.

CHAPTER 7

1. United Nations, "Image and Reality . . . About the UN, Chapter 5: Is the UN Good Value for the Money?" http://www.un.org/geninfo/ir/index.asp?id =150#q8 (accessed Dec. 3, 2007).

2. Joseph Kahn, "If 22 Million Chinese Prevail at UN, Japan Won't," *New York Times*, April 1, 2005, A4.

3. Richard McGregor, "Beijing in Dilemma over Protestors," *Financial Times*, April 12, 2005, 5.

4. Chris Buckley, "China Blames Anti-Japan Riots on Tokyo," *International Herald Tribune*, April 12, 2005, 5.

5. Joseph Kahn, "Beijing Finds Anti-Japan Propaganda a 2-Edged Sword," *New York Times*, May 3, 2005, A3.

6. Kahn, "If 22 Million Chinese Prevail at UN, Japan Won't."

7. Yasuharu Seki, "Young Dominate Anti-Japan Rally; China's Patriotic Education System Spawns Demonstrations," *Daily Yomiuri* (Tokyo), April 6, 2005, 3; McGregor, "Beijing in Dilemma over Protestors."

8. Gabriel Almond, *The American People and Foreign Policy* (New York: Praeger, 1950), as quoted in Ulf Bjereld and Ann-Marie Ekengren, "Foreign Policy Dimensions: A Comparison between the United States and Sweden," *International Studies Quarterly* 43, no. 3 (September 1999): 504.

9. Bjereld and Ekengren, "Foreign Policy Dimensions," 504–505.

10. Thomas Risse-Kappen, "Public Opinion, Domestic Structure, and Foreign Policy in Liberal Democracies," *World Politics* 43, no. 4 (1991): 480.

11. Risse-Kappen, "Public Opinion," 481.

12. Ole Holsti, *Public Opinion and American Foreign Policy* (Ann Arbor: University of Michigan Press, 1996), 31.

13. Holsti, *Public Opinion*, 110.

14. Shibley Telhami, "Arab Public Opinion and the Gulf War," *Political Science Quarterly* 104, no. 3 (1993): 437–52.

15. Telhami, "Arab Public Opinion," 440.

16. Telhami, "Arab Public Opinion," 445.

17. Telhami, "Arab Public Opinion," 450–51.

18. Telhami, "Arab Public Opinion," 451.

19. John F. Burns, "Mubarak Meets Arafat and Avoids Publicly Pressing Him to Meet Demands of Israel," *New York Times*, October 10, 2000, A17; "Arab Nations Stage Wave of Protests," *The Times* (London), October 9, 2000, Lexis-Nexis; and "Violence Threatens Yom Kippur," *Seattle Times*, October 9, 2000, A1.

20. Risse-Kappen, "Public Opinion," 510.

21. Risse-Kappen, "Public Opinion," 510.

22. Risse-Kappen, "Public Opinion," 511.

23. Risse-Kappen, "Public Opinion," 492 (table 1), 510–11.

24. John W. Dietrich, "Interest Groups and Foreign Policy: Clinton and the China MFN Debates," *Presidential Studies Quarterly* 29, no. 2 (1999): 285.

25. Yossi Shain, "Multicultural Foreign Policy," *Foreign Policy*, Fall 1995, 69–87.

26. Shain, "Multicultural Foreign Policy," 75–76.

27. Shain, "Multicultural Foreign Policy," 78.

28. Joseph S. Nye Jr., "Redefining NATO's Mission in the Information Age," *NATO Review* (Winter 1999): 13.

29. For an excellent summary of the views of policy makers, journalists, and scholars on the CNN effect, see Eytan Gilboa, "Global Television News and Foreign Policy: Debating the CNN Effect," *International Studies Perspectives* 6, no. 3 (August 1999): 325–41.

30. Jonathan Mermin, "Television News and American Intervention in Somalia: The Myth of a Media-Driven Foreign Policy," *Political Science Quarterly* 112, no. 3 (1997): 387; emphasis added.

31. Mermin, "Television News," 386.

32. Mermin, "Television News," 387.

33. Mermin, "Television News," 387.

34. Mermin, "Television News," 388.

35. Mermin, "Television News," 388.

36. Mermin, "Television News," 389.

37. Tony Shaw, "The British Popular Press and the Early Cold War," *History* 83, no. 269 (1998): 66–85.

38. Shaw, "British Popular Press," 78.

39. Warren P. Strobel, *Late-Breaking Foreign Policy: The News Media's Influence on Peace Operations* (Washington, D.C.: U.S. Institute for Peace Press, 1997), 6.

40. Strobel, *Late-Breaking Foreign Policy*, 211.

41. Strobel, *Late-Breaking Foreign Policy*, 5.

42. Strobel, *Late-Breaking Foreign Policy*, 212.

43. Robert M. Entman, *Projections of Power: Framing News, Public Opinion, and US Foreign Policy* (Chicago: University of Chicago Press, 2004), 2.

44. Entman, *Projections of Power*, 13.

45. Entman, *Projections of Power*, 5.

46. Entman, *Projections of Power*, 6.

47. Entman, *Projections of Power*, 15.

48. Entman, *Projections of Power*, 29.

49. Entman, *Projections of Power*, 29.

50. Entman, *Projections of Power*, 31.

51. Entman, *Projections of Power*, 20.

52. Entman, *Projections of Power*, 21.

CHAPTER 8

1. National Intelligence Council, "Mapping the Global Future," Report of the National Intelligence Council's 2020 Project, NIC 2004-13, December 2004, 10.

2. National Intelligence Council, "Mapping the Global Future," 12.

3. National Intelligence Council, "Mapping the Global Future," 10.

4. National Intelligence Council, "Mapping the Global Future," 47.

5. National Intelligence Council, "Mapping the Global Future," 47.

6. National Intelligence Council, "Mapping the Global Future," 37.

7. National Intelligence Council, "Mapping the Global Future," 73, 77.

8. Kenneth N. Waltz, *Man, the State and War* (New York: Columbia University Press, 1959), 159.

9. Waltz, *Man, the State, and War*, 160.

10. Charles Kindleberger, "Dominance and Leadership in the International Economy: Exploitation, Public Goods, and Free Rides," *International Studies Quarterly* 25, no. 2 (1981): 249–50.

11. Robert Gilpin, *U.S. Power and the Multinational Corporation: The Political Economy of Foreign Direct Investment* (New York: Basic, 1975), 24, as quoted in James E. Dougherty and Robert L. Pfaltzgraff Jr., *Contending Theories of International Relations: A Comprehensive Survey*, 5th ed. (New York: Longman, 2001), 72.

12. One of the classic treatments of this is in Thomas C. Schelling, *Arms and Influence* (New Haven, Conn.: Yale University Press, 1966).

13. For an excellent study comparing peacekeeping and peace enforcement operations in the 1990s, including those launched in Somalia, see Donald C. F. Daniel and Bradd C. Hayes with Chantal de Jonge Oudraat, *Coercive Inducement and the Containment of International Crises* (Washington, D.C.: US Institute of Peace Press, 1999).

14. Mark Bowden, *Black Hawk Down* (New York: Penguin, 1999).

15. Graham Evans and Jeffrey Newnham, *The Penguin Dictionary of International Relations* (New York: Penguin Putnam, 1998), 210.

16. Evans and Newnham, *Penguin Dictionary of International Relations*, 209.

17. Edward N. Luttwak, "Where Are the Great Powers? At Home with the Kids," *Foreign Affairs* 73, no. 4 (1994): 26.

18. Luttwak, "Where Are the Great Powers," 26.

19. Luttwak, "Where Are the Great Powers," 23.

20. Luttwak, "Where Are the Great Powers," 23.

21. As quoted in Ian Lustick, "The Absence of Middle Eastern Great Powers: Political 'Backwardness' in Historical Perspective," *International Organization* 51, no. 4 (1997): 659.

22. Lustick, "Absence of Middle Eastern Great Powers," 657.

23. Lustick, "Absence of Middle Eastern Great Powers," 660.

24. Mary Ann Tétreault, "Autonomy, Necessity, and the Small State: Ruling Kuwait in the Twentieth Century," *International Organization* 45, no. 4 (1991): 565–91.

25. Robert J. Art, *A Grand Strategy for America* (Ithaca, N.Y.: Cornell, 2003), 1.

26. Christopher Layne, "From Preponderance to Offshore Balancing: America's Future Grand Strategy," *International Security* 22, no. 1 (1997): 86–124.

27. Benjamin Schwarz, "Why America Thinks It Has to Run the World," *Atlantic Monthly*, June 1996, 96.

28. Schwarz, "Why America Thinks," 101.

29. Layne, "From Preponderance to Offshore Balancing," 88.

30. Benjamin Schwarz and Christopher Layne, "A New Grand Strategy," *Atlantic Monthly*, January 2002, 36.

31. Stephen M. Walt, "A New Grand Strategy for American Foreign Policy," *Boston Review*, February–March 2005, 1, available online at http://www.boston review.net/BR30.1/walt.html (accessed June 13, 2006).

32. Walt, "A New Grand Strategy for American Foreign Policy," 1.

33. Walt, "A New Grand Strategy for American Foreign Policy," 1.

34. Walt, "A New Grand Strategy for American Foreign Policy," 3.

35. Walt, "A New Grand Strategy for American Foreign Policy," 3.

36. Art, *A Grand Strategy for America*, 2.

37. Art, *A Grand Strategy for America*, 8.

38. Art, *A Grand Strategy for America*, 7.

39. Art, *A Grand Strategy for America*, 9.

40. For an explanation of neoconservatism that is not from a neoconservative, see Gore Vidal, *Perpetual War for Perpetual Peace: How We Got to be So Hated* (New York: Nation Books, 2002).

41. Francis Fukuyama, *America at the Crossroads: Democracy, Power, and the Neoconservative Legacy* (New Haven, Conn.: Yale University Press, 2006).

42. George W. Bush, "Inaugural Address by President George W. Bush," January 20, 2005, http://www.whitehouse.gov/news/releases/2005/1/10050120-3.html (accessed Nov. 1, 2005).

43. National Intelligence Council, "National Intelligence Estimate: Iran: Nuclear Intentions and Capabilities," November 2007.

44. Keir A. Lieber and Daryl G. Press, "The Rise of Nuclear Primacy," *Foreign Affairs* 85, no. 2 (March–April 2006): 42–54.

45. Keir A. Lieber and Daryl G. Press, "The End of MAD? The Nuclear Dimension of US Primacy," *International Security* 30, no. 4 (Spring 2006): 7–44.

46. Lieber and Press, "The Rise of Nuclear Primacy," 47, 48.

47. Benjamin Schwarz, "The Perils of Primacy," *Atlantic Monthly*, January/February 2006, 33, 36–37.

48. Josef Joffe, "How America Does It," *Foreign Affairs* 76, no. 5 (1997): 16.

49. Richard Falk, "Walt's Obsolescent Foreign Policy Is Deeply Rooted in the Statism of a Bygone Era," A Response to Stephen Walt, *Boston Review*, February–March 2005, 2, available online at http://www.bostonreview.net/BR30.1/falk.html (accessed June 13, 2006).

CHAPTER 9

1. James N. Rosenau, "Pre-theories and Theories of Foreign Policy," in *Approaches to Comparative and International Politics*, ed. R. Barry Farrell (Evanston, Ill.: Northwestern University Press, 1966), 147–48.

2. Rosenau, "Pre-theories," 147, n. 75.

3. Rosenau, "Pre-theories," 153.

4. John Mueller, *Retreat from Doomsday: The Obsolescence of Major War* (New York: Basic Books, 1989), 11, quoted in Christopher J. Fettweis, "A Revolution in International Relation Theory: Or, What If Mueller Is Right?" *International Studies Review* 8, no. 4 (December 2006): 678.

5. Fettweis, "A Revolution in International Relation Theory," 680.

6. Stephen Blank, "India's Rising Profile in Central Asia," *Comparative Strategy* 22, no. 2 (April–June 2003): 141.

7. Blank, "India's Rising Profile in Central Asia," 140.

8. Blank, "India's Rising Profile in Central Asia," 140.

9. Blank, "India's Rising Profile in Central Asia," 145.

10. Blank, "India's Rising Profile in Central Asia," 146.

11. Eric Heginbotham and Richard J. Samuels, "Mercantile Realism and Japanese Foreign Policy," *International Security* 22, no. 4 (1998): 172.

12. Richard N. Rosecrance, *The Rise of the Trading State: Commerce and Conquest in the World of Warlord States* (New York: Basic, 1985).

13. Michael Loriaux, "Realism and Reconciliation: France, Germany, and the European Union," in *Unipolar Politics: Realism and State Strategies after the Cold War*, ed. Ethan B. Kapstein and Michael Mastanduno (New York: Columbia University Press, 1999), 358.

14. William Wallace, "The Collapse of British Foreign Policy," *International Affairs* 82, no. 1 (2005): 53.

15. Wallace, "The Collapse of British Foreign Policy," 54–55.

16. Wallace, "The Collapse of British Foreign Policy," 65–66.

17. F. Duchêne, "A New European Defense Community," *Foreign Affairs* 50, no. 1 (1971): 82, 43, 19, as quoted in Ian Manners, "Normative Power Europe Reconsidered: Beyond the Crossroads," *Journal of European Public Policy* 13, no. 2 (March 2006): 183–84.

18. Helene Sjursen, "What Kind of Power?" *Journal of European Public Policy* 13, no. 2 (March 2006): 170.

19. Sjursen, "What Kind of Power?" 172.

20. Sjursen, "What Kind of Power?" 170.

21. Manners, "Normative Power Europe Reconsidered," 184.

22. Sjursen, "What Kind of Power?" 172.

23. Manners, "Normative Power Europe Reconsidered," 191.

24. Manners, "Normative Power Europe Reconsidered," 189, 190.

25. Sjursen, "What Kind of Power?" 170–71.

26. Carsten Holbraad, *Middle Powers in International Politics* (New York: St. Martin's, 1984).

27. Andrew F. Cooper, Richard A. Higgott, and Kim Richard Nossal, *Relocating Middle Powers: Australia and Canada in a Changing World Order* (Vancouver: University of British Columbia Press, 1993), 19.

28. John W. Holmes, *The Shaping of Peace: Canada and the Search for World Order, 1943–1975* (Toronto: University of Toronto Press, 1982); Bernard Wood, *The Middle Powers and the General Interest* (Ottawa: North-South Institute, 1988).

29. J. L. Granatstein, "Peacekeeping: Did Canada Make a Difference? And What Difference Did Peacekeeping Make to Canada?" in *Making a Difference: Canada's Foreign Policy in a Changing World Order*, ed. John English and Norman Hillmer (Toronto: Lester, 1992), 224–25.

30. Cooper, Higgott, and Nossal, *Relocating Middle Powers*.

31. Laura Neack, "The Retreat of Western Powers and the Potential Unraveling of U.N. Peacekeeping," 2007, unpublished manuscript.

32. Maria Papadakis and Harvey Starr, "Opportunity, Willingness, and Small States: The Relationship between Environment and Foreign Policy," in *New Directions in the Study of Foreign Policy*, ed. Charles F. Hermann, Charles W. Kegley, and James N. Rosenau (Winchester, Mass.: Unwin Hyman, 1987).

33. Davis B. Bobrow and Steve Chan, "Simple Labels and Complex Realities: National Security for the Third World," in *National Security in the Third World: The Management of Internal and External Threats*, ed. Edward E. Azar and Chung-in Moon (Aldershot, UK: Edward Elgar, 1988), 56–57.

34. Mary Ann Tétreault, "Autonomy, Necessity, and the Small State: Ruling Kuwait in the Twentieth Century," *International Organization* 45, no. 4 (1991): 565.

35. Tétreault, "Autonomy, Necessity," 572.

36. Tétreault, "Autonomy, Necessity," 567.

37. Tétreault, "Autonomy, Necessity," 588.

38. Tétreault, "Autonomy, Necessity," 573.

39. Tétreault, "Autonomy, Necessity," 577.

40. Tétreault, "Autonomy, Necessity," 579.

41. Tétreault, "Autonomy, Necessity," 582.

42. Martin W. Sampson III, "Exploiting the Seams: External Structure and Libyan Foreign Policy Changes," in *Foreign Policy Restructuring: How Governments Respond to Global Change*, ed. Jerel A. Rosati, Joe D. Hagan, and Martin W. Sampson III (Columbia: University of South Carolina Press, 1994), 93.

43. Sampson, "Exploiting the Seams," 93–94.

44. Sampson, "Exploiting the Seams," 94–95.

45. Sampson, "Exploiting the Seams," 95.

46. Sampson, "Exploiting the Seams," 99.

47. Sampson, "Exploiting the Seams," 98–99.

48. Sampson, "Exploiting the Seams," 107.

49. Michale T. Klare, "The Geopolitics of War," *Nation*, November 5, 2001, 12.

50. Klare, "The Geopolitics of War," 12.

51. Ken Silverstein, "Saudis and Americans: Friends in Need," *Nation*, November 5, 2001, 15.

52. Silverstein, "Saudis and Americans: Friends in Need," 15.

53. Aram Roston, "A Royal Scandal," *Nation*, December 3, 2001, 16.

CHAPTER 10

1. This case can be studied in detail, including issues of British, Chilean, and international law, at the following websites maintained by Human Rights Watch: www.hrw.org/hrw/reports/1999/chile/Patrick.htm and www.hrw.org/complaints/chile98/index.html. See also Marc Cooper, *Pinochet and Me: A Chilean Anti-Memoir* (London: Verso, 2001).

2. "Should Kissinger Be Tried for War Crimes?" *Statesman* (India), Global News Wire, March 2, 2001, Lexis-Nexis.

3. Jonathan Kandell, "Augusto Pinochet, 91, Dictator Who Ruled by Terror in Chile, Dies," *New York Times*, December 11, 2006.

4. "Vatican Plea on Pinochet's Behalf Prompts Outrage," *Boston Globe*, February 20, 1999, A20.

5. Marc Cooper, "Now the U.S. Must Face Its Past on Chile," *Los Angeles Times*, December 5, 2000, B9.

6. Kandell, "Augusto Pinochet, 91, Dictator Who Ruled by Terror in Chile, Dies."

7. Karen Mingst, "Uncovering the Missing Links: Linkage Actors and Their Strategies," in *Foreign Policy Analysis*, ed. Laura Neack, Jeanne A. K. Hey, and Patrick J. Haney (Englewood Cliffs, N.J.: Prentice-Hall, 1995), 235.

8. See the European Court of Justice website at http://curia.eu.int/en/index.htm.

9. As quoted in "When Tyrants Tremble: The Pinochet Case," Human Rights Watch online www.hrw.org/hrw/reports/1999/chile.

10. Andrew Sparrow and Bruce Johnston, "Pope Backs Call to Free Pinochet," *Daily Telegraph* (London), February 19, 1999, 1. See also "Vatican Plea on Pinochet's Behalf Prompts Outrage," *Boston Globe*, February 20, 1999, A20.

11. For a time line detailing the events depicted in this tale, see "Events Leading to Hearings on Stripping Pinochet's Immunity," Agence France Presse, April 26, 2000, Lexis-Nexis.

12. David White, "Straw to Send Pinochet Home," *Financial Times*, January 12, 2000, 1.

13. "Events Leading to Hearings on Stripping Pinochet's Immunity."

14. Karl Vick, "Former Chad Dictator Faces Pinochet Test," *Washington Post*, January 27, 2000, A22.

15. John Lichfield and Jan McGirk, "Kissinger 'Too Busy' for Chile Murders Inquiry," *Independent* (London), May 30, 2001, 14.

16. Ricardo Lagos and Heraldo Muñoz, "The Pinochet Dilemma," *Foreign Policy*, Spring 1999, 27–28.

17. Lagos and Muñoz, "Pinochet Dilemma," 28.

18. Lagos and Muñoz, "Pinochet Dilemma," 27.

19. "Globalization Is No Excuse for States to Shirk Their Human Rights Responsibilities: Amnesty International Outlines Human Rights Violations in 149 Countries," Amnesty International news release, May 30, 2001; available online at www.amnesty.org.

20. "Globalization Is No Excuse."

21. Lagos and Muñoz, "Pinochet Dilemma," 37.

22. Lagos and Muñoz, "Pinochet Dilemma," 37.

23. Margaret E. Keck and Kathryn Sikkink, "Transnational Advocacy Networks in International Politics: Introduction," in *Essential Readings in World Politics*, ed. Karen Mingst and Jack Snyder (New York: W.W. Norton & Company, 2001), 335.

24. Mingst, "Uncovering the Missing Links," 231.

25. Mingst, "Uncovering the Missing Links," 237, quoting Peter Haas, "Introduction: Epistemic Communities and International Policy Coordination," *International Organization* 46, no. 1 (1992): 3.

26. Karen DeYoung and Michael Dobbs, "Bin Laden: Architect of New Global Terrorism," *Washington Post*, September 16, 2001, A8.

27. Jonathan Curiel, "The Rise of Global Anger: Why They Hate the U.S. So Fiercely," *San Francisco Chronicle*, September 16, 2001, D4.

28. Sam Dillon, "Indictment by Spanish Judge Portrays a Secret Terror Cell," *New York Times*, November 20, 2001, A1.

29. Sam Dillon with Donald G. McNeil Jr., "Spain Sets Hurdle for Extraditions," *New York Times*, November 24, 2001, A1.

30. T.X. Hammes, "Fourth Generation Warfare Evolves, Fifth Emerges," *Military Review*, May–June 2007, 14–15.

31. Intergovernmental Panel on Climate Change, http://www.ipcc.ch/about/index.htm (accessed Dec. 16, 2007).

32. Mark Sappenfield, "Alongside Al Gore, An Indian 'Climate Control' Engineer," *Christian Science Monitor*, October 15, 2007, 1, 11.

33. Thomas Fuller and Andrew C. Revkin, "Climate Plan Looks Beyond Bush's Tenure," *New York Times*, December 16, 2007.

34. Fuller and Revkin, "Climate Plan Looks Beyond Bush's Tenure."

35. Fuller and Revkin, "Climate Plan Looks Beyond Bush's Tenure."

Glossary

accommodation strategy a strategy in which leaders attempt to bargain with a vocal opposition, accommodating or adopting some of its demands, in order to avoid controversy; associated with a restrained, non-controversial foreign policy

agent-structure problem the question of how best to understand the relationship between international actors and the international system, especially in terms of which—actor (agent) or system (structure)—is autonomous of the other

alliance an association or formal agreement between two or more states made in order to further similar foreign policy objectives such as security

anticolonialism the sentiment that the settlement of foreign territories is illegitimate and that subordinate populations have the right of self-determination and statehood

anarchy the general condition of the international system in which no ultimate authority (such as a world government) exists to govern relations between states and other international actors

autocratic describing a form of government in which a leader (or an autocrat) wields unlimited power

belief set an organized, relatively integrated, and persistent set of perceptions that an individual, group, or state holds about a particular universe

bilateral state to state; refers to a relationship or policy between two states

bipolar system   an international system in which power is fairly evenly distributed between two significant powers (states) or two power blocs (groups of states)

centre   also known as the core; a term derived from the Marxist, dependency, or structuralist worldviews; the world's wealthiest, most powerful states that work together to construct international institutions that serve to maintain their mutual interests and predominance over the majority of the world's states (which together compose the periphery)

civil society   the public realm "located" between households and government in which interest groups of all sorts protect individuals from the government (and from the free market)

cliency relationship   a reciprocal and strategic relationship between a strong state and a weak one (or between a great power and a small power); also known as a patron–client relationship

CNN effect   an explanation of the media's role in foreign policy making that posits that media broadcasts of unsettling international images incite the public to demand foreign policy action by the government; foreign policy makers, then, must take under consideration issues that they may not have otherwise considered and/or they must make foreign policy decisions without full and appropriate deliberation

coalition building   the bringing together of diverse actors and groups who share an interest in a common policy outcome; because the coalition is loosely built on a narrow issue-base, it requires constant maintenance and rebuilding by coalition leaders

coalition government   in a parliamentary system, an arrangement to govern between two or more political parties that together control sufficient votes to be the majority group in parliament; the leader of the party with the greatest number of seats in parliament is the head of the government formed

cognition   the study of the mental process or faculty of knowing

cognitive consistency   the idea that the images in a belief set must be logically connected and fairly well integrated

cognitive miser   the idea that individuals are assumed to be limited cognitive managers who rely on shortcuts to interpret and understand new information

constructive engagement   a policy of long-term involvement meant to change or influence the policy and behavior of a target state through offering incentives rather than threats and punishments

constructivism   a view that proposes that our understanding of world politics is a social creation (construction); for instance, constructivism holds that the international system is not anarchic but is *understood* and accepted to be anarchic

crisis a circumstance in which a threat exists that requires immediate action by decision makers

democracy a type of government in which power is exercised by the people through freely contested, open, and regularly held elections in which representatives are selected for government office

democratic peace the theory that democracies are less likely to go to war with other democracies

democratization the process in which constitutional limits are placed on the exercise of power by central authorities while free and openly contested elections for political office, with universal suffrage, are regularized as the norm

deterrence a situation in which one's enemy is stopped from initiating a military attack because of the threat of disproportionate retaliation and/or punishment

elite individuals who exercise great influence in the policy-making process (or individuals who have greater access to decision makers)

escalation-deescalation strategy a strategy in which (1) an actor plans a series of moves that are contingent on the reactions/moves of an opponent, (2) each move is undertaken in order to maximize relative gains, and (3) the actor intends to back away before incurring any significant loss at the hands of the opponent

EU (European Union) formed by the 1992 Maastricht Treaty; most recent integration of the European community along political, economic, and foreign policy lines

failed state a country in which no central government exists that can exercise effective control over the country's recognized territory; generally characterized by a stalemated civil war and the lack of international recognition for any group of would-be national leaders

game theory a mathematically based method for evaluating interactive choices that assumes that each player in the "game" (1) operates under the same assumptions and rules for interaction, (2) is aware of the payoff system, and (3) holds a clear understanding of "winning"

global free trade system a system in which all or a significant majority of the world's states engage in unrestricted trade with one another

globalization the growing internationalization of culture and economics, accompanied by increased interdependence between individuals, states, and nonstate international actors

governance the act, process, or power of governing

grand strategy a global vision and set of operating principles that frame the foreign policy of a major power, especially in its use of force

grassroots mobilization a linkage actor strategy in which public education and publicity efforts create widespread public engagement in favor of a cause or policy outcome

humanitarian intervention military involvement in the internal affairs of a state by another state, group of states, or international organization for the purpose of stopping massive human rights violations and/or preventing a humanitarian disaster such as widespread famine

ICC (International Criminal Court) an international tribunal formally created in July 2002 for prosecuting individuals charged with crimes against humanity and/or war crimes; based in The Hague

insulation strategy a strategy in which leaders deflect attention from and otherwise protect their foreign policy through suppressing, overriding, or co-opting the opposition

international organization (IO) a formal organization created by an agreement among states in order to facilitate cooperation on matters of mutual concern; may be regionally based or global

international political economy the study of the relationship between international politics and economics, or study that proceeds from the assumption that politics and economics are indivisible in the international system

international system as a descriptive term (rather than as a level of analysis), refers to the totality of international actors, distribution of resources, and the (written and unwritten) rules and (formal and informal) institutions that govern relations among the actors

internationalism a foreign policy orientation that favors cooperation and mutual empowerment over the narrow pursuit of immediate national interests

isolationism, isolationist a foreign policy orientation that attempts to disconnect the state from international obligations and entanglements in order to "go it alone" and pursue near-total self-reliance

leader a person, usually the head of a government, who makes policy choices affecting the international and domestic environments

leadership the top decision makers in a national government; regime

legitimacy the recognition or acceptance by citizens and/or international actors, including other states, that a government has the right to exercise power and make decisions on behalf of the country

leverage the use of a group's or state's unique circumstances to strengthen its position relative to another group or state

liberal economic regime the international agreements and institutions that together construct, protect, and maintain a global free trade system

liberal economic theory a theory that posits that free trade between countries will increase overall wealth and make conflict between those countries less likely

linkage the direct or indirect interconnectedness of two policies, groups, ideas, and so on, originating in one system and reacted to in another

linkage actors individuals, government representatives, and nonstate actors who work across national boundaries to influence public policy

MAD (mutual assured destruction) the idea that because both the Americans and Soviets possessed nuclear second-strike capability (the ability to sustain a first attack and retaliate in kind), any war between the two initiated by either side would destroy both

methodology the approaches and practices used in the study of a subject

MFN (most favored nation) refers to the extension of beneficial trade terms (usually in the form of lowered tariffs) to a country that reflect the best terms extended to third parties in the past or in the future

MNC (multinational corporation) a business nonstate actor whose production and/or service operations (not just marketing and sales) can be found in many countries

mobilization strategy a strategy in which leaders use assertive and sometimes risky foreign policy behaviors and calls to nationalism to assert their government's legitimacy against a vocal opposition

multilateralism, multilateralist acting in cooperation with other states to achieve a common international objective

multinational force a coercive military group composed of troops from three or more states whose purpose is to create orderly, secure conditions within a conflict zone; often deployed with U.N. approval, but not under U.N. command and control

multipolar system an international system in which power is fairly evenly distributed among four or five major powers (states)

nation a sociocultural group with a common language, common cultural institutions, and sometimes a common religion; a group whose members have a sense of a common history and destiny as a "people"

nation building within a state, refers to efforts by the national government to facilitate political and economic development; also refers to international efforts to facilitate political and economic development within a target state

national interest the interests of a state that are of primary importance for protection and enhancement

national self-image the concept or image of the country that is shared among a country's elite and mass public and guides the country's foreign and domestic policies and behaviors

nationalism strong, positive feelings about a group that are shared among its members and lead the members to want to preserve the group at all costs

NATO (North Atlantic Treaty Organization) an international organization (alliance) established for the mutual defense of its member states—the United States, Canada, and initially the countries of Western Europe;

originally designed to counter the military threat of the Soviet Union and its allies in Central and Eastern Europe; today its members include many of the former Soviet allies; now an organization designed in part to offer peace support operations

negotiation   the process through which international actors interact with and engage one another in order to achieve common objectives

neoimperialism   the idea that the Western, or advanced industrialized states, use indirect means—usually with some moral justification—to impose their political and economic structures on less-developed countries

nested game   *see* **two-level game**

NGO (nongovernmental organization)   a nonstate international actor whose members are not states, and whose membership and interests transcend national boundaries

nonstate actor   an international actor that is not a state or a representative of a state

nuclear deterrence   the condition in which opposing nuclear-weapons states refrain from using such weapons against one another because of the mutual threat of unacceptable damage

partisanship   devotion or commitment to a political party, group, or cause

peacekeeping   the use of a neutral, noncombatant multinational armed force for the purpose of enforcing a cease-fire, maintaining a demilitarized zone, and/or overseeing the return to normal politics, generally under the command and control of the United Nations

periphery   the states that are economically and politically dependent on the centre or core; also called the developing world

pluralist model   the theory that public policy results from bargaining, negotiating, and politicking among many distinct and autonomous interests within a society

policy coalition   a group composed of diverse interests formed by political leaders in order to get a certain policy program accepted and executed

political opening   within domestic politics, the lifting of barriers on political participation at all levels; associated with democratization

positivism/positivist   an approach to studying social phenomena that is founded on science-based ways of knowing

power approach   a linkage actor strategy in which the highest diplomatic circles or ultimate power resources are tapped in order to influence a policy outcome

preponderance of power   a condition in which one state possesses disproportionate political, military, and economic power, thereby giving that state a disproportionate voice in international affairs

public opinion the general views of the majority of individuals about some idea, person, policy, or action

rational actor model an approach to studying the behavior of actors in the international system that assumes that all actors will select the course of action that they perceive as most likely to bring about the preferred outcome while maximizing benefits and minimizing costs

regime the central, primary decision makers within a national government

security the absence of threat to acquired core values or national interests

security dilemma a cyclic situation in which actions undertaken by a state to increase its security ultimately decrease overall security because other states (mis)perceive the defensive actions to be hostile and threatening and so they respond in kind

self-determination the right of a group, generally a nation, to govern itself and determine the nature of its own political system

siege mentality when members of a group, nation, or state share the belief that the outside world holds hostile behavioral intentions toward the group

soft power the ability to persuade others to pursue common goals; also understood as the "pull" of an attractive culture

sovereignty the ultimate decision-making and decision-enforcing authority within a defined territory; only states are said to be sovereign in the international system

state a legal-political concept denoting a sovereign actor in the international system with a recognized territory, a population, and an effective government

state building the historical process whereby the institutions of government are constructed and the authority of the government is extended over territory and population

structuralism an approach to the study of international politics and economics that focuses on the structure of the world system—especially the world economic system—and how that structure influences the distribution of power and resources and state behavior

technocratic approach a linkage actor strategy in which expert knowledge is utilized to influence a policy outcome

terrorism the focused use of violence for the purpose of intimidating victims and their societies in pursuit of political objectives

transnational actors individuals or organizations in the international system that conduct activities across national borders

two-level game a concept that national leaders must divide their attention between the domestic and international environments, sometimes using one arena to further agendas in the other; also known as a **nested game**

UN (United Nations)   global international organization created in 1945; designed to prevent war and maintain international peace primarily through collective security but secondarily through a wide range of activities

unilateralism, unilateralist   when a state acts alone in its pursuit of its own narrowly defined foreign policy goals

unipolar system   an international system in which one state holds a preponderance of political, military, and economic power

Index

About the Author

Laura Neack is professor of political science at Miami University, Oxford, Ohio. She teaches courses in world politics, comparative foreign policy, and international security. She is the author of *Elusive Security: States First, People Last* (2007), the first edition of *The New Foreign Policy: U.S. and Comparative Foreign Policy in the 21st Century* (2003), and coeditor of two books, *Global Society in Transition* (2002) and *Foreign Policy Analysis: Continuity and Change in Its Second Generation* (1995). Neack is also the author of numerous journal articles and book chapters on foreign policy behavior and U.N. peacekeeping. She is the former editor of the quarterly journal *International Politics* and sits on the editorial boards of the *Bulletin of the Atomic Scientists, Foreign Policy Analysis,* and Rowman & Littlefield's New Millennium Books in International Studies. She received her doctorate in political science in 1991 from the University of Kentucky. She lives in Kentucky with her husband, son, and a very old pup who has heard every word of this book read several times over.